FROM A DARK SKY

Books by Orr Kelly

Never Fight Fair!
Brave Men—Dark Waters
Hornet
King of the Killing Zone

FROM A DARK SKY

The Story of U.S. Air Force Special Operations

ORR KELLY

PRESIDIO

For my brother, Jack Kelly

Published by Presidio Press
505 B San Marin Drive, Suite 300
Novato, CA 94945-1340

Library of Congress-in-Publication Data

Kelly, Orr.
    From a dark sky : the story of U.S. Air Force Special Operations / Orr Kelly.
        p. cm.
    Includes bibliographical references and index.
    ISBN 0-89141-520-3 (hardcover)
    1. United States. Air Force—Commando troops—History.
I Title.
UG633.K42   1996
358.4'14—dc20   96-8208
                                              CIP

All photos courtesy USAAF except where noted.
Printed in the United States of America

Contents

Foreword   vii
Preface   ix

Part 1: Birth of the Air Commandos   1
1: The Day Thursday Came on Sunday   3
2: The Reluctant Warriors   8
3: A "Grandiose Scheme"   17
4: Deep in Enemy Territory   26
5: Aerial Invasion of Germany   36

Part 2: Behind the Lines in Europe   41
6: The Carpetbaggers Are Born   43
7: Enemy Territory—in the Dark   50
8: D-day and Beyond   61
9: Jack of All Trades   70
10: Action in the South   82
11: The Final Days   94

Part 3: Korea and Beyond   101
12: Drawdown and Rebuilding   103
13: Rebirth and Decline   112

Part 4: The Longest War   121
14: They Called It Jungle Jim   123
15: Leading the Way   133
16: Death From the Sky   150

Part 5: Through the Looking Glass   163
17: The Secret War   165
18: Butterflies and Ravens   174
19: The Third War   193

Part 6: Son Tay and the *Mayaguez*   207
20: Destination: Hanoi   209
21: "Utter Chaos" at Tang Island   223

Part 7: Hostage Rescue Efforts   233
22: Operation Rice Bowl   235
23: Back to Teheran   253
24: Not Quite Ready   263
25: Panama—Getting It Together   274

Part 8: New Challenges   287
26: The Gulf War and Beyond   289

Glossary   315
Sources   321
Index   334

Foreword

In the more than half a century that we have been in business, we in Air Force special operations have made contributions to our nation's security far out of proportion to our small numbers.

But in the process we have, more often than not, failed to leave behind a clear record of where we have gone and what we have done—if we left any record at all.

When Col. Phil Cochran was preparing to leave for India in 1944, he noticed the packing list included half a dozen typewriters. He crossed them off the list, taking literally Gen. Hap Arnold's order: "To hell with the paperwork; go out and fight."

In Korea, Henry "Heinie" Aderholt kept a single record, in bookkeepers' ledger books, of single-plane flights far behind enemy lines. When a book was filled, it was tossed in a corner, later to be discarded. Fortunately, Aderholt brought home a few of those handwritten records of an important, but little known, chapter in special operations history.

Our concentration on getting the job done, rather than on keeping records, is one reason our history is so little known to the public, and even to many in the Air Force itself.

Another reason, of course, is that, by the very nature of our business, many of the things we do must be highly classified. Not only are our operations secret, but they are often shrouded by cover stories and deceptive actions to make sure that enemy gunners, waiting there in the dark, will not get a shot at us.

In 1970, to deceive the enemy about our raid on the suspected prisoner-of-war compound at Son Tay, we orchestrated what appeared to the North Vietnamese to be a major air attack from the east as we sneaked in from the west. In all, 116 aircraft taking off from seven airfields and 3 carriers were involved in the operation. But almost all of them were part of the deception, keeping the enemy from detecting our small force of 6 helicopters and 7 fixed-wing planes that went into North Vietnam on the actual raid.

Our reluctance to keep records, coupled with the secrecy and deception that are an essential part of our tactics, poses a special challenge to anyone trying to put together a coherent account of the history of Air Force special operations.

It is a tribute to Orr Kelly's skill as a reporter and researcher and his persistence that he has been able to gather together the bits and pieces of information we have left behind—a written reminiscence here, the declassified fragment of an old record there—and meld them, with the help of a series of probing interviews, into this sweeping record of the often unheralded accomplishments of some very special people.

For the present and future members of the Air Force special operations community, this volume will prove an invaluable guide to who we are, where we came from—and what lies in our future. For members of the larger Air Force community, who have often regarded special operations with suspicion, if not hostility, this history will provide insight into the vital role Air Force special operations will play in the broader Air Force mission.

Essentially, of course, this is an adventure story—a gripping, suspenseful account of very special people doing very unusual, and often very dangerous, things. In recounting our history, Orr Kelly has done an admirable job of not just telling the facts but bringing the experiences of Air Force special operations to life. *From a Dark Sky* is not only an important story but a highly readable one as well.

Lt. Gen. LeRoy J. Manor, USAF (Retired)

Preface

Special operations has ranged in size, over the years, from a small part of the bigger Air Force down to a virtually invisible part. But whether they called themselves Air Commandos or Carpetbaggers, Ravens or Butterflies, Nimrods or Spectres, whenever the going got tough, the special operators made their mark. They were the ones called on to do the unusual jobs—often the "impossible" jobs—that other Air Force units couldn't, or wouldn't, do, whether it involved flying low, slow, and alone in the dark behind enemy lines or introducing unique new weapons such as the fixed-wing gunship or the Pave Low helicopter.

Two things have struck me most in my research on the half-century history of Air Force special operations. One is how remarkably rich and varied that history has been. The other is how the history of special operations has so often been the story, not of groups or wings or squadrons, but of resourceful, innovative, and often strikingly courageous individuals or very small groups of individuals.

Almost always the story quickly focuses down to the exploits of individuals—whether it is the extraordinary adventure of John Carney, alone in the dark Iranian desert preparing a landing site for the attempt to rescue American hostages from Teheran in 1980, or Bob Leonik, thinking of himself as an orchestra conductor as he piloted his helicopter and its small crew into Iraq to begin the Desert Storm offensive a decade later, or Ron Terry, bucking the opposition of the brass and using his own credit card to get the fixed-wing gunship into combat.

Unfortunately, this volume can give credit to only a small number of the many men who have made their mark on special operations over the years. I have chosen to highlight the accomplishments of a few to give the reader a sense of the accomplishments of the many who have also served with distinction.

Because their units are small and their assignments special and often very secret, the special operators have never fit comfortably into the bureaucratic structure of the big Air Force. Traditionally, a career in special operations has been one of the surest ways to avoid becoming a general. That tradition may be changing now, and perhaps that change is to be regretted. The history of special operations offers plentiful evidence that those who are best at this special work are often those who don't aspire to become generals and are genuinely surprised on those rare occasions when they find stars on their shoulders.

Most military histories focus on the actions of the generals because they are the ones who make the large decisions and have the most influence on the course of events. The reader will find this history different. Much of what special operators do is done by enlisted men and relatively junior officers, and this is their story.

The reader may be especially intrigued to read of the little-known combat controllers, or special tactics teams, as they are now called. Trained to swim like a Navy SEAL, fight like a member of the Army's elite Delta Force, and parachute with the Rangers, they also have the special skill to set up and run a busy airfield in the dark behind enemy lines. Recently, they have taken on the added responsibility of caring for the wounded and injured during airfield assault operations. Most of the combat controllers and all of the pararescuemen, or PJs, as they are called, are enlisted men.

Probably to the discomfort of many of those mentioned in this book, I have followed the Air Force practice of using the words *air commando* as a kind of convenient blanket term for all of special operations. But many men identify themselves with their own specialty rather than the broader blanket term. A Carpetbagger considers himself a Carpetbagger, a Raven considers himself a Raven, and a Nimrod prides himself on being a Nimrod.

The Carpetbaggers and the Ravens have their own separate reunions. The Nimrods attend the annual air commando reunion but tend to remain off by themselves. And even the Air Commandos of World War II, who gave their name to the concept, seg-regate themselves into two groups—the 1st Air Commandos, who served in Burma, and the 2d and 3d Air Commandos, who came later and served as more traditional military units in the Pacific.

I have tried to keep the use of military designations and acronyms from being any more burdensome to the reader than it has to be, inserting explanations—or translations—of military terminology wherever necessary.

Some confusion is unavoidable, however. A prime example is the Douglas Invader aircraft. Known in World War II as the A-26, it was called the B-26 during the late 1940s and the 1950s, only to revert to the A-26 designation during the war in Southeast Asia. It was always basically the same plane—not to be confused, of course, with the World War II-era Martin B-26 Marauder. I have used the designation current at the time. There are other terms, unfortunately, which have dual meanings. The acronym *CAS,* for example, stood for *Controlled American Source*—a term for Central Intelligence Agency operations in Laos—but also means "close air support." For the reader still in doubt despite context and ex-planatory notes, I have included an extensive glossary.

For help in research for this volume, I owe a debt of gratitude to a number of people.

Mrs. Yvonne Kincaid, librarian at the Air Force history center at Bolling Air Force Base in Washington, D.C., guided me through the voluminous microfilm and paper records on file there. My re-search there was supplemented by a visit to the Air Force Histor-ical Research Agency library at Maxwell Air Force Base, Mont-gomery, Alabama, where the originals of many of the records duplicated at Bolling, plus additional records, are available. Essie Gay Roberts was most helpful during my visit to Maxwell.

Herb Mason and his assistant, Clay McCutchan, at the Air Force Special Operations Command history office at Hurlburt Field, Florida, at first apologized for having so little material—and then began pulling detailed reports off their shelves going back to World War II. Of particular value were reports and original doc-uments saved and collected by Col. Robert Fish, a commander of the Carpetbaggers in Europe during World War II. Fish and his neighbor, Col. J. W. Bradbury, USAF retired, who served with the Carpetbaggers and has collected a good deal of information about their contacts with the resistance force, were particularly helpful during interviews in San Antonio, Texas, where they now live.

Another invaluable source of anecdotal information was the past issues of the *Air Commando Association Newsletter,* in which many special operators had told their personal stories.

For my account of the operations of the Air Resupply and Communications Service in the 1950s I am indebted to Carl H. Bernhardt, Jr., of Cheshire, Connecticut, who sent me a complete file of the Air Resupply and Communications Association's newsletter on a computer diskette.

Air Force public affairs officers at Hurlburt and Kirtland Air Force Base in Albuquerque, New Mexico, were particularly helpful in setting up interviews. At Hurlburt, I had the help of Shirley Sikes, Lt. Sean McKenna, and Sandy Henry, who keep their office running. At Kirtland, a week of interviews was ably managed by Senior Airman Jim Fisher, whose performance far exceeded his pay grade.

For an insight into what it is like to do the kind of flying special operations crews routinely do, I am indebted to Lt. Col. Michael E. Homan, Maj. Robert Abernathy, and Capt. Ed Meyer and their crews. With them, in a series of flights, I spent more than nine hours in the air in the Pave Low helicopter, flying through the New Mexico mountains in the dark at two hundred feet, refueling from an HC-130 Combat Shadow tanker—again in the dark—and flying formation and landing at rough landing zones in the mountains with the aid of night-vision goggles.

I am indebted to MSgt. Timothy Hadrych, with whom I flew at Kirtland, for permitting me to use the remarkable pictures he took during the rescue of Lt. Devon Jones during Desert Storm.

Particular thanks are due to Col. William Hudspeth, Chair of the Department of Special Operations Forces at the Air University at Maxwell Air Force Base, for reviewing my manuscript for accuracy. The opinions expressed and any remaining errors are, of course, my responsibility.

Thanks are due, too, to my wife, Mary, for her patience; to my agent, Mike Hamilburg; to my new editor at Presidio Press, E. J. McCarthy, and to Cary Ryan, a most meticulous copy editor.

PART 1
Birth of the Air Commandos

CHAPTER 1

The Day Thursday Came on Sunday

At 6:12 P.M. on Sunday, 5 March 1944, a twin-engine C-47 transport plane lumbered down the grass airstrip at Lalaghat, near the eastern border of India. Behind it bounced a glider, attached to the plane by a three-hundred-foot nylon towrope.

Thus began one of the most imaginative and daring exploits in military history, an enterprise that was to foreshadow many of the successes—and some of the failures—that lay in the future for Air Force special operations.

By the time the plane had completed a full circle and come back over the airfield, it was still only 2,500 feet in the air. From Lalaghat, it had to struggle up to 8,000 feet to cross the Chin Hills and then penetrate 160 miles into the center of Japanese-occupied Burma.

The goal of Operation Thursday, as it was called, was to deliver three brigades of British and colonial troops far behind the Japanese lines to carry out a series of raids, cutting rail lines and roads, blasting bridges, and generally making life miserable for the Japanese, who had driven the British out of Burma with remarkable speed two years before.

The first plane was quickly followed by two more planes, with their gliders in tow. It was the job of the glider crews in these

3

pathfinders to land in the dark at a rough clearing in the jungle that had been named Broadway, after the New York boulevard, and prepare as best they could for the arrival of sixty more gliders. Forty minutes after the first takeoff, the rest of the force began rolling down the runway at one-minute intervals, with each C-47 towing two gliders. The gliders were seriously overloaded—with men, mules, bulldozers, food, ammunition, and other supplies.

Even before the first pathfinder left the ground, Operation Thursday had already gone badly wrong. The original plan had been to dispatch eighty gliders during the long moonlit night, half of them carrying part of the force to Broadway, the other half carrying the rest of the force to another landing site a few miles away code-named Picadilly, for the London avenue. But a bare fifteen minutes before 5 P.M.—a takeoff time that would permit the first pathfinder to land just after dark—last-minute photographs revealed that the planned landing strip at Picadilly was blocked by large teak logs.

A worried group of officers gathered around the photos. On hand for the start of the operation were British Maj. Gen. William J. Slim, Air Marshal Sir John E. A. Baldwin, commander of the third tactical Air Force, American Maj. Gen. George Stratemeyer, the top American air commander in the area, and Brig. Gen. William D. Old, commander of the United States Troop Carrier Command. But the major burden of deciding how to respond to this bad news fell on three lower-ranking officers, one an eccentric Briton recently promoted to brigadier, and two American Army Air Forces colonels.

Brigadier General Orde C. Wingate was the driving force behind Operation Thursday. It was his dream to insert a fighting force deep behind enemy lines in a position to cause damage and disruption far out of proportion to its numbers. He had tried his plan in Burma the year before. It had failed, with serious losses. Colonel Philip G. Cochran and Col. John R. Alison had been personally selected by General of the Army Henry H. Arnold, commander of the Army Air Forces, to put together an air organization to support Wingate on a second try. With a small, dedicated air force to move his men and keep them supplied, to provide air cover, harass the enemy, and—most important—pluck his wounded men out of the jungle and hurry them to hospitals in India, Wingate's plan might have a chance this time.

As the officers studied the photographs, taken that afternoon from a B-25 bomber, there was no doubt that the airstrip was not usable. Did that mean the Japanese had learned what was coming and blocked Picadilly? Did the fact that Broadway and Chowringhee, another potential landing spot named for the main thoroughfare in Calcutta, appeared clear mean they were safe landing zones? Or did it mean the Japanese had purposely left Broadway and Chowringhee undisturbed, planning to ambush the Allied force as it landed?

Within the hour, a decision had been made: the operation would go ahead. But the Picadilly landing was scrubbed and twenty of the forty gliders scheduled for that site were added to the forty scheduled for Broadway. If the Japanese were lying in wait there, it would be a very bloody night.

While Cochran and Wingate waited at Lalaghat, Alison took the controls of the third glider scheduled to land. Although he had flown almost every type of plane in the American inventory, he had practically no experience in the cockpit of a glider. Despite his unfamiliarity with the craft, he landed safely and immediately took charge of the airfield operation at Broadway, preparing for the stream of gliders that would soon come sliding noiselessly out of the dark sky.

The pathfinders landed safely. But they quickly found that the aerial photographs showing a smooth landing field were dangerously deceptive. The even surface shown in the pictures was formed by waist-high grass. It covered ruts made by logs as they were dragged across the clearing, holes where water buffaloes wallowed, and the stumps of trees cut down to form the clearing.

At this point, there was nothing the pathfinders could do about the condition of the airstrip. Their radio was broken, so all they could do was put out marker lights and await the arrival of the follow-on gliders.

Smudge pots outlined a diamond-shaped landing area. Off in

the jungle, a single flare was set. The pilots were told to cut loose from the tow plane as they passed over the flare, then hold their speed at a steady eighty knots, aiming to land within the diamond-shaped field. Without engines, they had little control over their trajectories, although one pilot had enough momentum to hop his glider over one that had landed in his path.

Virtually every landing was a crash landing. Gliders tore off their landing gear on the ruts or stumps and stopped abruptly. Following gliders, dropping onto the dark field, smashed into those already on the ground. Two gliders crashed into the jungle short of the field, killing all aboard. Another, carrying a small bull-dozer, overshot the runway and crashed, but the crew survived.

After each pair of gliders landed, Alison and his crew frantically worked to avoid collisions on the ground by rearranging the smudge pots they had set out to mark the diamond-shaped landing area.

Before the pathfinders had taken off, two code words had been agreed upon. If all was well, the signal would be a cryptic *PORK-SAUSAGE*. If there was trouble, the signal would be *SOYA-LINK*—the name of a meat substitute despised by the British troops.

For hours, there was no word at all. Cochran, Wingate, and their superiors waited through the night as additional gliders took off toward an unknown fate. One of Alison's radios had been destroyed in the landing. His other radio was badly damaged. When it was finally repaired, he sent the code word *SOYA-LINK*—the bad news message—and it was received back at Lalaghat at 2:27 A.M.—more than eight hours after the first gliders had departed. Cochran, assuming the airstrip was under attack, recalled the aircraft that were still in the air.

In the darkest hours, just before dawn, Operation Thursday had all the earmarks of a major disaster. The commanders back in India, their fears reinforced by the cryptic message from Broadway, fully believed they had sent the force into a Japanese trap. On the ground at Broadway, there was wreckage everywhere. Of the thirty-seven gliders that had landed, only four were still flyable.

But what later came to be called "the luck of special operations" was intact. Casualties were surprisingly light. Twenty-four men were killed and thirty-three were injured badly enough to require evacuation. But the gliders had managed to deliver five hundred thirty-nine men, three mules, and nearly fifteen tons of supplies during the night. And, best of all, there was no sign the Japanese knew of the landing.

CHAPTER 2
The Reluctant Warriors

Americans remember Pearl Harbor. But often forgotten are the scope and speed of the Japanese advance through Southeast Asia. Within little more than two months of the attack on the Hawaiian Islands on 7 December 1941, they swept south to the islands bordering Australia.

The attack on Burma (now Myanmar) began on 23 December 1941 with air raids on the capital of Rangoon (now Yangon). The British force in Burma was small, poorly supplied, and poorly trained for the kind of war it would have to fight in the jungle-covered mountains of Southeast Asia. But commanders counted on the rugged north-south mountain ranges, the thick jungle, and the broad rivers to slow the Japanese advance until it bogged down in the rains and floods of the annual monsoon.

They also counted on their naval stronghold at Singapore to prevent a seaborne invasion of Burma, and on neighboring Thailand to provide a protective buffer to the east. But Singapore fell to the Japanese on 15 February 1942, a month ahead of schedule, and the defense of Thailand collapsed after only eight hours of fighting.

If the Japanese had played by the British rules and stuck to the roads, the British might have held on until the monsoon. But the

Japanese refused to be pinned down to the roads and rail lines. Instead, they sent small units through the jungles to slash away at the British in hit-and-run raids and ambushes. Their tactic was so successful that they beat the monsoon, driving the disorganized British before them.

On 8 March, the British abandoned Rangoon. Major General William J. Slim, the commander of a two-division British corps, fled north along the Irrawaddy River valley and crossed into India on 16 May with twelve thousand troops. He left behind another thirteen thousand men, many of whom managed later to escape into India.

American Lt. Gen. Joseph W. Stilwell, commanding a Chinese force in northern Burma, slipped across the border into India with a ragtag collection of one hundred soldiers on 19 May.

Stilwell gave a blunt appraisal of the outcome of the battle for Burma: "We got a hell of a beating. We got run out of Burma and it is humiliating as hell."

For the British, it was the biggest and longest retreat in history—and one of the most mortifying.

The British, strained by war in Europe, North Africa, and the Pacific, might still have made a more effective defense of Burma if they had seen it as the Japanese did—as both more vulnerable and more important than it seemed to the British.

For the Japanese, Burma was a plum well worth plucking, especially since it fell so easily. The nation's 12 million acres of rice paddies produced a crop of 8 million tons, of which 3 million tons could be diverted to feed the far-flung Japanese force.

By capturing Burma, the Japanese also came into control of the southern terminus of the Burma Road. Built in 1937, the 717-mile road wound its way over rugged mountains between Lashio, in Burma, and K'un-ming, in southern China. It provided the main route for supplies destined for the armies of Chinese Generalissimo Chiang Kai-Shek. Although Chiang and his corrupt warlords often seemed more intent on fighting other Chinese than on ousting the Japanese, who controlled much of the country, or inclined not to fight at all, the threat of Chinese opposition kept thousands of Japanese troops pinned down. By cutting off this last trickle of supplies from the outside world, the Japanese hoped to free more of their men to carry on the war elsewhere.

Most ambitious was the Japanese plan to seize India, then the major British colony, and link up with the Germans moving eastward from North Africa.

While this disaster for the Allies was unfolding, Wingate, then a colonel, arrived in India on 19 March with an unorthodox plan in mind for dealing with the Japanese in Burma. With his full black beard, gleaming eyes, and irascible temperament, Wingate had the look and manners of an Old Testament prophet—and received much the same kind of welcome traditionally accorded to prophets.

Generals much his senior had ambitious plans—most of which came to naught—for cranking up a major frontal offensive to drive the Japanese back out of Burma. But Wingate brought with him a reputation gained from his command of guerrilla units operating against the Italians in Libya and the Arabs in Palestine. Perhaps because the situation in southern Asia was so desperately bad, Wingate was listened to more seriously than a relatively junior officer with such unorthodox ideas might otherwise have been.

General Slim said of him that he was "a strange, excitable, moody creature, but he had a fire in him. He could ignite other men."

Although the conventional wisdom was that British soldiers could not live and fight in the jungle as the Japanese did, Wingate insisted that properly trained soldiers could not only take advantage of the jungles but could beat the Japanese at their own game.

He was given command of a brigade of British and colonial troops and set about training them to operate alone far behind enemy lines, moving stealthily through the jungle to chip away at the enemy's supply lines—and his morale. As Wingate supervised the training, he acted as a model. Whenever he moved about the training ground, he ran from one point to another at full tilt, leaving panting aides trailing in his rear. When the time for putting his force into action neared, he marched them overland from the railhead at Dimapur to Imphal—a distance of 133 miles. They carried no rations; instead, he arranged for supplies to be dropped to them from the air during the eight-day march.

To this unorthodox force, Wingate gave a distinctive, unorthodox name. He called them the Chindits—a corruption of the Burmese word *chinthe,* the fierce dragonlike creature whose likeness guards Burmese temples.

Between 8 and 10 February 1943, in an operation code-named Longcloth, three thousand Chindits of the 77th Indian Infantry Brigade crossed into Burma on foot and penetrated deep into the country. Their first few weeks were a distinct success. They cut the key rail line between Mandalay and Myitkyina in more than seventy-five places.

But two key elements of Wingate's plan were missing. Since his soldiers, traveling on foot, could not provide their own artillery support, Wingate counted on the Royal Air Force to provide him with close air support. Whether because of inability or lack of willingness on the part of the air arm, he didn't get the support he needed. Wingate had also counted on linking his operation to an offensive by conventional forces. He didn't get that either.

As Wingate pictured the situation, the Japanese would be so busy dealing with the conventional assault that they wouldn't be able to turn and swat at him as he chewed on them from the rear. But without an offensive to keep them busy, the Japanese were able to turn their attention to the Chindits.

Operation Longcloth turned into a disaster. Without a source of supplies, the men were forced to live on the meat of their pack mules. When that ran out, they subsisted on snakes and rats. If a Chindit was wounded or sick and couldn't keep up with his colleagues, he was left behind with a rifle, a canteen of water, and, sometimes, a Bible.

Wingate and his Chindits made it back across the border into India in early June. He brought out 2,182 of his original force, but most of them were unfit for duty because of their cruel ordeal in the jungles of Burma.

It is more a measure of how bad things were for the Allies in mid-1943 than any significant successes Wingate achieved that he and his Chindits became public—and official—heroes. Despite the licking they had taken, the Chindits had, for a time at least, showed that the Japanese were not the only soldiers who could use the jungle to their advantage.

British Prime Minister Winston Churchill, who had often battled his nation's tradition-bound generals and admirals in support of his own unorthodox schemes, became Wingate's most enthusiastic admirer. When he departed in late August for the Quadrant Conference in Quebec, where he met with President Franklin D. Roosevelt to plan the future course of the war, Churchill took Wingate along and had him explain his plans for a renewed assault against the Japanese in Burma.

Roosevelt and Churchill were guided by quite different objectives in their planning for the war on the Asian mainland. Churchill was primarily interested in restoring and strengthening the British Empire. This included driving the Japanese back out of Burma. But it also involved keeping China relatively weak and thus less of a threat to the empire in the future. Roosevelt, on the other hand, wanted a stronger wartime China—as a possible base for air attacks on the Japanese homeland and a staging area for an invasion of the home islands.

Wingate's plan, with its potential for weakening the Japanese hold on portions of the British Empire and providing the opportunity to reopen the Burma Road into China, appealed to both Churchill and Roosevelt.

As Wingate outlined his plan in Quebec, what he had in mind was basically a larger-scale repeat of Longcloth. He proposed a force of four brigades—two to march into Burma and two in reserve to relieve the first two after ninety days in the field. And, mindful of the lack of support Longcloth had received from the Royal Air Force, he insisted on his own little air force—sixteen C-47 transport planes to move men and supplies, one bomber squadron to serve as flying artillery for each brigade, and a light-plane force to evacuate the sick and wounded.

Roosevelt, whose enthusiasm for the unusual and unorthodox rivalled Churchill's, seized upon Wingate's plan. He gave the task of providing Wingate's air support to General Arnold. For Arnold, World War II was not only a war to be won but also an opportunity to demonstrate how victory could be achieved through air power. His primary goal was to build a giant armada of planes to carry the war to Germany and later to Japan, destroying the enemy's ability, and will, to fight. He was impatient with anything that detracted from this goal. But he had his orders from Roosevelt, and he set about carrying them out.

To set up the organization to support Wingate, Arnold turned first to the ranks of the veterans of the prewar Army Air Corps, men he had served with, or at least knew by reputation. At some point, Arnold worked up a real enthusiasm for this project, seeing in Wingate's proposal the chance to demonstrate yet another aspect of air power—the ability to support sizable Army units behind enemy lines. But, whatever enthusiasm he had in the beginning, he had trouble communicating it to potential commanders of the special unit.

Phil Cochran, then a lieutenant colonel, had joined the Air Corps after graduating from Ohio State University in 1935. He became a fighter pilot and advanced to become a squadron commander before the war. Twice, he roomed with another young pilot, John Alison, and they became good friends.

When the United States entered the war, Cochran was assigned to take thirty-five pilots into North Africa as replacements for pilots lost in the Allied invasion. They were ordered to deliver their planes and themselves by catapulting their P-40s off the deck of a British carrier. Neither Cochran nor his pilots—many of them barely out of flying school—had ever seen a catapult, let alone been launched by one. Four planes and two pilots were lost in the operation.

Cochran fought in North Africa until June of 1943, sometimes flying as many as five missions a day against Field Marshal Erwin Rommel's tanks and supply lines. When he returned to the States, he was badly worn out. He was also a public hero. A fellow Ohio State graduate, Milton Caniff, had become a popular cartoonist. He made Cochran—or Flip Corkin, as he called him—the hero of his comic strip, *Terry and the Pirates.*

After a brief rest, Cochran got what he wanted most: orders to Europe, where the new P-47 fighters were being introduced into the "real war." Then he received a telegram ordering him to report to General Arnold. When he arrived in Washington, he learned for the first time that he was under consideration to command a new air force unit in Burma.

"If ever I was going to shoot myself, it was then, because I just couldn't see it," he recalled later. "I just couldn't stomach it. I rebelled so strongly against that thing. I probably made a damn fool of myself, but I no longer wanted to go to Burma than anything. . . . I screamed like a stuck hog right off the bat when I heard what they had in mind."

Cochran went to the Pentagon and was escorted in to see Arnold—"the rankingest person I ever would get to see." He came as close as he could to outright defiance.

Arnold let him blow off steam and then dismissed him: "That's enough for now. I'll see you later."

As he headed for the door, Cochran recalled a chance meeting earlier. He had run into his old friend Alison and rightly surmised that he was one of the five other officers rumored to be under consideration for the Burma post.

"I'm not supposed to know who the other five are," he told Arnold, "but I ran into a guy in the Pentagon yesterday, and I know he is here for the same thing. That's the guy you ought to take. He is a grand person, and that's Johnny Alison."

The next day, Cochran saw Alison after he had had his own interview with Arnold.

"We walked down the hall together, and he was as close to crying as any tough little fighter pilot I ever saw in my life," Cochran recalled. "He was just terribly discouraged, and he had refused it, too. But he was afraid that he was going to get it. I told him that I told Arnold to give it to him."

Alison had had a distinguished and unusual wartime career. A veteran of the prewar Air Corps, he was sent to England in 1941, before the United States entered the war. He then went on to Russia with Harry Hopkins, President Roosevelt's personal representative, and remained to test-fly P-40 fighters being delivered under the lend-lease program. With that job completed, he received a promise from Lt. Col. Townsend Griffiss, who was returning to Washington. He said he would arrange a combat command for Alison as soon as he arrived back in the States.

Alison started home but stopped over in Teheran, Iran, expecting word from Washington any day. While waiting, he helped assemble A-20 light bombers being shipped to the Russians through Iran.

He ended up remaining there for six months. Only later did he learn that Griffiss's plane had been misidentified while crossing the English Channel and shot down by Spitfire fighters, with the loss of all aboard.

Finally, in the spring of 1942, Alison received the combat assignment he had been seeking. He was ordered to fly directly from Teheran to China. He flew the "hump" from India into China and became deputy commander of the 75th Squadron—part of what, before the war, had been the "volunteer" Flying Tigers—American pilots supporting the Chinese. Alison distinguished himself in combat, shooting down six Japanese planes to become an ace and destroying another Japanese plane on the ground.

When Arnold called Alison in, he reacted just as negatively to the Burma assignment as Cochran had. Both he and Cochran understood the job to be primarily providing a force of light planes to carry supplies and evacuate the casualties for Wingate's operation. Both wanted command assignments with real airplanes in a real war. Alison told Arnold he had just the man for him: Phil Cochran.

Arnold settled the matter by choosing both men, making them cocommanders of the project.

He told them: "To hell with the paperwork; go out and fight." Cochran and Alison took him much more literally than he probably imagined. At one point, when Cochran saw a dozen typewriters among the items to be shipped to their new headquarters in India, he simply crossed them off the list.

Quickly realizing that having two heads for a military organization was a dumb idea, Cochran and Alison agreed that Cochran would be the commander and Alison his deputy. But they were so closely attuned that decisions made by one man were almost automatically backed by the other. Together, they set out to build a force unique in Air Force history, in the process enlarging it far beyond what Wingate, Churchill, Roosevelt, and, probably, Arnold, had envisioned.

CHAPTER 3

A "Grandiose Scheme"

Cochran and Alison set up shop with offices in the Pentagon and in the Hay Adams House, a hotel just across Lafayette Square from the White House. Tentatively, they called their operation Project 9.

To learn just what it was they were getting into, Cochran flew to London to meet with Wingate and Lord Louis Mountbatten, who was preparing to take over as the new supreme Allied commander in Southeast Asia. It quickly became apparent to Cochran that what was required was a substantially bigger and more capable force than the relatively modest air arm that Wingate had in mind.

Barely a month after getting their orders from Arnold, Cochran and Alison had put together the outline of the force they thought was needed to do the job and had it approved by both Arnold and his boss, Gen. George C. Marshall. Not only did it include the transport planes, bombers, and light aircraft desired by Wingate, but it also called for fighter planes and gliders. Project 9 even included some experimental helicopters Alison had obtained over the objections of everyone involved in their development.

The two young officers presented their plan to Arnold at the Pentagon with some trepidation. They had gone far beyond the original concept of a small force of light planes to evacuate wounded Chindits and built it into what Cochran admitted was a "grandiose scheme."

Arnold read the plan, gave Cochran and Alison a sly look, initialed the plan, and said: "All right, do it!"

There was only one major modification to their plan. They asked for P-38 Lightning fighters. When they were not available, they substituted P-47 Thunderbolts. Those were not available either, so they finally settled for the P-51 Mustang.

Instead of limiting themselves to supporting Wingate's Chindits once they had marched through the jungles and set up bases in Burma, they planned to bring the commandos themselves in by air and plunk them down far behind the enemy's front lines.

While Cochran was sketching out the broad outlines of the force to support Wingate, Alison was busy rounding up the men and equipment they would need. With the authority given them by Arnold and their wide circle of acquaintances in the Air Corps, they were able to reach out and bring in the best people they could find to get the job done.

Members of the new organization were all volunteers. They were not told where they were going or what they were going to do. They were simply told that the operation would involve combat, that it would last no more than six months—and that they shouldn't expect any promotions.

Training began on 1 October 1943 at two North Carolina airfields. The fighters and gliders were based at Seymour-Johnson field, the light planes at Raleigh-Durham. The force was rapidly growing to its eventual size of 346 aircraft. That was as many aircraft as one would normally find in a full air force wing. But the ground and aircrews totalled only 523 men—far fewer than the 2,000 normally found in a wing.

The light planes were the older L-1 Vigilant and the more modern L-5 Sentinel. Although the L-5 was newer and faster, the L-1 was in some ways more desirable because it could carry more wounded and operate from a shorter field than the L-5. Both were single-engine, high-wing monoplanes.

The L-1 had a fixed, rather than a variable-pitch, propeller, limiting the control the pilot had over the plane. It also had an unorthodox combination flap-aileron system that permitted the plane to fly very slowly. But it also made the plane awkward to handle. One pilot likened it to "dancing with a fat lady."

From the first, training focused on low-level flying. When residents of Raleigh-Durham complained that the planes were buzzing their rooftops at one hundred feet, their commander ordered them to fly lower.

For the American Army, the use of gliders as troop carriers was an untested concept. What was known about their use was not very encouraging. The Germans had used gliders in the invasion of Crete with disastrous results. But the United States Army was still feeling its way along.

The Waco gliders assembled at Seymour-Johnson were equipped with a special new gyro towing device, similar to an autopilot, to make it easier for the pilot to maintain the proper position behind the tow plane. To recover the gliders for reuse, the C-47 tow planes were fitted out with a reel designed to "snatch" a glider from the ground—a maneuver in which the transport plane flew slowly overhead, snagged a line attached to the glider, and plucked it off the ground.

Crews practiced both day and night with both single and double tows. Emphasis was placed on nighttime operations because the plan was to deliver Wingate's Chindits at night, with no lights on the planes or gliders.

The pilots had a difficult choice: If they flew in the high tow position, behind and above the tow plane, the air was smoother and it was easier to maintain tension on the tow line. But, at night, it was almost impossible to see the unlighted tow plane against the dark earth.

If they flew in the low tow position, behind and slightly below the tow plane, they could see the glow of the plane's exhaust, but there was more turbulence and it was much more difficult to maintain the proper tension on the tow line. If the glider pilot overtook the tow plane, the line could get tangled up. If he took up the slack too abruptly, he could tear the cable attachment loose.

Gliders were not the only unorthodox flying machines to capture the attention of the Project 9 leaders. Through their connections in the Air Corps, Cochran and Alison learned that a few experimental helicopters were being tested at Wright-Patterson field near Dayton, Ohio. To the fledgling air commandos, the helicopter—if it worked as promised—seemed ideal as a way of plucking wounded or sick Chindits out of the jungle, from spots where even a light plane could not land and take off again.

They asked for the helicopters, but at every step, they were turned down. Finally, they appealed to Arnold himself.

"All right," Arnold replied, "I got you everything. Now, I did what I promised you guys, but there is no way you can get those helicopters. I just can't do it. . . . They are all taken."

A short time later, Alison ran into Harry Hopkins, with whom he had traveled to Russia before the United States entry into the war. He mentioned the helicopter problem to Hopkins. A few days later, word came through that they would get four helicopters to try out in the jungle operation.

Arnold asked Cochran how they had done it.

"Well, General, you just have to know the right people," Cochran replied.

The schedule called for two and a half months of intensive training—a dauntingly short period for such a pioneering endeavor. But in late October, the training period was abruptly cut short by forty-five days. The crews were ordered to pack up and head for India.

Cochran left on 3 November 1943 while Alison remained behind to manage the move. The C-47s and most of the men followed quickly behind Cochran. Their route took them from Miami to Puerto Rico, Trinidad, British Guiana, Brazil, Ascension Island, the Gold Coast of Africa, Nigeria, Sudan, Aden, Masirah Island, and thence to Karachi, India.

The light planes, fighters, and gliders were packaged up and sent by sea. Cochran commandeered a dirigible hangar at the Karachi airport to assemble the fighters. He was disappointed to find that the first load of P-51s, which had been lashed to the deck of the transport ship, were so badly damaged by the seas and salt corrosion that they had to be replaced. A similar assembly operation for the gliders was set up at Barrackpore field near Calcutta.

For a brief time after the planes and men of Project 9 arrived in India, the unit was known as the 5318th Provisional Unit (Air). But General Arnold had taken to calling them air commandos, and on 29 March 1944, the designation was changed once more, to the 1st Air Commando Group. From the beginning, this unorthodox military unit was viewed with a mixture of envy, distrust, and covetousness by the commanders of other military units in the area. Their first inclination was to absorb the new unit into their existing organizations. And, if they couldn't do that, they certainly wanted to strip the new outfit of its new planes and equipment. With strong support from Arnold, Cochran fended them off. As his ace in the hole, he carried a "Dear Dickie" personal note from Arnold to Mountbatten urging him to support this unusual outfit and let it do its job.

Late in December 1943, Alison joined Cochran in India, and on Christmas Eve, they flew to the Assam region, on the eastern border of India, adjoining Burma, to look for a base of operations. They chose two sites. The field at Lalaghat, with a sixty-three-hundred-foot runway, was chosen for the transports and gliders. The field at nearby Hailakandi, with its forty-five-hundred-foot runway, was chosen for the fighters and the bombers later added to the force. The light planes were divided between the two fields. Both had grass airstrips that would turn into lakes, or at least swamps, when the monsoon rains came. The few buildings at each field were bamboo huts.

On 29 December, the American glider and transport crews began training with the Chindits. Ten days later they conducted a twenty-glider operation in which four hundred men were landed on a mud field near Lalitpur. The operation was successful, but when it was over, the gliders remained where they had landed, stuck in the mud. One by one, tow planes swooped down low over the field and "snatched" the gliders out of the mud and into the air. It was very much a case of on-the-job training.

For the Chindits, the glider-borne operation was a daunting challenge. It was probably better than walking for days through the jungle with heavy packs, hacking away at vines and always on the alert for an enemy ambush. But the idea of dropping out of the night sky into a rough clearing in the jungle in a powerless balsa-wood glider was not much better. If anything went wrong, there was no chance to pull up and go around again. If the craft went down in the jungle, it meant almost certain death for all aboard.

On 15 February 1944, such an accident occurred during a night towing operation. Four of the British troops and three Americans were killed. The Americans feared the Chindits might decide it was better to walk after all. But a message came from Wingate's headquarters: "Please be assured that we will go with your boys any place, any time, any where." Even if redundant, that vote of confidence was seized on by the Americans, and the phrase "Any Place, Any Time, Any Where" remains a motto of the air commandos today.

Even though the Americans were in the process of making aviation history, they faced a problem as old as armies: how do you get a mule to do what you want him to? In this case, the question was how to get a big British army mule into a glider and keep him from kicking the craft apart. Once the Chindits arrived at their forward bases behind Japanese lines, they would need the mules to help them carry the food, ammunition, light artillery, and other supplies for their hit-and-run attacks on the enemy's lines of communications. The mules had already been de-brayed so they would not give the Chindits' position away as they sneaked through the jungle.

The glider floors were reinforced to carry the weight of the mules. Their legs were hobbled to keep them from kicking. Their heads were tied down to keep their long ears out of the control cables, and they were confined in slings to keep them from moving around.

The question still remained: how do you coax a mule into something as unfamiliar as a glider?

Cochran recalled how they attacked the problem as a terrible, insurmountable thing and had "all manner of wild schemes of how we were going to do this."

But then it occurred to them to see if there were any farm boys who knew anything about mules.

"One of these kids, not from his experience, but just from his plain, practical mind, set us all on our ear," Cochran said. "This kid just . . . said, 'Why don't we just try walking them in and see what they do?' Lo and behold, that's what we did, and the mules took to it just like they take to everything else. It didn't concern them one bit. It amazed us, the wisdom of this youngster, after all our planning, that the simplest thing was, 'Well, why don't you ask the mule, really?' So we asked the mule, and we asked him to go in the glider."

The first test mule-lift occurred on the night of 10 January. The mule handlers were told that, if a mule acted up, they were to shoot him.

The mules, as the farm boy had predicted, walked docilely into the glider and took their places. When the glider trundled down the runway and became airborne, they seemed unconcerned. And when the glider banked, the mules banked, too, just as though they were veteran frequent fliers.

As the time for the Chindits' foray into Burma approached, the air force supporting them grew to impressive proportions.

Worried they would not get the air support they needed from the British, the American commanders requested—and got— twelve B-25H bombers from the United States Tenth Air Force. In reality, the twin-engine B-25 in this configuration was a combination fighter-bomber. It carried six .50-caliber machine guns and a forward-firing 75mm cannon. It carried a crew of five. But only one of them was a pilot, and he flew it like a fighter plane, aiming through the same kind of gunsight used in fighters for air-to-air combat and squeezing a trigger on the control wheel to fire his guns. In fact, many of the bomber pilots were fighter pilots, and they switched back and forth, flying one mission in a bomber and then strapping into a fighter for the afternoon sortie.

At its peak, the unit had 346 aircraft: 150 CG-4A troop gliders; 25 TG-5 training gliders; 100 L-1 and L-5 light planes; 30 P-51A fighters; 13 C-47 transports; 12 UC-64 small transports; 12 B-25H bombers; and 4 YR-4 helicopters.

While the glider and transport crews trained with the Chindits, the bomber, fighter, and light-plane crews pitched in to help out in the war.

On 3 February 1944, Cochran took a flight of five Mustangs into combat for the first time, and on 12 February, the newly arrived B-25s went to war. Wingate flew along in one plane and was visibly impressed when the pilot fired his 75mm cannon and blew the roof off a large building. The pilot didn't tell Wingate he was aiming at a railway switch two hundred yards from the building he had hit.

From 3 February until 4 March, the day before Operation Thursday, the unit flew fifty-four fighter-bomber missions.

On one mission, Cochran led a flight of sixteen Mustangs in an attack on a Japanese supply depot in Mandalay. As they began their attack, they got careless and were surprised by what Cochran described as "a horde" of Japanese Zero fighters. Because the Japanese had the jump on them, Cochran shouted orders by radio to his men to get "down and out"—dive for the ground and run for home. He stayed over the target to make sure his men had broken off the engagement. When he headed for home, he ran into the Zeros that had been chasing the other American fighters.

One of the Americans had been shot down. It was mistakenly reported that the downed pilot was Cochran. Before he could clarify the report, his hometown newspaper had printed a headline reporting his death in action.

When Cochran returned to his base, he was grounded. It had belatedly occurred to Wingate and others that he knew too much about the forthcoming operation to risk having him taken prisoner by the Japanese.

The light-plane pilots also got the opportunity to practice exactly the kind of operations they were slated to perform as they supported the Chindits in their foray into Burma. A British army, attacking the Japanese on the Arakan front, along the Burma-India border, suffered a number of casualties. Within three weeks, seven hundred wounded or sick British troops were flown by the American light-plane pilots from the Arakan front to airfields in the rear, where they could be transferred to C-47s and moved back to hospitals in India.

Even the gliders got a chance at on-the-job training. One glider was called upon to insert a British patrol behind Japanese lines. They landed safely, but the glider was damaged, so the crew had to walk back to India. In another instance, on 29 February, two gliders carried folding boats, outboard motors, and gasoline to British troops preparing to cross the Chindwin River. They landed on a sandbar. The gliders were later snatched off the sandbar and flown back to Lalaghat.

By this time, the "snatch" technique had been improved to the point where it was possible for a C-47, flying at twenty feet altitude at night, to pick up a fully loaded glider. This was done through the use of a boom, with a hook attachment, extending from the plane. As it flew overhead, the hook caught the glider tow rope, which was suspended in a frame about twelve feet off the ground. Wingate was so intrigued that he insisted on being one of the passengers in the first test of this technique.

As the date neared for the beginning of Operation Thursday, it was only five months since the American aircrews had begun their training back in North Carolina and little more than three months since they had begun working with the Chindits. But, despite the brief time for preparations and training, everyone was ready to go—except for one thing. Wingate had insisted that it would be foolhardy to send his men into combat unless there was a major offensive to draw attention away from his small force. Despite many aborted plans, there was no Allied offensive ready to go.

The entire operation might have been called off. But the Japanese obliged by launching an offensive of their own, known as U-Go. Wingate gave the go-ahead for Operation Thursday.

CHAPTER 4
Deep in Enemy Territory

In the first hours of the landing at Broadway, the officers waiting back in India became convinced that the Japanese knew about the operation and had attacked the troops as they glided down to a rough landing. But the Japanese had not discovered the landing at Broadway—in fact, were not even aware of the Allies' effort to insert a powerful military force deep in territory they thought was theirs.

The Japanese knew that something was up, but they were badly mistaken in their assumption about what was going on.

What had happened was this:

As they boarded the gliders for Operation Thursday, the Chindit veterans of the Longcloth disaster the year before were determined not to be stranded again deep in enemy territory. Each man packed a little extra—extra food, extra ammunition. Somehow, even an extra horse was carried along. The gliders were supposed to take off carrying seventy-five hundred pounds—and that was stretching it. Instead, Cochran later estimated in a note to General Arnold, they were badly overloaded, carrying nine thousand pounds.

Almost as soon as they took off, the extra weight made itself felt. Two gliders crashed shortly after takeoff. Four more broke loose and landed in India without even crossing into Burma. As the tow planes struggled up over the Chin Hills, the glider pilots had difficulty maintaining the proper tension on the tow ropes. Even though there was a bright moon, haze in the air gave the sky a silvery glow that made it difficult for the pilots to see the tow planes. When word of the problems reached him, Cochran ordered the tow planes to turn on their lights and told the glider pilots to move up into the high tow station, where it would be easier to maintain the proper position.

By the time the new orders went into effect, nine gliders had broken loose and descended into Japanese-held territory on the eastern side of the Chindwin River.

The survivors of one of the gliders that landed in Japanese territory set out for India on foot. As they crossed the Chindwin River, Cpl. Estil I. Nienaber, who could not swim, was swept away in the swift current. He didn't call for help. Instead, he went silently to his death, avoiding a sound that might have alerted Japanese patrols. He is still remembered as one of the earliest air commando heroes. Most of the crews and passengers of the gliders that went down in enemy territory managed to return to India or make it on to Broadway.

Almost as though it had been planned that way, seven of the gliders landed close to various Japanese command posts. Two came down near the 31st Division headquarters. Two more landed near the 15th Division headquarters, and three were near regimental headquarters. The Japanese understandably assumed these landings were part of a small commando force assigned to knock out the Japanese leadership rather than part of a full-scale airborne invasion. They thus focused all their attention on defending their bastions of strength against this phantom threat rather than going out to look for the something bigger that was really going on. At least partially because of this unplanned diversion, it was a week or more before the Japanese understood the situation.

This diversion of the enemy's attention gave Alison and the men at Broadway the respite they needed to prepare their defenses and turn their rough clearing in the jungle into an airstrip that would soon become the busiest airport in the world. They had a big job ahead of them.

One of the two gliders that had crashed in the jungle carried the leader of the engineering team that was supposed to prepare the airstrip. He and all the others in the glider were killed. Alison turned to the senior surviving engineer officer, an inexperienced young second lieutenant.

When Alison asked how long it would take to make the airfield usable, he replied: "If I have it done by this afternoon, will that be too late?"

With help from the Chindits, the Americans set about clearing the wreckage of the gliders and, using bulldozers and mules, to smoothing the grassy field and turning it into a strip capable of handling C-47 transports.

At 4:30 P.M., they flashed word that a lighted, forty-three-hundred-foot runway would be ready to receive transport planes that night. An hour later, six planes took off from India, headed for Broadway. During that night, flying a virtual nonstop shuttle, the transports delivered sixty-two planeloads of men, mules, equipment, and supplies to Broadway.

The whole operation went so well that an elated Wingate moved up, by two days, his plans to deliver the 111th Brigade to the clearing code-named Chowringhee. As with the operation at Broadway, a glider-borne force was sent in to secure the field and prepare it for the landing of transport planes. But the glider carrying the sole bulldozer destined for the operation crashed, destroying the bulldozer and killing all onboard.

Another bulldozer was hurriedly flown over from Broadway, and a second was ordered flown in from Calcutta. Word came that the field would be cleared and lit late on the night of 7 March. At midnight, twenty-four planes took off, destined for Chowringhee. But then a radio message reported that only a twenty-seven-hundred-foot section of runway was lit—too short for the C-47s. The planes were recalled, although four of them didn't get the word and managed to land safely at Chowringhee despite the short runway.

Because of the problems with the Chowringhee operation, Cochran diverted all the transports to Broadway. During that night, Broadway received ninety-two planeloads—an average of sixteen planes an hour, or more than one every four minutes, all night long.

While the buildup continued, the other half of the air force Cochran and Alison had assembled was also busy. On 8 March, intelligence reported that the Japanese were massing aircraft in the Shwebo area, north of Mandalay. Twenty-one Mustangs took off from Hailakandi, each armed with one five-hundred-pound bomb. They found seventeen fighters on the ground at the Japanese airfield at Anisakan. After dropping their bombs, they roared back and forth across the field, raking it with machine-gun fire.

On the way home, the fighters passed over two other airfields, at Shwebo and Onbauk. At the two fields, they counted some sixty fighters, bombers, transports, and trainers, either landing or already on the ground. The Mustangs dove on the fields, firing their machine guns until their ammunition ran out. When they arrived back at Hailakandi, many of the same pilots climbed into the cockpits of the twelve B-25 bombers and headed back to the attack.

When the series of attacks was over, the airfields were ablaze and fourty-eight Japanese aircraft had been destroyed. In that one day, the air commando pilots had accounted for more than forty percent of all the Japanese aircraft destroyed in the entire China-Burma-India theater of war during the month of March and severely crippled both the Japanese offensive and the enemy's ability to strike back at the Chindits.

As soon as their bases were secure, the Chindits of the 3d Indian Division fanned out from Broadway and Chowringhee to begin harassing the Japanese in their hit-and-run raids. Operation Thursday—the movement of Wingate's force deep into Burma—officially ended on 11 March. But Broadway remained as a major staging area for the Chindits' operations.

It was in this phase of the operation that the light-plane force proved its worth. Flying from Broadway and a new base named Aberdeen (Wingate had closed down Chowringhee just before the Japanese hit it with a powerful force), small planes were able to land and take off from sandbars and tiny clearings in the jungle, delivering supplies and ferrying sick and wounded Chindits back to the jungle bases, where they were loaded into the bigger C-47s for evacuation to hospitals in India.

The pilots of the little planes—all enlisted men—flew literally at treetop level.

Stam Robertson of Plainville, Connecticut, who was a staff sergeant pilot, says, "I grin sometimes, what the FAA would think about me doing that. It got to the point when I came to a tree, I'd just raise one wing and go over it. One Brit I took out, he said: 'Gee, mate, don't these birds go any higher? I can see the bird nests down there.' I said: 'If we get higher, we're a target. Down here, we're hard to see.'"

Flying at such low altitudes made it very difficult to navigate, especially in the early days before the pilots learned their way around the area in which they were operating.

"It was hard to navigate," Robertson says. "I don't know if you've ever seen a hunting dog; he'll jump up to look around. I'd do the same thing: pull up to a hundred foot just to get a look around, and then I'd come right down again."

The maneuverability of the little planes and their ability to fly so low was their major protection against Japanese fighters. In a test before Operation Thursday began, a light plane was matched against a Mustang. The pilot of the speedy fighter never was able to get the little plane in his sights.

Richard D. Snyder, of Cumming, Georgia, was one of the young light-plane pilots.

"The first guy I flew out," he recalls, "had both of his testicles shot off. I felt so sorry for that man. When I picked him up, he was sitting over there drinking a cup of tea. That guy got up and walked to my plane, with both of his testicles shot off.

"When I was flying an L-1, if you put stretchers in it, you could only haul two. But I have hauled as many as seven if they were able to sit up. On one mission, I had a load of them in there; I had six or seven in there, and I thought they were Gurkha soldiers. When I got back to Broadway to unload 'em, this doctor said, 'Why are you bringing me these Jap prisoners?' I had a load of

Japanese prisoners and didn't know it. I had one sitting in there with his legs over my shoulders. Hell, I never saw any Japs before. I didn't know they were Japs. Some of them were wounded, but some of them weren't. I never could understand it. They just loaded 'em in there and said, 'take 'em out.'

"I hauled one Japanese officer out one time. I tied his thumbs together with strings and then tied them to the top of the airplane. And I was talking to him in pidgin English: 'No gun. You no shoot. I shoot you.' I flew him back to the base, and when I let him out of the airplane, he turned around and said, 'Thank you very much for the ride.' He could speak English better than I could, but he never said a word until he got out of the airplane."

Flying through the trees, landing on sandbars and on tiny strips in the jungle, often overloaded, the small planes were responsible for evacuating as many as fifteen hundred casualties, providing an enormous boost to the morale of the Chindits.

But there were some places that even the tiny planes couldn't go. Late in April, one of the light planes crashed near a road in Japanese-controlled territory. The pilot and his three injured passengers hid in the jungle. If they could not be rescued, they would have to try to walk the thirty miles or so to Aberdeen, hoping to avoid capture along the way.

James Phelan, a helicopter mechanic who had just arrived a few days before, recalls Cochran saying, "Let's try the eggbeater."

Lieutenant Carter Harman loaded the cabin of his little YR-4 helicopter with five-gallon cans of gasoline and took off from Lalaghat on 21 April and flew by stages to Aberdeen. Light planes carrying fuel met him on sandbars along the way. On 23 April, with Stam Robertson, in his L-1, leading the way, he flew out to the downed plane and ferried the pilot and the three casualties— one at a time—back to Aberdeen.

His exploit was the first use of a helicopter in combat. In the next few days, he flew another eighteen combat sorties. But the experimental craft was so badly underpowered that the engine finally failed, and the helicopter was taken out of service. The helicopter played a historic, but minor, role in these early days of the air commandos.

The Japanese finally found Broadway, a bustling air base deep in their territory, on 11 March. On that day, fighter-bombers made thirteen attacks on the base, and ground forces also arrived to try to put Broadway out of commission.

"When there was an attack going on, they'd call us on the radio and say, don't come home, they were under attack," Snyder recalls. "We'd fly out five or six miles, stay away from the base, and watch them while they were doing it, and when they'd leave, we'd go in and land."

The Japanese attacks did relatively little damage and never did succeed in knocking out Broadway.

The enemy did cause the Allies considerably more trouble near the city of Mawlu. On 17 March, a brigade of Chindits fortified a hill north of the city in a position to block traffic on the main north-south rail and road link between Mandalay and Myitkyina. While setting up shop in a fixed position was a violation of the Chindits' basic hit-and-run strategy, the fact that the air commandos were available to keep them supplied made it possible for them to remain there and deny the Japanese use of the road and rail lines.

The base came under almost constant attack by the Japanese, but, with help from the air commandos, the soldiers on the ground were able to beat them off.

So many bundles were dropped into the Chindit position that the hillside became covered with abandoned parachutes, and the pilots quickly nicknamed the position White City.

On 24 March, the operation received its most serious setback as the result of an accident rather than enemy action. Returning from a visit to Broadway, Wingate's B-25 flew into a hill, and he and the other eight men onboard, including two war correspondents, were killed.

Raymond J. Ruksas, of Phoenix, Arizona, who was one of the flying sergeants, and, half a century later, president of the Air Commando Association, recalls that day well:

"Wingate, the day he died, called us together and said they were so happy with the work we were doing he would do his very best to see we got commissions. I wondered, how is a guy in the British army going to get us commissions in the American Army? And then I figured, being Wingate, he just might do it. Six hours later, he was dead."

As Ruksas recalls, only a handful of planes were sent out to look for Wingate's plane when he was overdue at his next destination. From experience, they knew that, whenever someone was missing, they were likely to lose someone else looking for him. As it turned out, SSgt. Lloyd I. Samp found Wingate's plane—and then he crashed in the jungle. Robertson spotted Samp's plane and arranged for his rescue. They found him in a Burmese village.

"The headhunters were very nice to him," Robertson says.

Instead of replacing Wingate with one of his aides who shared his enthusiasm for long-range penetrations, General Slim put Maj. Gen. W. D. A. Lentaigne in charge. Lentaigne did not like Wingate personally and didn't agree with his hit-and-run tactics. He ordered the Chindits to combine into larger groups and assault major Japanese defensive positions. The troops had neither the training nor the heavy weapons needed for such operations.

By that time, however, the Chindits had already achieved a major goal of their operation: to disrupt Japanese plans for an invasion of India. In their U-Go operation, the Japanese hoped to cross the border near the town of Imphal, defeat the British IV Corps, and march across India to establish a puppet government. But the offensive was repulsed, and the Japanese were forced to retreat back into Burma, eventually giving up the northern portion of the country.

After the war, comments by Japanese officers and messages sent at the time revealed how much the airborne invasion had disrupted plans for the offensive.

General T. Numata, chief of staff of the Japanese southern army, said: "The difficulty encountered in dealing with the airborne forces was ever a source of worry to all the headquarters staffs of the Japanese army and contributed materially to the Japanese failure. . . ."

Even more telling was the message traffic from the headquarters of Lt. Gen. K. Sato, commander of the 31st Division. By May, his men were short of ammunition and almost all other supplies.

The food shortage was so severe that the troops were subsisting on grass and black slugs and suffering from sickness. Sato revolted.

"Since leaving the Chindwin, we have not received one bullet from you, nor a grain of rice," he said in a message to 15th Army headquarters. When he prepared to withdraw his forces from the front, he was threatened with court martial. He sent back a rebellious response: "Do what you please. I will bring you [the commander of the 15th Army] down with me. . . . The 15th Army has failed to send me supplies and ammunition since the operation began. This failure releases me from any obligation to obey the order—and in any case it would be impossible to comply."

By the time the Japanese were feeling the full effect of the attacks by the commando forces, the entire operation was already over. At the end of March, Alison was called back to Washington to begin the formation of two more air commando units—the Second and Third. Arnold had visions of these new units going back in the next dry season to conquer Burma. But, by the time they were formed, the war had changed, and they were incorporated into conventional units fighting in the Pacific.

By the end of April, the Chindits had been pulled back out of Burma, and the airfields at Lalaghat and Hailakandi, already knee-deep in water from the monsoon rains, had been abandoned for the monsoon season.

In a period of less than two months, the air commandos had demonstrated convincingly that it was possible to fly a significant force deep into enemy territory, set up and defend a base of operations, and cause major damage to the enemy's ability and will to fight.

The light-plane pilots thought their portion of the war was over—at least for the time being—but they were wrong.

"We thought we were going to come home," Richard Snyder recalls, "but they told us, since we didn't lose as many people as they thought we would, they were going to leave us there to go with the British troops the rest of the war. We did such a good job, they just said we could stay and help the British finish the war, thank you very much. We stayed on and supported the British troops all the way down to Rangoon. That took another year and a half. As they moved down, the British army would build a strip, and we'd move a squadron in there. We'd get their wounded and drop them supplies. And we did some artillery spotting for them."

Arnold called Cochran back to Washington and put him to work setting up an operation in Europe that would make Thursday seem like a little sideshow.

CHAPTER 5

Aerial Invasion of Germany

W
hen Cochran arrived back in the United States in the late spring of 1944, at about the time of the Normandy invasion in Europe, he was badly in need of a rest. He had either been in combat or in demanding command positions for more than two years. And he also suffered from hypoglycemia, a blood-sugar disorder that causes extreme fatigue. Although he had hidden the nature of his problem from his superiors so he could remain on flight status, he could not hide his fatigue. An officer from the inspector general's office, on a swing through India, had seen how run-down he was and recommended that he be relieved of his job.

Cochran managed to hang on in India until Operation Thursday was all wrapped up and then flew home. General Arnold hustled him off to a rehabilitation center in upstate New York and, in effect, offered him his choice of his next job.

Before Cochran had completed his stay in the rehab center—and before he had decided what he would like to do next—Arnold called him in and gave him an intriguing new assignment.

Having been impressed by the success of the airborne invasion of Burma, Arnold was eager to put this new technique to use—not only to help bring World War II to an end but also to demonstrate a new facet of air power that might be used in any future war. What he had in mind was an aerial invasion of Germany.

Cochran later described his conversation with Arnold: "General Arnold could foresee an aerial invasion of Germany that would preclude the agonizing, arduous advancement across France and the lowlands up across Holland, and in the invasion of Germany. . . . Wouldn't an air invasion hasten the end of the war and make the tough, tough ground action—the World War I kind of ground action, creeping forward and forward, the lines, and all that sort of thing—wouldn't it make that unnecessary if in fact you could invade a country that was as strong and defensible as Germany? Could you do that? His mind was searching for that."

Cochran flew to England to begin preliminary work for the aerial invasion of Germany. The project was given the code name Arena. He didn't need to be told to be as quiet as possible about what he was doing. Many, if not most, generals would see the whole project as a pie-in-the-sky operation that would simply waste the resources they needed to get on with fighting the war the old-fashioned way.

Quietly gathering intelligence about the Allied and German forces and the geography of Germany, Cochran settled on a site for the aerial invasion of Germany. Even now, half a century later, it is awe-inspiring to look at a map and envision the audacious plan he had in mind. The site Cochran picked was the valley surrounding the industrial city of Kassel, deep inside Germany, 120 miles east of the Rhine River and hundreds of miles beyond the Allied armies fighting their way across France in the summer and fall of 1944, as they were already worried about the battle that faced them at the Rhine, Germany's natural defense line on the western front.

The Kassel Valley is about thirty miles long and about eleven miles wide. It is surrounded by hills, with easily defended passes through the hills. Cochran counted eleven landing strips, including one fairly good-sized civilian airport.

A major drawback to the use of the Kassel Valley was that a dam at one end of the valley contained a large reservoir. If the Germans opened the floodgates, they could flood a good part of the valley, thwarting the Allies' plans to use it as a base. The planners decided this was not an insoluble problem. Either they could send airborne troops or commandos in just before the operation to seize the dam, or they could send bombers ahead of time to blow a hole in the dam and release the water so the valley would have time to dry out before the invasion.

With his plans beginning to jell, Cochran sought an audience with Gen. George Patton. Of all the generals in Europe, Arnold had told him, Patton was the one who would be quickest to see the advantages of the aerial invasion. Cochran had never met Patton personally, but he had seen his formations from the air in North Africa and knew how he liked to dash, with his tanks, deep behind enemy lines, relying on the air force to protect his flanks.

They met at a dinner party in the headquarters of Gen. O. P. Weyland, whose aircraft were providing the flanking protection for Patton's dash across France. Cochran told Patton why he was there. Patton drew him off to the side, and the two men sat on a stairway, where they couldn't be overheard. Years later, Cochran's enthusiasm for the plan he outlined to Patton was still obvious:

"They were planning this thing of crossing the Rhine. It looked like it was going to be a terrific confrontation, and the casualties and the losses would be horrendous. . . . Why not get Patton around in behind . . . and supply him with an area that was a hundred times as big as the stronghold that Wingate built in Burma? Make it a large stronghold, the whole Kassel Valley, and pour in enough troops in there, enough infantry, enough artillery, and enough tanks to hold the area. Then build it, and build it with the biggest aerial invasion anyone ever saw, and use every airplane the air force could find and just launch a massive, massive effort and make it the deciding effort, the final effort."

As Cochran saw the plan, the Allied armies would get behind the Germans and race to Berlin, leaving the enemy cut off and surrounded.

Patton's style of hell-for-leather warfare was plagued by one serious weakness: his tanks moved so fast that, when they ran out of gas, the whole offensive stalled until the fuel trucks caught up with them. The aerial invasion concept promised to solve this problem by giving Patton a sanctuary to head for—a friendly enclave deep in enemy territory where he could refuel, rearm, and rest his tank crews.

"That's a hell of a good idea. . . ." he told Cochran. "Let's get going on this. . . ."

Before letting Cochran get back to work, Patton provided a bit of battlefield hospitality. He invited him out to see how the ground war was fought—and to get shot at.

Cochran had plenty of combat hours in the air, but he had never been involved in a battle on the ground. Patton took him to a point on the front lines where the Army was trying to bridge a narrow stream. What Cochran saw reinforced his resolve to leapfrog behind the German army and avoid a head-on collision.

Just across a small river, Cochran could see German snipers, picking off American soldiers who were trying to bridge the stream. As he watched, several of the men toppled into the water. Cochran was appalled. He told his hosts that trying to build a bridge in the face of such fire was the stupidest thing he had ever seen.

With Patton's blessing, Cochran came out into the open and began developing detailed plans for the operation, working toward a full-scale briefing for Gen. Dwight D. Eisenhower, the overall commander. The planners gathered a growing number of supporters. But there was also serious and determined opposition. The British supported a dash across the north German plain to swoop down on Berlin from the north. The aerial invasion didn't fit into their plans. The strategic bomber command wanted nothing to detract from their effort to crush Germany from the air. And even some in the fighter community, who might be expected to support such an audacious undertaking, raised objections.

Do you realize, the fighter pilots asked, that the biggest air battle in history will take place over this valley?

Cochran agreed. But, with the Germans low on fuel, low on pilots, and with few planes left, he argued that the plan to leapfrog behind the Nazi lines would force the Luftwaffe into a battle in which it would be destroyed. The Allies would then have total control of the air over the battlefield.

"Many of the air people and the troop people thought our plans were too ambitious, that we couldn't load and take off airplanes and tow gliders that fast," Cochran recalled. "Our answer

to that was to show them what we had done in the jungle, for
heaven's sake, and how fast we could go."

Eisenhower seemed favorably impressed. He noted that Cochran had been involved in Wingate's operation in Burma and
asked: "What do you think of this plan?"

"General, I dreamed it up," Cochran replied.

Eisenhower chuckled, slapped the papers outlining the plan,
and said: "I like this plan. I think it ought to be done."

But the war on the battlefield outran the planning. After the
Germans' last big effort in the Battle of the Bulge, in the winter
of 1944–45, it was apparent that their ability to defend the Reich
was rapidly disintegrating.

Patton crossed the Rhine at several points and dashed northeast, through the Fulda Gap, past the Kassel Valley, and on toward
Berlin.

While plans for a Burma-style aerial invasion of Germany by air
commandos were being prepared, another breed of air commandos was fighting its own brand of warfare in Europe. They
called themselves the Carpetbaggers.

PART 2
Behind the Lines in Europe

CHAPTER 6

The Carpetbaggers Are Born

I f the air commandos in Burma suffered from disease, jungle, monsoons, and Japanese guns, they at least had one great advantage: strong and unwavering support in the person of General Arnold.

In western Europe, life tended to be a bit more comfortable than in Southeast Asia, but there was little support from on high for those attempting to develop a special operations capability. In some cases, there was active opposition, both in the field and in Washington.

The lack of support and even hostility would be very familiar to later generations of air commandos. In that sense, the special operators in Europe were more truly the forebears of younger air commandos than were the more favored units in Burma.

That the predecessors of today's air commandos were able to mount major special operations campaigns in both northern and southern Europe was due to persistence, changing circumstances as time went by, and, in no small measure, luck.

The first to see the need for special operations were the imaginative officers of the Office of Strategic Services. Formed in July 1941—five months before the United States entered the war— the wartime spy agency was at first known as the Office of the Coordinator of Information (COI). It was headed by Gen. William J. Donovan, a World War I hero and New York lawyer. In June of

1942, the COI was reorganized and became the Office of Strategic Services. Unlike the Central Intelligence Agency, which emerged as the successor to the OSS after the war, Donovan's outfit was organized along military lines and was an agency of the military's Joint Chiefs of Staff.

At least as early as the beginning of 1943, the OSS began pressing for the creation of special units to operate behind the lines in German-occupied Europe. One goal was to insert spies to gather intelligence. The other goal was to provide help, in the form of supplies, technical support, and leadership, to resistance movements so they would be able to do their part, behind enemy lines, when the invasion of Europe came in the spring of 1944. This classic guerrilla warfare would have been impossible—at least on such a large scale—without the support of air power. The OSS interest focused on two broad areas.

In the north, within reach of planes based in England, were France, Holland, Belgium, Denmark, and Norway. One estimate prepared by the OSS calculated that there would be 160,000 resistance fighters—the equivalent of about ten divisions—available in France alone to disrupt the German response to the Allied invasion. In Norway, it was estimated that, by the beginning of 1945, there would be 30,000 people actively involved in the resistance movement and another 20,000 who could be activated during an Allied effort to liberate the country.

In the south, interest focused primarily on Yugoslavia, although there were also significant resistance movements in northern Italy, Greece, and Albania. Portions of southern France were also reachable by planes flying out of North Africa and Italy. In Yugoslavia, Josip Broz, known as Marshal Tito, was building a force that would eventually grow to a significant army—big enough to tie down seventeen German divisions.

The British had begun clandestine flights into German-occupied parts of Europe and were operating, at least on a small scale, from Norway to the Balkans. But many of their flights to deliver agents and supplies were made with small, single-engine Lysander planes, capable of carrying only a couple of people or a small amount of supplies. The Americans carried out a few experiments with B-25 medium bombers, but quickly concluded that they were too small and had too short a range to be effective.

What was needed to do the job, as the British had learned, were big, long-range four-engine bombers. But in early 1943, as Donovan and his people pressed their case for aid to the resistance movements, such bombers were in desperately short supply. Lieutenant General Ira C. Eaker, commander of the Eighth Air Force, based in England, had only 337 B-17 and B-24 heavy bombers in his arsenal, far fewer than the numbers he needed for the sustained daylight raids against Germany that Arnold and other advocates of victory through air power demanded.

Bomber production began to surge in 1943 (the United States eventually produced more than eighteen hundred B-24 bombers alone), but losses to enemy antiaircraft guns and fighters also mounted alarmingly. On 1 August, fifty-four B-24s were lost in an attack on the Ploiesti oil fields in Rumania. On 17 August, sixty B-17s went down in a raid on industrial plants in Schweinfurt and Regensburg.

By the fall of 1943, with preparations for the invasion of the Continent well underway, key officers in England were becoming increasingly convinced that the OSS was right: well-armed, properly led resistance fighters could make a dramatic contribution to the success of the Allied landings. But they remained convinced it would be a mistake to pull bombers out of the effort to carry the air war to Germany in order to aid the resistance. It was then that a bit of unexpected luck came into play. It happened this way:

During the decade of the 1930s, the navy spent heavily on aircraft carriers and carrier-based planes, but it simply didn't buy the long-range, land-based planes needed for finding and destroying enemy submarines lurking off the coasts of the United States and Europe. The job of antisubmarine warfare (ASW) patrols fell to the air force.

One of the units assigned to this task was the 479th Anti-submarine Group, with four squadrons of B-24 Liberators. It first patrolled off the United States coasts and then moved to England in 1943 to hunt for German subs in the waters near the British Isles and the Bay of Biscay.

It was not until the fall of 1943, nearly two years after the United States entered the war, that the Navy took delivery of its own version of the B-24—a model with a single tail rather than the twin tail of the air force model—and declared itself ready to begin assuming the ASW role in October.

Suddenly, the air force found itself with extra B-24s that, at first glance, weren't good for much of anything. Many of them lacked the oxygen system and other equipment needed for high-altitude bombing, and their crews were trained to fly alone at low altitudes rather than up in the stratosphere in formations with hundreds of other bombers. But those limitations made them almost ideal for the neglected job of aiding the resistance in northern Europe.

Once the potential value of these units was realized, the air force moved with a speed that seems almost unbelievable to one accustomed to the lethargic pace of the peacetime military. In late August, Lt. Gen. Jacob L. Devers, the senior American officer in England, signed off on the plan to set up two special operations squadrons and quickly received an okay from the Joint Chiefs of Staff. On 12 October 1943, an OSS colonel produced a detailed memo outlining plans for aid to the resistance. Actually, such plans had been sitting on the shelf in the OSS London headquarters since January. Although the original OSS plans had called for eighteen planes, flying out of both England and North Africa, there would now be two squadrons, with thirty-two planes, available in England for this special mission.

On 24 October, officers of the antisubmarine unit met with OSS officials at the Bovingdon air base, west of London, to be told of their new mission. Among those attending were Col. Clifford J. Heflin, commander of the 22d Anti-submarine Squadron, and Maj. Robert W. Fish, his deputy.

It was at that meeting that the name Carpetbagger was picked at random from a list of approved code names.

The very next day, a small group of Americans was assigned to the Royal Air Force base at Tempsford to learn about British flights into the Continent. By that time, the British were using not only the Lysanders, for landing to deliver or pick up agents, but also twin-engine Whitley bombers and four-engine Halifax bombers to parachute agents and supplies. They were ranging all over the western part of occupied Europe, from Norway to Greece.

The Americans quickly began flying with the British—and learning of the dangers of their new assignment. On the night of 3 November, eight Americans took off with the British, one in each of eight Halifax bombers. One crew failed to return, and Capt. James E. Estes was listed as missing in action—the first Carpetbagger lost to enemy action.

While the Americans learned their new role, their planes were sent to a depot for modifications. The ball turret, in the belly of the plane to the rear of the bomb bay, was removed, and a hole was prepared for use by agents parachuting. It quickly became known as the Joe hole. The men who were dropped were known as Joes and the women as Janes. The Joe hole was fitted with a metal shroud through which the parachutist slid out of the plane. The shroud was forty-four inches in diameter on the inside and flared to forty-eight inches at the exit. During flight, the hole was covered with a plywood panel that could be folded back out of the way.

Flame arresters were installed over the exhaust ports so they could not be seen. Similarly, the muzzles of the machine guns were masked so, if they were fired at night, they would not give away the position of the plane to a night fighter.

The instrument panel was reconfigured to place the instruments the pilot would need for flying at night at three hundred or four hundred feet off the ground directly in front of his face. Special navigation and communication equipment was installed to help the crews find delivery zones and communicate with those on the ground.

At first, the planes were painted a dull black to make them harder to see at night. Later, however, it was determined that a glossy black paint made them more difficult to pick up on radar, so the paint scheme was changed.

The planes were stripped of their armor plate and their nose and waist guns, as well as the lower ball turret. The few remaining guns were left on more for morale purposes—so the crews wouldn't feel entirely defenseless—than for fighting. The crews were told to avoid firing their weapons so as not to give away their position and to rely on their low altitude to avoid German radar, which was ineffective below about three thousand feet. By flying low, they were also relatively safe from night fighters. Even during the day, German pilots were reluctant to fly as low as the Carpetbaggers.

The removal of the guns permitted reducing the crew from the ten men normally carried on a heavy bomber to eight: pilot, copilot, bombardier, navigator, engineer, radio operator, dispatcher—as the waist gunner was called—and tail gunner. The ball turret gunner and one of the waist gunners were eliminated.

The crews were, at least in theory, volunteers. Fish, who now lives in an Air Force retirement village outside San Antonio, had the job of welcoming new members to the squadron.

The new crew members gathered in a Quonset-hut briefing room. Fish took the podium and described their new mission. The crews had been trained to fly in formation at high altitude during the daytime. In their new assignment, Fish told them, they would be flying their four-engine B-24s at three or four hundred feet above the ground . . . alone . . . at night.

"You're going to be flying that airplane at that altitude with the wheels and flaps down to slow it down so people can jump out. You're going to do this alone in the dark of night, flying at ten miles above stalling speed," Fish continued. If any of the crew members didn't want to be involved, he told them, they could simply get up and walk out. There would be no black marks in their records. Then he left the room for a few minutes.

Every time he returned, all the young fliers were still sitting there. Later, some of them told him they were ready to walk out but didn't want to be first. "So," he says, "they all got sucked in."

The two new special operations squadrons were called the 36th and 406th Bombardment Squadron (Special) and attached to the 482d Bombardment Group (Pathfinder) as the "special project" at the Alconbury airfield, north of London. Heflin was named the commander. In March, the unit, by then known as the 801st Bombardment Group (Provisional), settled in at its "permanent" home at the Harrington airdrome. Later, on 13 August 1944, the designation of the unit was changed again and it became the 492d Bombardment Group. Carpetbaggers usually refer to their unit as the 801st/492d Bombardment Group.

By the beginning of 1944, the Carpetbaggers were ready to go to war.

CHAPTER 7
Enemy Territory—in the Dark

Even before Heflin's crews flew the first mission on their own, on 4 January 1944, the Carpetbaggers thought of themselves as something special—and they were. While most bomber crews flew in huge formations—as many as a thousand planes—of B-17s and B-24s penetrating deep into Germany in daylight at twenty to twenty-five thousand feet, the Carpetbagger crews flew by themselves, at night, close to the ground.

Heflin was given extraordinary authority over his command. On 9 April 1944, he was given full authority to accept or reject missions for the Carpetbagger group. No other group commander in the Eighth Air Force had such control over his operations.

The Carpetbagger commanders, working with the OSS, picked their own targets. Once airborne, each aircraft commander was in charge, selecting his route and his altitude and deciding whether to make his drop or abort the mission. The Carpetbaggers even had their own weather experts and sometimes flew when the rest of the Eighth Air Force was grounded.

"We had three weather people," Fish recalls. "The captain was an artist. The lieutenant was a mathematician. The master sergeant was just a plain career weather guesser. When those three guys got together, we could almost always bank on their forecast being true."

Their skill was tested in the winter of 1944, when the weather was so severe that the entire Eighth Air Force was grounded. The Carpetbaggers looked at the weather map. The storms flowing in off the Atlantic were losing ferocity as they moved down over the Continent. Many of the places in southern France where agents and supplies were to be delivered were clear. Unlike the Eighth Air Force bombers, the Carpetbaggers didn't have to worry about forming up in large formations. Even with the weather socked in, they could take off and get to their targets. The problem was finding a place to land when they returned to England.

The three weather experts studied the storm pattern and found there was usually a break of at least a few minutes as one front followed another across England. There would be some airfields open, at least for brief periods of time.

Heflin and Fish decided to fly. They laid on a dozen single-plane missions the first night. All of them returned safely—although none of the planes got back to its home field.

"We did that the second night, same damn routine," Fish recalls. "Got everybody back safely. On the third night, the weather stayed the same. We had missions we could have flown, but I lost my nerve. I figured, if we do this a third time and we do lose an airplane, I've had it."

On many of their missions, the Carpetbaggers dropped both cargo and people—Joes and, occasionally, Janes. The relationship between the aircrews and their passengers was a strange one.

The Joes were delivered to the airfield about four hours before the scheduled flight time. Each person was carefully searched by an officer from the British customs office and required to sign a sworn statement that he or she was not carrying anything not approved by the OSS. A memo to Heflin gave this reasoning behind the security precautions:

"The personal safety of every resistance worker demands that he should not carry on his person articles which betray his stay in England. As the time for action approaches [the D-day invasion], it also becomes more and more important to prevent leakage of information to the enemy. A careless word in a private letter or even in an official document might give the enemy valuable information."

Many of those scheduled to be dropped onto the Continent were natives of the area where they would land, and some had been brought out to England to receive special instructions or training. Later in the Carpetbaggers' operations, they delivered many "Jedburgh teams," whose job was to work with the resistance, providing training, leadership, and a link to England. Jedburgh was a randomly selected code word that had no particular meaning. The three-man teams were made up of one OSS officer, one member of the British Special Operations Executive, and a Free French officer or enlisted man. Still later, larger sabotage teams of as many as thirty men were delivered to the Continent.

When the agents arrived at Harrington, they were taken to dressing huts near the flight line. There, the plane's dispatcher was in charge of getting them ready for the jump. The dispatchers had all received special training for their job—including two low-level parachute jumps. They were warned not to question the agents about themselves or their mission—or to let the Joes think they were new at this business. They were also told not to talk about the flight—what their route would be or how high they would fly.

The agents first donned a baggy pair of coveralls that looked more like a clown suit than apparel for a mission behind enemy lines. It was covered with pockets and pouches to store knives, guns, a compass, money, and other items. The rear of the suit was padded with sponge rubber to protect the jumper on a hard landing. The suit was topped off with a rubber helmet and goggles. Special boots were padded to cushion the shock of landing. The parachute harness was fitted over the coveralls. By that time, according to one account, the person "is a grotesque, top-heavy figure who lumbers about like a Frankenstein monster."

Some of the agents sat by themselves, quietly smoking, thinking not only of the dangers that lay ahead but, sometimes, of the reunion, a few hours later, with family, loved ones, and friends. Others worked off nervous energy, clowning around in their cumbersome garb.

Before going to the plane, the agents were briefed again and provided with a handful of pills. Some were for air sickness; some were to help a person sleep and others to keep him awake. And some were lethal, in case the person fell into enemy hands.

Packages, weighing up to 150 pounds, were delivered to another section of the base by the OSS. They were fitted with parachutes, carefully sorted to make sure each package went to the right plane, and then loaded into the planes in the afternoon before the flight.

Before each flight, the navigators carefully plotted their planned course to avoid known antiaircraft—or "flak"—positions. In this, the Carpetbaggers were better off than the bomber crews. While the bombers routinely attacked heavily defended targets, the Carpetbaggers made their drops in fields away from cities and military targets. But they shared with the bomber crews the problem of penetrating the German coastal flak belts.

The Carpetbaggers' standard tactic was to approach the coast only a few hundred feet off the water, under the German radar, climb rapidly to about eight thousand feet to get over the coastal guns, and then drop back down to low level.

Most, if not all, operations before D-day, in June of 1944, were conducted on moonlit nights to make it easier to navigate and to identify the target.

Fortunately, the crews had excellent maps, showing woods, streams, even individual houses. Lakes and streams stood out particularly well, shining silver in the moonlight. Forests appeared as distinctive black blobs. The bombardier, sitting in the Plexiglas nose, watched the scenery unfold a few hundred feet below and was primarily responsible for identifying checkpoints. But the rest of the crew members kept up a constant watch for significant terrain points and for other aircraft—especially enemy night fighters. The navigator, in his own compartment in the nose, kept track of the plane's progress by estimating the time and distance that had been flown and ticking off checkpoints as they were spotted by other members of the crew.

Navigation was aided by the Gee box, a system that pinpointed the plane's position by comparing signals from three radio stations in England. It was accurate to within a quarter of a mile in

England but less accurate over the Continent. The Gee box doesn't measure up to today's standards for navigational accuracy, but in World War II, a navigator could claim a perfect mission if he ended up within three miles of his destination and within three minutes of his estimated time of arrival. The new radar altimeter, just becoming available, told the pilots how far they were from the ground and also helped to identify prominent terrain features.

In some cases, the agents insisted on being dropped into unmarked and unmanned drop zones. That way, they could be almost certain not to be greeted by German soldiers. But, in most cases, drops of Joes and cargo were made where members of the resistance movements were waiting on the ground. Finding the right place and making sure that the right people were waiting down there in the darkness were critical.

The planes had several systems for communicating with those down below. The most primitive was an exchange of coded signals by flashlight or small signal lamp. But there were two more sophisticated means of communicating between the approaching plane and those waiting on the ground.

The S-phone was a kind of powerful walkie-talkie radio with a range of eight to ten miles. As soon as the ground operator heard the plane, he could talk to the crew, guiding them into the drop zone. An advanced version of the S-phone, known as the homing S-phone, sent out a signal that permitted the navigator, using his radio compass, to home in on the transmitter.

During 1944, the Carpetbagger planes were gradually equipped with the Rebecca-Eureka system, which used radar pulses reflected off the ground system—Eureka—to guide the plane, with its Rebecca device, to the target. The Eureka operator could also vary the intensity or frequency of the radar blips to transmit a coded identification signal to the plane.

The reception committees on the ground used three different systems of signal lights to mark the drop zones. The first system consisted of a triangle formed by three white lights with a single red light at the apex of the triangle flashing the recognition signal for the day. The red light was placed downwind, and the plane would approach from that direction, against the wind.

The second system was similar, except that one white light flashed and three red lights formed the triangle.

In the third and most commonly used system, three red torches were set out in a line with a flashing white light at the downwind end. Sometimes, bonfires were used instead of torches.

In an ideal situation, the pilot spotted the lights, lined up properly, and swooped over the drop zone, delivering Joes and cargo in one pass.

As the plane lined up on the lights, the pilot spoke over the intercom to the dispatcher in the waist of the plane: "Running in." This meant the plane was about two minutes from the drop zone. The dispatcher folded back the covering over the Joe hole and signaled the agent to scoot up to the edge of the hole.

Just before the plane reached the drop zone, the bombardier or the pilot toggled the salvo switch, dropping the cargo. At the same moment, the pilot told the dispatcher: "Action station." This meant the drop signal would come in two to five seconds. The Joe swung his legs into the hole and prepared to jump.

The pilot said, "Go" and switched on a green light in the waist. The Joe dropped through the hole in the floor. If he hesitated, the dispatcher gave him a helping shove. In some cases, more than one Joe was dropped in a matter of seconds, so there was no time for the Joe to sit in the hole and have second thoughts.

The system was dangerous both for those being dropped and for those doing the dropping. Fish recalls one tragic incident:

"Down in France one night, I killed the leader of a team. We were coming in, in the hilly country in southeast France. We came to the drop zone. The lights and everything were there. We went in to drop. We got the packages out. The first parachutist went out and he landed okay. The second parachutist went out and he broke a leg. The third went out and he hit the ground before his chute got open.

"What had happened was, when you've got the B-24 sitting there at 135 miles an hour, with flaps and wheels down, you've got zero maneuverability. These people had put the drop zone on a hillside, so I was going into the rising hillside as we made the drop. I couldn't see that until we got into it.

"About the time the first guy went out, I saw my atmospheric altimeter was constant, but my radar altimeter showed I was getting closer to the ground. There's only one possible answer for that: the ground's coming up to meet me.

"I poured the coal to it, but, shucks, you had no maneuverability. I probably didn't pick up five miles an hour. By that time, things were happening fast. They had been told to go! And they went: bang, bang, bang. By that time, the ground had come up to where he didn't have the six hundred feet he thought he had. When he hit the ground, it killed him. Our biggest enemy was the ground, not the Germans."

On a number of occasions, planes circling in the darkness met up with that deadly enemy.

On the night of 27–28 April 1944, a B-24 piloted by Lt. George W. Ambrose approached a drop zone in a mountainous area near the village of Saint-Cyr de Valorges in France. According to accounts later pieced together from survivors and members of the resistance party on the ground, the plane circled three times and then clipped a tree or the ground with one wing. Ambrose managed to keep the plane flying for a few more moments and then lost control and crashed.

Ambrose and four other members of the crew were killed, but three members of the crew either jumped or were thrown from the plane in the seconds before the crash and survived. One of them was so badly injured that he was turned in to the Germans so he could receive medical treatment. But the other two survivors—Sgt. George W. Henderson and SSgt. James J. Heddleson—escaped from the crash area, linked up with the resistance, and managed to avoid capture until mid-July, when they were picked up by a British bomber and returned to England.

Even though the ground was the ever-present enemy, the crews could never stop worrying about the danger posed by enemy guns and fighter planes. On every flight, there was the possibility that it was the enemy, not a friendly group of resistance fighters, waiting down below in the darkness.

On 5 April 1944, a plane piloted by 2d Lt. William W. Nicoll took off from Harrington at 10 P.M. and followed the usual routine of crossing the channel at about five hundred feet, under German radar, and then climbing over the coast. Suddenly, the bombardier, sitting in the Plexiglas nose, saw a burst of flak directly in the plane's path and shouted: "Hard right!" But it was too late; they were caught in a flak trap. The first blast hit the tail, killing the tail gunner. Then the nose was hit. The bombardier shouted: "Get out! Get out!" By then, the plane was out of control and on fire. Two men managed to parachute at about eight hundred feet and survived, but the others died in the wreckage.

On the night of 28 May 1944, a Carpetbagger crew made a routine drop of supplies to a Belgian resistance group. The next night, Lt. Ernest B. Fitzpatrick and his crew took off from Harrington at 11 P.M. with another load of supplies destined for the same group. They reached the drop zone at 1 A.M. and began to circle, looking for the expected signal lights. Suddenly, gunfire erupted from a mobile flak battery, and the plane was hit. Fitzpatrick banked sharply to escape the antiaircraft fire and flew right into the path of a waiting JU-88 night fighter, which raked the B-24 with 20mm cannon fire.

With the plane on fire, Fitzpatrick sounded the bail-out alarm, pulled up to about seven thousand feet, struggled to hold the plane level until his crew jumped, and then put the craft on autopilot and jumped himself.

The Germans, alerted by the drop on the previous night, had set a deadly trap for Fitzpatrick and his crew, moving in so quickly that the Belgians did not have time to flash a warning to the Carpetbaggers. Fitzpatrick and his crew were fortunate, however. They parachuted safely and then were hidden by the Belgians until Allied forces liberated the area later that summer.

Attacks by night fighters against the Carpetbaggers were relatively rare, for two reasons. The major reason was that the fighters were engaged in a desperate battle to fend off the Royal Air Force's nightly raids on German cities. As the British attacks mounted in intensity, the Germans built thousands of radar-equipped ME-110, JU-88, and DO-17 night fighters and laid out a string of ground control intercept radar sites to guide the fighters to their targets. In 1943 alone, the night fighter pilots were credited with 2,882 confirmed kills of Allied aircraft. Most of the night fighters were deployed along the primary route followed by bombers flying toward German cities—over Belgium, Holland, and Denmark. This left few of the fighters to patrol the areas in France where the Carpetbaggers conducted many of their missions.

The Carpetbaggers also gained a good deal of protection from the fact that they flew so low—below the coverage of the German radar, which was focused primarily on the high-flying bombers.

It thus came as a very bad surprise when a Carpetbagger crew learned—usually by the impact of cannon shells—that they were under attack.

On the night of 27 June 1944, a Liberator crew was conducting a training mission near their base in England when the plane suddenly shuddered violently. It was not until that moment that the crew realized they were under attack by a night fighter that had penetrated almost into their home landing pattern. The bombardier, 2d Lt. Robert L. Sanders, scrambled back through the nose of the plane to reach his parachute, which was lying behind the pilots' cockpit. Normally, bomber crews wore only a parachute harness rather than the more cumbersome back or seat packs. In an emergency, a chest pack could be snapped quickly to fasteners on the front of the harness. But when Sanders tried to reach his chute, his way was blocked by fire. He turned and saw the navigator, 2d Lt. Robert Callahan, preparing to jump through a hatch in the nose of the plane. Callahan sensed Sanders's predicament and motioned to him to hang on to his back.

"I sat down and slid out of the plane with the bombardier on my back," Callahan later told the United Press. "I pulled the ripcord as soon as we left the plane, and there was only a slight jolt when the 'chute opened."

As they floated down, Sanders worked his way around in front of Callahan so the two could hold on to each other. They hit the ground hard. Callahan suffered a broken ankle and Sanders a sprain. But they were fortunate. Only one other crew member, the badly burned radio operator, managed to escape before the plane crashed.

The incident involving Callahan and Sanders occurred in the days immediately after the 6 June Normandy invasion, a period when the Carpetbagger operations were reaching a crescendo. The crews were hearing dramatic accounts of how their support for the resistance, and the earlier British operations, were paying off.

On 15 January 1944, the London *Daily Express* carried an item under a Geneva dateline with a headline saying, "Patriots Wreck Railways." It reported:

"French patriots last night attacked the German-held Annecy railway depot and blew up several locomotives. At Rumilly, in Savoy, patriots stopped a train, forced the passengers to alight, then sent the train rushing uncontrolled along the line until it overturned. In Belgium, patriots, complying with directions given them by the Allied Command, carried out forty-one acts of sabotage in one week on the railway tracks in the province of Hainaut. They stopped trains and started them again without drivers, placed bombs on the tracks, unbolted rails, destroyed signal boxes, and put pumping stations out of action."

On 17 May 1944, a leader of a French Maquis unit in the Haute-Savoie Department of south-central France visited the Carpetbagger base at Harrington. He was a short, slightly built man in his thirties, wearing horn-rimmed glasses.

Crew members crowded into the ready room to hear his first-person account of the situation on the Continent. He told them that all trucks on main or subsidiary roads were stopped and searched and about 40 percent of what the crews dropped ended up in German hands. The danger of this happening increased, he said, when a drop was not made directly on the target, disrupting the plans for moving the material from the reception site.

Most of the material, such as weapons, was distributed almost immediately; ammunition and explosives were stored, but they were broken up into small amounts as quickly as possible, he told the airmen.

One of the crew members asked if trucks seen on the road after the 10 P.M. curfew could be assumed to be German. The Maquis chief said they could—but in a convoy, one or two of the trucks could also be assumed to be driven by members of the resistance.

With support from the air, the French resistance movement eventually came to control entire regions of the country. As the time for the D-day invasion approached, the resistance was a significant force to be reckoned with by the Germans. And the Allied high command, at first reluctant to provide the planes and aircrews for the Carpetbaggers, became wholeheartedly supportive. On 2 May 1944, a little more than a month before the landing in France, General Eisenhower ordered the Eighth Air Force to make another twenty-five B-24s available for the Carpetbaggers, increasing their force to sixty-four bombers.

CHAPTER 8
D-day and Beyond

I n mid-May, three weeks before the Normandy invasion, the tempo at Harrington was clearly on the upswing. The two new squadrons assigned to the group by General Eisenhower arrived on 17 May, one of them fresh from the States, the other reassigned from high-altitude bombing.

With the sudden doubling of crews and aircraft, the base was overcrowded. The newcomers were assigned, grumbling, to tents, while the crews already present lived in relative luxury in Nissen huts—dome-roofed structures that looked like half of a giant corrugated metal barrel.

On the night of 3 June, three nights before D-day, the Carpetbaggers flew seventeen successful missions, the largest number in a single night thus far.

On 6 June, the secret warriors gathered around radios to follow the course of the invasion. The group diary noted:

"H-hour of D-day is arrived at last! The Allied invasion of northern France is the sole topic of conversation. All men of the Group are in a state of high excitement over this latest and greatest step toward Victory. And there is a new determination to deliver a maximum of supplies to the resistance groups, who are bound to play an important role in the liberation of the occupied countries."

Even before the invasion, a listener to the BBC could have guessed that something was about to occur. Strange little coded messages began to fill the airwaves, signaling to resistance movements to prepare to strike at the enemy from behind when the Allies hit the Normandy beaches.

The assignment of two more squadrons of B-24s was only one indication of the seriousness with which the top brass now took the potential of the resistance movement to disrupt the German defense while they were trying to respond to the Allied landing.

In the weeks after D-day, with the suddenly intensified fighting, many of the resistance units were running dangerously low on supplies.

By that time Gen. James Doolittle, the leader of the famous bombing raid on Tokyo two years before, had replaced Ira Eaker as commander of the Eighth Air Force. He diverted 180 four-engine B-17 Flying Fortress bombers from the bombing campaign to bolster the Carpetbaggers' effort to deliver supplies to the resistance movement. The crews were given a crash course in Carpetbagger techniques for parachuting supplies.

On 25 June, in an operation code-named Zebra, the 180 bombers took off, with fighter escort, and made a daylight drop of supplies at four drop zones behind enemy lines. Each of the five wings involved in the operation was able to deliver enough rifles, machine guns, rocket launchers, ammunition, grenades, and small weapons to arm one thousand to thirteen hundred men.

The second mass drop, code-named Operation Cadillac, took place on 14 July as the battle for Saint-Lô was reaching its climax. In this operation, nine wings of 36 B-17s—a total of 324 planes—accompanied by 524 P-51 and P-47 fighters, dropped supplies at seven points in three regions. The goal of this mass infusion of supplies was not only to hamper the German defense at Saint-Lô but also to disrupt the movement of men and supplies from other areas to the battle zone.

A third mass drop—Operation Buick—was conducted on 1 August when 192 B-17s delivered 2,281 containers to resistance units in eastern France. A final drop, by 72 bombers, occurred on 9 September.

In an implied criticism of the Carpetbaggers, a report by the 3d Air Division, which conducted the mass daylight drops, concluded that such missions were "not only possible but were more economical and practical than nighttime operations conducted for the same purpose."

This would not be the last time that the big, conventional Air Force looked down its nose at the unconventional special operators.

In this case, the Carpetbaggers had clearly filled a role that would have been inappropriate for the massed bombers, even if large numbers of bombers could have been diverted from the bombing campaign against Germany. In the months preceding the invasion, the Carpetbaggers had helped build the nucleus for an uprising against the Germans. In that period, daylight drops by large formations of planes would have been like a beacon, calling attention to the location of resistance units. Once the uprising occurred and resistance units were out in the open, the demand for supplies outstripped the capacity of the Carpetbaggers, with their single-plane nighttime missions.

For the Carpetbaggers, the invasion was the signal for a much greater effort devoted to delivering agents—Jedburgh teams and other larger teams—to France.

With the delivery of larger numbers of agents, the Carpetbaggers were faced with a new challenge for which they were not equipped: picking up agents, downed fliers, and members of the resistance and bringing them back to England. The four-engine bombers flown by the Carpetbaggers were too big to land in the rough open fields and cow pastures that served as airfields behind enemy lines. The British had been carrying on a small-scale airline service using their single-engine Lysanders and twin-engine Hudson bombers. But something better was needed.

The Carpetbaggers turned to the C-47—the same rugged twin-engine workhorse that was doing such a good job serving the Chindits at Broadway, Aberdeen, and White City. The officers of the Troop Carrier Command were reluctant to give up any of their planes for this new operation. General Doolittle broke the impasse by giving up his personal C-47. Someone forgot, however, to spread the word that the plane no longer carried the general. When a Carpetbagger crew picked up the plane and flew it to a depot for modifications, they were met by an honor guard of colonels, ready to welcome General Doolittle to their base.

In preparation for their C-47 operations, the Carpetbaggers experimented and practiced for more than two months. Heflin began the tests on 1 May by taking off from Harrington and landing on a short stretch of the runway marked only by seven men holding ordinary flashlights. Captain Wilmer L. Stapel made as many as twenty landings a day to determine how short a landing field could be used for landing and takeoff with a C-47.

Meanwhile, reconnaissance planes photographed potential landing sites so the crews could familiarize themselves with the fields they would have to approach in the dark.

The night of 6 July was chosen for the first flight, code-named Mixer One. Heflin took the controls as aircraft commander with Stapel as his copilot. Major Edward C. Tresemer, probably the most skilled navigator in the group, flew as navigator. A bombardier and radio operator filled out the five-man crew. The cargo consisted of eleven agents trained to disrupt German operations plus three thousand pounds of supplies. Since no fuel would be available where they landed in France, an extra fuel tank was installed in the fuselage so the plane could carry a total of 906 gallons of gasoline for its thousand-mile round-trip.

The destination for the flight was a partially harvested wheat field near the town of Nantua in a Maquis-controlled region in southeastern France only about twenty-five miles west of the Swiss city of Geneva. That meant flying diagonally across France, much of which was still under German control.

Because of the distance involved, Heflin flew from Harrington to the Bolt Head airdrome southeast of Plymouth to refuel before taking off at 11 P.M. and heading out across the Channel. They crossed the coast at eight thousand feet without seeing any sign of enemy activity and entered what they knew to be the enemy's night-fighter belt.

The C-47 had no armor and no guns, and its fuel tanks were not self-sealing. Most worrisome of all, the plane, unlike a bomber, did not carry a tail gunner who might detect and fend off a night fighter. Instead, Stapel, the copilot, stood in the astrodome—a Plexiglas dome on the top of the plane normally used by the navigator to observe the stars while relying on celestial navigation. This gave him a 360-degree view of the sky above the plane.

As the plane approached the mountainous area of eastern France about 3 A.M. on 7 July, Heflin held his altitude at one thousand feet above the terrain. They flew closer and closer to their destination, until they were only minutes away. And still, because of the low altitude and surrounding mountains, Tresemer was unable to pick up a signal on his Rebecca receiver. Finally, when they were only four miles from the landing site, the signal came through. Moments later, they picked out four lights on the ground. A beacon down below flashed the coded signal, *N* (dash-dot). The plane responded with an *R* (dot-dash-dot). Heflin swung around and made a perfect three-point landing on the rough field.

As Tresemer jumped down to guide the plane to a parking place, the first words he heard were: "Jesus Christ, Yanks, am I glad to see you!" It was a Canadian gunner whose plane had been shot down over France. An American lieutenant, who used only the name Paul, emerged from the darkness and directed the plane to a spot near a grove of trees at the foot of a thousand-foot cliff. As soon as Heflin parked, Maquis troops moved in and placed small trees in holes that had already been dug. Within minutes, the plane disappeared into the woods.

For the next two days, the Carpetbaggers were honored guests of the French resistance. They toured the area controlled by the Maquis, distributing a resistance newspaper. And they ate and drank. At one party, they and their hosts did away with thirty-eight bottles of champagne.

On the first afternoon of their visit, the Americans attended a ceremony at which Heflin reviewed Maquis troops marching by and then placed a wreath at the base of a monument to those who had died in the resistance movement. Standing by dejectedly at the ceremony was a group of German prisoners. The Americans were told of a Maquis policy: for each member of the resistance killed or tortured by the Germans, three prisoners would be killed. The previous day, they were told, fifty-seven Germans had been shot.

On the first night, the Americans listened to the BBC for a signal giving them the go-ahead for takeoff. Their flight was canceled. The next night, they received the okay to return home, and Heflin made an instrument takeoff in a driving rain at 11:15 P.M. The passengers on the return trip were two American aviators; the Canadian gunner who had greeted them on their arrival; two British fliers; a British major who had been organizing the resistance; a young French girl and a Frenchman who were slated to attend a school for saboteurs in England; and two Hindus who had been rescued from the Germans by the Maquis.

The plane came in for a landing at Harrington at 4:30 A.M. on 9 July.

The Carpetbaggers soon received another C-47 and then, in mid-August, two more. Full-scale operations began late in August, with two to four planeloads of Joes and supplies delivered each night. By mid-September, when the advancing Allies had occupied most of the area served by the Carpetbaggers, the C-47s had carried out thirty-five missions to twelve different fields and delivered 78 Joes and 104,000 pounds of arms and ammunition. On the return trips, they brought back 213 Joes along with cargoes of mail.

Almost all the deliveries made by the Carpetbaggers were warmly received. However, the reception committee at Nantua let it be known that they would just as soon have more arms and ammunition and not necessarily so many Joes. The resistance fighters also reacted with derision to one brilliant idea cooked up by someone in the OSS. The OSS produced thousands of one-shot .45-caliber pistols. The pistol cost two dollars to make and was called the Liberator. The theory was that, on D-day, each Frenchman and -woman would rise up and shoot one German. The word quickly came back: "If you can't drop us something that shoots more than once, don't bother." Long after the war, Fish came upon thousands of the pistols stored at a military base in Washington.

During these missions, only one plane was damaged, when it ran into a ditch on a rough field in France on 6 September. The propellers were bent and the nose was crushed, but no one was injured. The next day, a maintenance crew was flown in from England to repair the plane so it could be flown home five days later.

During the hectic months of 1944, the Carpetbagger crews, whether flying B-24s or C-47s, knew they were making a significant contribution to the war effort and had heard anecdotal accounts of the activities of the resistance. But it was not until much later that a full picture emerged of what they had accomplished.

In June, July, and August, special-forces agents and sabotage team members, who had been dropped onto the Continent by the hundreds, were credited with making 885 rail cuts and destroying 322 locomotives. German records indicated 295 locomotives were destroyed by sabotage in June alone.

A major contribution by the saboteurs was to cut telephone and telegraph lines. This forced the Germans to communicate by radio—with the Allies listening in.

While the battle raged in Normandy, major elements of eight German divisions were tied down in antiguerrilla campaigns. Several crack German divisions were specifically targeted by the saboteurs. When the 2d SS Panzer Division moved north from Toulouse toward Normandy on 8 June, sabotage teams dogged its heels all the way, delaying its arrival on the battle front by at least five days.

Although it was certainly not their job, a few of the Carpetbaggers became actively involved in the guerrilla movement on the ground after crashing behind enemy lines. Perhaps the most notable was Lt. John B. "Johnny" Mead.

He was a bombardier on the crew of Lt. Murry L. Simon. Their plane was caught by flak guns mounted on a blacked-out troop train a little after midnight on 5 May 1944. The plane was hit repeatedly and burst into flames, but all the crew members managed to parachute to safety. They landed near the town of Roanne, about forty miles northwest of Lyon in central France.

Mead hid in a farmhouse for four days until a British agent

known as Victor came for him. They bicycled to a Maquis headquarters in Roanne. The agent asked if Mead would stay and help
him train a resistance unit. Mead agreed, and, later that month,
they received a coded message of approval from London.

At first, Mead was assigned to teach the French members of the
unit how to use American equipment being dropped to them by
the Carpetbaggers. On 29 May, he was at the drop zone for a delivery and talked over the S-phone to the crew of the circling B-
24. Apart from the earlier secret message from the British agent,
it was the first word the Carpetbaggers had received that Mead
and other members of the crew were alive.

Mead's duties rapidly expanded beyond training and coordinating air drops from the Carpetbaggers. In late June, he was
made commander of his own small guerrilla outfit—code-named
Maquis Violette—operating out of a mountain headquarters
southeast of Roanne. At one point, in late July, Mead's unit was
attacked by German police and French Milice working for the
French puppet government in Vichy. Instead of standing to fight,
they simply faded away, to rendezvous a week later. Their next assignment was to an area northwest of Roanne, where they carried
out a series of attacks on German roads, telegraph and telephone
lines, and railways.

On one of their operations, a band of twenty-eight men led by
Mead found themselves on a hill surrounded by what they
thought were thirty or so Germans. He decided to stay and fight.
But their information was wrong. Rather than facing a widely scattered force of thirty, they found themselves confronting an estimated six hundred Germans.

As the enemy soldiers moved up the hill, Mead and his men
slipped through their ranks down the hill. But there, they
found their path blocked by a road patrolled by armored cars.
Waiting until the cars were at the greatest distance, the men
scooted across the road. One armored car turned and sprayed
them with machine-gun fire, but one of the Maquis stood up with
his submachine gun and silenced the enemy weapon.

As soon as they crossed the road, the small group split up. Mead
and one aide reached the Loire River, with the Milice close be-

hind. The two men dove in and swam the river while their pursuers raked the water with bullets. They later joined up with other members of their group.

On 20 August, the Germans abandoned the Roanne area. Mead received instructions to rejoin his unit in England and set off on a circuitous route that took him to Lyon and then down to Italy.

When Mead reached Italy, he was finally able to send off a wire to his wife, Dorothy, telling her that he was alive. She had been informed that he was missing in action, but, because of the secrecy surrounding the Allied work with the resistance, she was not informed that he had survived the loss of his plane even after members of his unit knew he was okay.

In Italy, Mead received orders to return to France to work with an air force recovery unit involved in finding aviators who had been shot down by the enemy. It was not until 4 November that Mead finally returned to England to find that he had been promoted to captain and recommended for a Silver Star.

With the Allies moving rapidly across France, the Carpetbaggers flew their last mission—for the time being—on 16–17 September and ceased operations over the Continent the following day. In their eight and a half months of almost nightly flights, they had dramatically increased their ability to deliver men and supplies to the Continent.

In January, the Carpetbaggers had attempted 17 sorties but completed only 8 of them. In July, when they reached the peak of their operations, they flew on twenty-eight nights—including nights when there was no moon and the weather was bad—and successfully completed 397 sorties. In that month, the four Carpetbagger squadrons dropped 4,608 containers, 2,909 smaller packages, 1,378 bundles of leaflets, and 62 Joes.

Although the Carpetbaggers ceased their nightly operations in September, the war for them was far from over.

CHAPTER 9
Jack of All Trades

With the liberation of most of the drop zones they had served during much of 1944, the Carpetbaggers found themselves in a situation that would be very familiar to later generations of Air Force special operators. They were called upon to carry out a variety of tasks, from ferrying gasoline to the fuel-starved tanks of General Patton to smuggling a German V-2 missile out of Norway to serving as bait for enemy night fighters so British bombers could get to their targets.

The fuel-lift to Patton began almost immediately after the cessation of flights to support the resistance. The last drop flight was flown on the night of 16–17 September. On 21 September, the first B-24 took off with fuel for Patton's tanks.

For these flights, the B-24s were quickly modified. Four five-hundred-gallon fuel bladders were installed in the bomb bay. Other tanks holding another thousand gallons were installed in the fuselage behind the bomb bay. The plane's auxiliary wing tanks were blocked off so they, too, could be used to carry fuel. With these modifications, each plane carried twenty-five hundred gallons of eighty-octane gasoline for the tanks. This was in addition to its own one-hundred-octane aviation fuel.

Although their routes carried them over areas already controlled by Allied armies and thus safe from enemy antiaircraft fire, the crews were still nervous with their highly inflammable cargo. The danger was increased by the fact that the fields they landed on in Belgium were either rough strips quickly prepared by army engineers or recently liberated German fighter-plane bases with short runways. At some fields, abandoned by the Germans only days before, the Army was still busy finding and exploding mines when the B-24s arrived.

The crews quickly got into the fuel-delivery routine. As soon as a plane landed and pulled off to the side, engineers moved in with pumps to transfer the gas to trucks of the Red Ball Express, which then roared off to supply the tanks of the Third Army.

Within a few weeks, the Carpetbaggers had delivered almost a million gallons of gasoline, preparing Patton's army to resume its march to the east.

The emergency fuel-lift was not cheap, however. Because the planes' auxiliary tanks had been used to carry the lower-grade gasoline, they could not be used again for aviation fuel. Before the planes could be put back in service, the contaminated tanks would all have had to be removed and replaced. Instead, with new B-24s coming off the production lines at the rate of one an hour, the group was simply issued new airplanes.

At about the same time the fuel operation was getting under-way, the Carpetbaggers were also tasked with returning Allied crewmen who had been interned in Switzerland and Sweden, two neutral countries bordering the war zone.

In the case of Switzerland, the 856th Squadron of the 492d Bombardment Group, the Carpetbagger unit, set up a processing center at the Hotel Beau Rivage on Lake Annecy in south-eastern France. This occurred on 5 October 1944, as soon as the Allied armies had cleared the Germans from the border area between France and Switzerland. At that time, there were an estimated twelve hundred Americans interned in Switzerland. Most of them were aircrew members whose planes had landed in Switzerland or who had made their way across the border after crashing in France.

With an Allied victory only a matter of time, the Swiss seemed unconcerned if the airmen escaped and might even have been happy to see them go.

As soon as a man crossed the border, a car was sent from Annecy to pick him up. At the Beau Rivage, the men were given a hot meal, a hot bath, and new clothes. They were then carefully questioned about their experiences in Switzerland and any information they had about traffic between Switzerland and Germany.

Some of the interned aviators had given their word that they would not flee the country. They were then free to move about as they wished. Fish, who was group commander at the time, recalls one visit he made to Annecy:

"After a night's rest at the Beau Rivage Hotel, we prepared to return to England. Several 'escapees' were brought to the field to return with us. One 'escapee,' a first lieutenant, informed me that he might not be a 'legal escapee.' After he was interned, he agreed to a Swiss parole which allowed him to attend the University of Zurich. He had left the university without resigning his parole. He was concerned. I told him not to worry. My job was to transport 'escapees' back to England, and he was obviously an 'escapee.' I took him to England and sent him to London for interrogation.

"Two days later, I received a telephone call from our embassy in London. The caller told me to get that lieutenant back into Switzerland as fast as I could. The Swiss government was vigorously protesting that he had broken his parole. I explained the situation to our London air force headquarters, and they sent him back to Harrington. The next day, we carried him back to Annecy, took him to the Swiss border, turned him over to the Swiss border guards, and they placed him back in an internment camp. His parole was revoked and the Swiss were satisfied.

"About five days later, he again escaped and came to Annecy. This time, he was a legitimate 'escapee' and the Swiss had no objection. We transported him back to Harrington, sent him to London, where he was processed and returned to the USA. The requirements of international neutrality had been satisfied."

Between October 1944 and mid-February 1945, the Carpetbagger mission at Annecy processed 783 persons. In February, as the Allies seemed on the verge of victory, the Swiss agreed to a repatriation plan according to which one American internee would be released for every two Germans. Since most of the Americans were highly trained aircrewmen and most of the Germans were middle-aged ground-force men, the United States got the better of the deal. On 17 February, a train carrying 512 former internees steamed from Geneva to Marseilles, and the Annecy mission was closed down.

Late in the war, the Swiss relaxed their neutrality stance even further and, in March of 1945, began permitting Allied planes to fly across their territory. In a memoir written after the war, Douglas D. Walker recalled his first such flight. Walker settled in Tacoma, Washington, after the war and has since died. On his mission over Switzerland, he was a waist gunner–dispatcher on a B-24 flying out of Lyon into southern Germany as part of a renewed Carpetbagger operation.

"By flying from Lyon to southern Germany over Switzerland, we cut the flying time considerably," he recalled. "More importantly, we avoided flying over a considerable portion of enemy territory bristling with antiaircraft guns and night-fighter pursuit planes.

"That night, as we flew over the jagged Swiss Alps, we were all spellbound by the majestic beauty of those lovely peaks glistening in the moonlight under their white mantle of snow and ice.

"We were all a little nervous about flying over neutral Switzerland—even with their permission. We were concerned that instructions from higher Swiss authority not to fire on us might not trickle down to the Swiss gun crews in time to insure us a safe over-flight.

"As we flew towards the city of Geneva, we were awed by the sight of the blazing lights of the metropolis, sparkling by the side of Lake Geneva. It was a peacetime scene which we had not seen in some time.

"We were accustomed to flying over totally blacked-out cities in the rest of war-torn Europe. It was such a drastic change to see brilliantly lit skies over neutral Switzerland's cities.

"We were all staring out of the Liberator's window at this startling scene when suddenly the interior of the Lib was illuminated to almost daylight intensity!

"The Swiss gun batteries around Geneva had thrown several

searchlight beams on us. We felt naked and vulnerable as we held our collective breath, waiting for 'friendly' flak to hit us.

"However, the word must have filtered down to the gun crews, and we flew on without a shot being fired.

"On the way back to Lyon, after we had dropped our agent in Germany, Lt. [Robert] Swarts [the pilot] carefully avoided the larger Swiss cities, just for added insurance. Needless to say, we were relieved that our Liberator did not get shot full of holes—like Swiss cheese."

In the north, the Carpetbaggers had several quite different assignments.

One of them was to fly a kind of off-the-record airline from Leuchars, Scotland, into Stockholm's Broma airport. The American planes were unmarked, and the crew members wore civilian clothes. Since Sweden was neutral and still carried on some commerce with Germany, the Americans had the strange experience of sharing the airfield with German planes.

The SONNIE Project, as it was called, carried supplies for the Norwegian underground. The planes also carried spare parts to repair Allied planes that had landed in Sweden. A major part of the work of the secret airline was to bring passengers back to England. From 1 April 1944, when the operation began, to 25 June 1944, 4,304 passengers were carried from Sweden back to the United Kingdom. They included interned airmen and a large number of Norwegians to be trained as aircrews.

One of the biggest intelligence coups of the war occurred with the cooperation of the Swedes. Operating from their test base on the island of Peenemünde, the Germans fired two test models of their secret weapon—the V-2 ballistic missile—northward to land in Swedish territory. So confident were they of Swedish fear of attack by Germany, they boldly inquired where their missiles had landed—and asked for them back.

"You fired two?" the Swedes asked. "We only found one. Maybe the other one landed in a lake or the sea."

The wreckage of the other one was carefully gathered up and hidden away. Word was flashed to London, and a Carpetbagger crew was dispatched to pick up the rocket and bring it back.

A B-24 was sent for the pickup, but the rocket wouldn't fit through the bomber's small doors. So a C-47 stationed at Prestwick, Scotland, was stripped down to the bare fuselage. Lieutenant Colonel Keith Allen flew the C-47 to Sweden, and the V-2 was loaded in through the plane's larger cargo door. Allen flew back to Scotland, and Maj. Dave Schreiner then flew the rocket on to a British laboratory in London.

The Carpetbaggers were thus able to boast that they had landed the first V-2 on British soil. Because of their exploit, the Allies were able to study the enemy's new weapon and understand how it worked.

Unfortunately, they couldn't do much about it. The V-2 was a much more difficult weapon to counter than the earlier buzz bomb. The buzz bomb was like a small airplane—in effect, an early-day version of today's cruise missile—and flew so slowly it could be shot down by a fighter plane. People on the ground could hear it coming and tell, when its engine shut off, that it was about to plunge to the ground.

But the V-2 was quite different, the predecessor of today's intercontinental ballistic missiles. Rocketing off from a base along the coast of the Continent, the V-2 climbed high into the stratosphere, following a path much like that of an arrow fired high into the air, and then plunged down toward its target without warning. The Allies had no defense against such a weapon, and the V-2 not only caused severe physical damage but battered the morale of the war-weary British people. Even today, defense against such a ballistic missile is a very difficult technical problem.

On 20 September 1944, a short time after the V-2 mission, Allen and Schreiner were on another operation that had a tragic ending. Schreiner described it in a memoir written after the war:

"Our intelligence people had ascertained that the German battleship *Tirpitz* was hiding in one of the fjords in the uppermost tip of Norway. Our intelligence headquarters wanted to keep it under surveillance. They proposed we parachute a two-man team in the mountains on the north tip of Norway. This team would have a radio with which they could notify British intelligence headquarters if the *Tirpitz* tried to escape.

"We installed two bomb-bay gas tanks in a B-24 to enable us to make the extremely long trip to the top of Norway and return. We were to take off at 3 P.M. on 20 September 1944 and return to Leuchars by 9 A.M. on 21 September 1944. All went well during the first half of the journey. We made the drop, but when we started to bring our wheels up and our flaps up for our return trip to Scotland, we lost power on our number-three engine. We had to feather the prop. Now what to do?

"Should we try to go back to England over the North Sea on three engines, which would be an eight-hour flight, or should we go to Russia, which was our ally and only two hours away? We had the proper flares in our signal pistol to identify ourselves as friendly to the Russians. We decided to go to Russia. We went out over the water and turned east. When we arrived at the Kola Inlet, we headed south for Murmansk, flying at fifteen hundred feet with our lights on.

"We had about ten miles to go to reach Murmansk. At Vaenga, the sky lit up. Every Russian ship in the harbor was firing at us. We caught fire. Colonel Keith Allen would not leave the aircraft. The rest of us bailed out, some landing in the water and some landing on land. I was in the water . . . for quite a while before the Russians picked me up."

Allen stayed at the controls while the other crew members got out. He died in the crash. Schreiner and the rest of the crew survived. They returned to Scotland on a British ship.

The mission on which Allen was lost was one of a series that proved among the most difficult of all the Carpetbagger operations: delivering agents and supplies to the Norwegian underground. The weather—especially in the winter of 1944–45—and the rugged Norwegian terrain were at least as much a challenge as the German defenses, although they also played a role.

Douglas Walker later recalled one such mission:

"Lieutenant [William H.] Hudson's crew and our crew—Lieutenant Swarts's—took off on a dual mission to drop American commandos of Norwegian descent, together with munitions and supplies, into the Jaevsjo Lake area northeast of Trondheim. This was a point near the Swedish-Norwegian border.

"The commandos were under the leadership of Maj. William E. Colby [later director of the Central Intelligence Agency], and their objective was to cut the north-south railroad line in that area, thus hampering Nazi troop movements. They were to blow up the rail lines and railroad bridges and then retreat into the mountains to evade the inevitable German pursuit."

The two planes flew to Scotland to pick up the commandos and refuel and then headed across the Norwegian Sea. As they neared the drop zone, they ran into severe snowstorms and turbulence. After trying for an hour to penetrate to the target, Swarts turned back and dropped off the commandos. He and his crew then flew on to their base at Harrington and waited in vain for Hudson's plane to return.

After several days of uncertainty, a radio message from the Norwegian underground reported that Hudson's plane had crashed into a mountain in the blizzard. The Norwegians located the wreckage the next day and buried the eight crew members.

"In all, two Liberator aircrews from Harrington crashed in the attempt to land those commandos in Norway, due to the severe winter weather conditions in January and February 1945," Walker wrote.

"Finally . . . sixteen of the original thirty-six commandos were successfully dropped near Jaevsjo Lake and, although outnumbered ten to one, they completed their mission with honor. They teamed up with a local group of Norwegian resistance forces and blew up several rail bridges and four miles of heavily guarded rail lines."

Fish made three attempts to deliver agents into Norway—and each time, he was forced to turn back by icing and impenetrable weather. On one mission, he came within thirty miles of his destination before finally swinging around and heading back to England.

Fish clearly recalls his first such mission in early 1945:

"We entered Norway at a point west of Oslo at an altitude of eight thousand feet. The night was very clear, and the moon was very bright. We would have been a very easy target for a night fighter in the moonlight. Fortunately, we encountered no fighters.

"I vividly recall the beautiful grandeur of the snow-covered mountains in the moonlight. It was almost as bright as day.

"About fifty miles short of our drop zone, we began to encounter scattered clouds. A few more miles and we were in solid cloud. We turned back to the clear area in an attempt to go in under the cloud. It was impossible because the clouds covered the mountains and filled the valleys. More cloud cover was rolling in from the west. There was no way we could get into the high valley to our target location. We had no choice but to return to England.

"The weather was turning bad as we flew southward toward the North Sea. We were flying at eight thousand feet as we crossed the coastline. Just as we crossed, there was a loud explosion in the number-three engine in the right wing. My first reaction was that we had taken an antiaircraft shell in that engine. We immediately pushed the propeller-feathering button and the propeller came to a full feathered position before the engine stopped."

While feathering the propeller, Fish threw the plane into violent evasive maneuvers to avoid further damage from antiaircraft. He quickly decided the problem was a blown cylinder in the engine rather than gunners on the ground and leveled off to check the condition of the plane.

"By that time, we were in clouds over the North Sea, and we began to pick up ice on our wings. Because we were now reduced to the power of only three engines, I knew we could not continue flying at eight thousand feet with a heavy load of ice forming on the aircraft," Fish says.

He dropped down to a thousand feet, skipping in and out of clouds. Between breaks in the clouds, the crew members caught glimpses of whitecaps on the water down below.

"Our navigator reported that we were flying into a seventy-mile-per-hour head wind," Fish says. "This wind would extend our flight time back to Leuchars by almost an additional hour. We just had to sit there and hope we didn't lose another motor. If we did, we faced the probability of a forced landing in a rough sea driven by seventy-mile-an-hour winds. Our chances of surviving such an event were practically nil."

Fortunately, the three remaining engines kept running. They landed in Scotland just at daybreak.

Even though the war was, by that time, going badly against the Germans and they were short on aviation fuel, they were still able to make life tough for the Carpetbaggers on occasion.

Walker, again flying as a gunner-dispatcher on Lieutenant Swarts's crew, recalled one moonless night in March 1945 when they dropped supplies to a Norwegian resistance unit:

"We made our first pass over the zone and dropped our large containers from the bomb bay. As we made our turn for the second pass to drop our smaller containers from the waist, the tail gunner, Ralph Schiller, reported in on the intercom and said, 'Tail gunner to pilot. Bright lights just came on over to our right—it looks like an airport—and there is a plane taking off with its landing lights on.'

"We had stirred up a real hornets' nest. The Nazi airfield was only a few miles away and they had obviously sent a night fighter pursuit plane to zero in on us.

"We completed our second pass in a hurry and turned toward the North Sea. When we were over the water a few minutes later, we began to relax, feeling the night fighter had missed us. Just then, Ralph spoke up again: 'There is a plane directly to our rear. I can see the glow of his exhaust and his faint silhouette.'"

Swarts, the pilot, threw the Liberator into a steep dive toward the ocean. He leveled off a few hundred feet above the water, zigzagging violently. After about five minutes, with no further sign of the fighter, he climbed back up to cruising altitude.

Another crew was less fortunate a month later, on the night of 20–21 April 1945. Twelve B-24s joined a flight of British planes in a large-scale drop of supplies to the Norwegians, preparing to force the surrender of the Germans in Norway.

One of the American planes was piloted by Lt. Ralph W. Keeny. Just after they crossed the coast, they were attacked by a night fighter and heavily damaged. Keeny set a course for the nearest point on the Swedish border, hoping to come down in neutral territory. But before they reached the border, they flew into a flak trap and were hit again. Keeny sounded the bail-out alarm.

The entire crew managed to get out of the plane before it crashed. But in an incident remarkably similar to that involving Lieutenants Sanders and Callahan, recounted in Chapter Seven, Lt. Stephen J. Marangus could not reach his parachute. He jumped while clinging to SSgt. H. H. Brobec. But Marangus lost his grip shortly before they reached the ground and fell to his death. The other crew members all survived, although some of them were injured, and remained in German custody until the war ended on 7 May.

Perhaps the most unusual task given to the Carpetbaggers was in the spring of 1945, when about a dozen of the unit's B-24s were assigned to assist the Royal Air Force. Since the Carpetbagger crews were used to flying at night—as distinguished from most of the other American bomber crews, who flew in the daytime—they were called on to serve as decoys for the RAF night bombers.

Flying without guns in the nose and lower ball turret—the normal Carpetbagger configuration—they were assigned to mingle in with a stream of RAF night bombers and then peel off toward targets of their own, hoping to lure the German night fighters away from the main bomber stream.

In most cases, the American planes were accompanied on their feint by a larger number of RAF bombers and planes carrying metal "chaff," which was dropped to make the formation look larger than it really was on German radar.

This was in the period when Allied air power reached its peak and German defenses were increasingly strained. The nightly raids by the RAF and the daytime attacks by the Americans were a deliberate attempt to undermine German morale and will to resist by crushing and burning down the enemy's cities. Feints such as those carried out by the Carpetbaggers against cities that were not the main target not only drew night fighters away from the bomber stream but also caused the German firefighters to rush down the autobahns to the wrong place.

The most famous such raid, carried out by both British and American bombers, was the destruction of Dresden, with the loss of more than thirty-five thousand civilian lives, on 13 and 14 February 1945. But Dresden was only one of many German cities subjected to massive bombing and firestorm as the war drew to a climax.

In March of 1945, the Carpetbaggers were involved in night-time raids against Münster, Dortmund, Emden, Freiburg, and Wiesbaden, which, ironically, later became United States Air Force headquarters in Europe.

Following a raid on the night of 9–10 April, a British air vice-marshal sent a teletype praising the American involvement: "The operations last night provided an outstanding example of the valuable degree of support that can be afforded to bomber command by our special operations. The enemy reacted strongly and with great determination but in the wrong place, with the result that the main force, despite its great strength, was unmolested, whilst the whole of the enemy's considerable fighter effort was expended on the feint force. . . . To add to his discomfort, he lost three night fighters destroyed and one damaged to British night fighters."

One of the Carpetbagger aircrew members took a more jaundiced view of the operation. In a memoir written after the war, James Darby recalled:

"The night-bombing pathfinder missions with the RAF were pretty grim. Four or five of our B-24s flew in trail with the RAF bomber streams of aircraft. We were mixed in with the RAF Lancasters and Wellingtons. As soon as the German Luftwaffe night fighters were committed, we were instructed to turn back to England. We were required to carry bombs and to drop them on German targets on the way home. We were required to do this just to say that the United States was engaged in twenty-four-hour bombing operations. This was stupid. We did no damage to speak of, and our lives and aircraft were in extreme danger for no reason except public relations."

Late in the war, the Carpetbaggers, using new planes and flying from bases in France, were to return briefly to their original job of delivering Joes to the Continent—this time into the heart of Germany itself. But, meanwhile, a similar operation had grown to major proportions supporting resistance movements in Italy, Albania, Greece, and, most important of all, Yugoslavia.

CHAPTER 10
Action in the South

Aid to resistance movements in southern Europe got off to a slower and rockier start than the operations conducted by the Carpetbaggers in northern Europe. Shortage of equipment, official indifference, if not outright hostility, and the diversity of the resistance movements, both politically and geographically, all played their part in the slower pace in the south.

But once the assistance to guerrilla fighters behind the German lines began to build momentum, it grew, especially in the case of Yugoslavia, into a major undertaking that vastly exceeded the efforts of the Carpetbaggers in the north.

There is still a tendency among Carpetbaggers, and even among some of today's special operators, to think of the operations carried on in the south of Europe during World War II as somehow outside the mainstream of the air commando tradition. Because the southern operations were slower starting and more widespread, they did not have the neat cohesiveness of the Air Commandos' Burma campaign or of the Carpetbaggers' nighttime flights in northern Europe. Perhaps the main reason that some tend to disregard the southern operations is that they involved a major contribution by the conventional air force, primarily in the form of hundreds of missions flown by C-47 crews of the Air Transport Command.

But, measured in terms of innovation and the bravery of those involved, the operations in the south of Europe fall well within the bounds of the air commando tradition, and, in geographic scope and sheer magnitude, they were significantly larger than those in Burma and northern Europe.

As early as December 1942, General Donovan and the OSS received permission from the Joint Chiefs of Staff to deliver men and equipment into southern Europe by both air and sea. The plan approved by the JCS provided for an average of three bomber-type airplanes available "per each moon night of the month."

The decision by the JCS was exactly what the OSS outpost in Algiers had been waiting for. This seemed to mean they could quickly begin conducting clandestine operations into southern France. But approval in Washington and what actually happened in North Africa were two different things. Lieutenant General Carl A. "Tooey" Spaatz, the highest ranking air force general in the European conflict and commander of the Northwest African Air Forces, simply said, "No." He didn't have enough planes for such diversions. An aide flatly labeled the OSS plan to create an American special operations unit "undesirable."

Opposition continued even after the OSS had carried out a spectacular bit of espionage. In February 1943, with no planes available, OSS in Algiers used a Free French submarine to land an agent code-named Tommy on the south coast of France. He obtained the complete German antiaircraft defense plan for France. But, even with this prize in his possession, there was still no aircraft available to land in France and pick him up. He returned the way he had come, by submarine.

For more than a month, during May and June of 1943, the OSS begged for a plane to insert Tommy back in France. Finally, they arranged for a British plane to deliver him.

In August, Spaatz finally agreed to provide three B-17 heavy bombers to operate as a special flight section under the Twelfth Air Force. Operating out of an airfield in Tunisia, bomber crews were retrained to fly the low-altitude, nighttime missions needed for this form of special operations. On the moonlit night of 20 October 1943, a single B-17 parachuted weapons, ammunition, and other supplies to a French resistance unit in the French Alps near Lake Geneva. The drop was successful. But on the way back to Africa, the plane was badly damaged by antiaircraft fire. With two of their four engines shut down, the crew limped back across the Mediterranean and landed at an emergency airstrip in Algiers.

In late October, Spaatz provided three more aircraft for OSS's special operations. But, instead of heavy bombers, he gave them B-25 medium bombers. Although the B-25s looked good on paper, the OSS quickly found that they were almost totally unsuitable for the type of missions they were flying into occupied France. They were too fast for personnel drops; they didn't have the range to reach most parts of France from North Africa, and they couldn't carry enough to make their dangerous flights worthwhile. They were also unsuitable for landing and taking off from the rough fields available in occupied France, so they could not be used to bring out agents and members of the resistance.

In December, the B-25s were moved to Manduria, Italy, where the OSS found other uses for them. The three B-17s remained in North Africa, operating out of the Blida airdrome in Algiers—the home base for the RAF's special operations unit. From there, they were able to make regular visits to drop zones in southern France, although on a limited scale.

Fish recalls that he and Heflin flew down to Algiers in one of their B-24s in late 1943 or early 1944 to share their experience in equipping and training the Carpetbaggers and flying missions with the British. He was not impressed: "They really didn't have any assets. We briefed a room full of people and then came home."

What stands out about that trip in his memory is the stop in Gibraltar to refuel on the way back to Britain. As they approached the runway in bumpy weather, the cover on the Joe hole came open, and the crew's B-4 bags, containing all the clothing they had brought with them, fell out the hole and into the sea.

At about this same time, General Ira Eaker was transferred from command of the Eighth Air Force in England to head of the Mediterranean Allied air forces. He had overseen the successful organization of the Carpetbaggers in England and was sold on the need for special operations support to resistance movements behind the enemy lines. What he found when he moved to the Mediterranean theater shocked him: only three B-17s and half a dozen B-25s available for special operations. In the previous four months, the B-17s had flown only twenty-six missions—and on only eleven of those did they make successful drops.

The situation was a shambles.

Eaker, fresh from England, knew that the invasion of the Continent was only a few months away. General Eisenhower, who was in charge of planning for the landing, desperately wanted full-scale support for the resistance movement, not only in the north of France, where the invasion would take place, but also in the south of France, as a diversion and to "hold" German divisions in place and away from Normandy.

On 31 January, Eaker sent a cable to Washington proposing what seemed a simple solution: he asked for permission to create a special operations unit with a total of fifteen heavy bombers, a unit similar in organization to the Carpetbaggers. His plan was to do this without any additional planes or crews, but something got lost between his headquarters and Washington.

General Arnold, who at the same time was so supportive of Cochran and Alison and their air commandos in Burma, interpreted Eaker's message as a request for more planes and crews. He turned down the request.

By this time, General Spaatz had been promoted to commander of United States Strategic Air Forces, an important one step up from Eaker in the air force pecking order. He didn't approve of the request for special operations aircraft when he was running things in the Med, and he didn't like them any better in his new position in overall command of both the Eighth and Fifteenth Air Forces.

Eaker kept pushing for approval of his plan, working the back channel through friends in the Pentagon. Pressure also came from Eisenhower, Winston Churchill, the RAF, and the United States State Department. Finally, after Gen. George C. Marshall, the Army chief of staff, became personally involved, Eaker got permission to put together his special operations squadron.

Approval came in a message on 9 March, five and a half weeks after Eaker's original proposal—not long by peacetime standards, but a terribly long time to wait, considering the fact that the Normandy invasion was only a few months away.

Once he received approval, Eaker moved quickly. He added twelve B-24s to the three B-17s and created a new unit that, after several changes of designation, became the 885th Bombardment Squadron (Heavy) (Special). Colonel Monro MacCloskey was named commanding officer. When the Balkan Air Force was created, with representatives of all the Allies, the 885th became a part of it, working not only with the British but with Polish, South African, Italian, and Russian units.

The new squadron concentrated on supporting the resistance movement in southern France through the late spring and early summer of 1944. And then, in late summer, with the Allies having landed both at Normandy and in southern France and having pushed the Germans back in both areas, the squadron switched to supporting partisan resistance fighters in northern Italy and the Balkans.

Aid to the Italian partisans was a relatively small part of the effort by the Allied air arm until relatively late in the war. Aid went to resistance movements in Albania and Greece and other parts of the Balkans, but by far the biggest part of the effort was focused on helping those fighting Hitler in Yugoslavia.

In the early years of the war, the Allies supported two rival movements. One consisted of the Cetnik forces headed by Gen. Draja Mihailovich, minister of war in the royal Yugoslav government, then operating in exile out of Cairo. The other was headed by Marshal Tito, a Russian-trained Communist who headed a growing movement that was giving the German forces severe problems. At one point, it was estimated that Tito's two hundred thousand or more partisans were tying down at least seventeen German divisions that might otherwise have been fighting the Allied forces on the eastern or western fronts.

In contrast, Mihailovich's forces were smaller and seemed, to many Allied officials, more concerned with battling their rivals within Yugoslavia—even if that involved cooperating with the Nazis during the war—than in fighting the German invaders. The evidence that they were in fact collaborating with the Germans became so convincing by the end of 1943 that, as of 1 January 1944, aid to Mihailovich's Cetniks was cut off.

That date not only marked the end of aid to the Cetniks but roughly coincides with a dramatic increase in aid supplied to Tito. In effect, the Allies provided Tito's logistical support and his air arm while his guerrilla fighters were the ground forces.

The decision to back Tito was highly controversial because of the fact that Tito was a Communist with strong links to the Soviet Union. But Prime Minister Churchill, speaking to the House of Commons on 24 May 1944, gave this rationale for the decision: "We have proclaimed ourselves supporters of Marshal Tito because of his heroic and massive struggle against the German armies. We are sending and planning to send the largest possible supplies of weapons to him and to make the closest contact with him."

Tito's partisans not only carried out extensive sabotage and harassment actions against the Germans but also had to defend themselves against repeated attempts to crush their movement. All this meant a growing demand for arms, ammunition, and other supplies, a demand the 885th Bombardment Squadron and other Allied special operations units could not meet by themselves. Particularly needed was the ability to land in the rough fields held by the partisans to deliver supplies and bring out downed Allied airmen and partisans who were sick or wounded or required specialized training.

Until the end of 1943, Tito obtained his arms from a variety of sources. A good deal of material became available when the Yugoslav army collapsed in 1941. More was captured from the Germans, and still more fell into the guerrillas' hands when the Italians capitulated in 1943. But by the end of 1943, with the size of Tito's forces growing rapidly, supplies and arms were running dangerously short. In November 1943, the British landed three thousand tons of supplies by sea. But that was only a trickle compared with what was needed in the face of an offensive launched by the Germans in December to solidify control of Bosnia and the Dalmatian coast.

The British, flying out of an airfield at Brindisi, where the heel of the Italian boot stretches out into the Adriatic Sea toward

Albania, stepped up their efforts to help Tito. But they managed to deliver only 524 tons of supplies even though they attempted more than five hundred sorties during the period between 1 December 1943 and the first of March 1944.

In February 1944, two American troop carrier squadrons, with their C-47s, arrived at Brindisi and began flying supply missions to northern Italy and the Balkans, with the bulk of the flights going into Yugoslavia and Albania. In February and March, they delivered a total of 187 tons in spite of persistently bad weather.

On 23 February, the Americans conducted an operation remarkably similar to the one the air commandos carried out a few days later halfway around the globe in Burma. Three C-47s took off from the Allied air base at Bari, Italy. Each towed a single Waco glider. The gliders carried a twenty-three-man Russian military mission and six British officers destined for Tito's headquarters. The C-47s brought the gliders into position for a safe landing and then parachuted 10,500 pounds of supplies, even though the visibility was practically zero over the target.

The original two American troop carrier squadrons were replaced in late March by four C-47 squadrons, and an additional RAF squadron was added in May. Between April and October 1944, the American troop carriers flew an average of thirty-five missions a night. As Tito's operations expanded, the partisans were operating more than three hundred drop zones. Most of the locations were known to the Germans, and they were often attacked by air or land. But there were so many of them, and so many were in inaccessible areas, that the enemy had little success in trying to cut off the Allied supply operation.

The first landing—as opposed to supply drop—came on the night of 2–3 April 1944, when two American C-47s landed on a rough strip near Tito's headquarters. By the end of April, there were three strips available, at least part of the time, in that same area. By July, there were sixteen strips in use, and by the end of the war, there were thirty-six strips in use in Yugoslavia alone. The number of landing operations increased dramatically in mid-1944. There were 13 landings in April; 50 in May; 125 in June; 194 in July; 145 in August; and 128 in September.

The Allies even organized a Balkan Air Terminal Service to coordinate activities on the receiving end. Each BATS team consisted of an officer and five or six enlisted men to select and prepare airstrips, guide planes to the strip, prepare cargo and personnel for evacuation, and organize the partisans to load and unload the C-47s. One group of partisans became so efficient they could unload a C-47 in ten minutes. The BATS teams were a forerunner of today's special tactics teams.

At the other end of the supply line, at the airfield in Brindisi, the Allies set up a businesslike system for feeding supplies to those fighting behind enemy lines. Stocks were gathered in a warehouse area known as Paradise Camp. Partisans who had been evacuated for medical treatment prepared packages for each plane under the supervision of British officers. Trucks picked up the packages, stopped at a special post office to gather up mail for those in the field, and then delivered their cargo to the planes. Each C-47 carried about 4,000 pounds of cargo, plus 150 pounds of leaflets— or "nickels," as they were called—to be dropped on each mission. The bigger bombers, which loaded from their own storage area, carried about 6,000 pounds of supplies and personnel plus 250 to 300 pounds of "nickels."

By the summer of 1944, the Balkan Air Force was able to provide fighter escort for the unarmed C-47s and suppress enemy defenses near the landing zones. This meant the supply planes could operate in the daytime as well as at night. In August, the 60th Troop Carrier Group made 145 successful landings in Yugoslavia. In one case, pilots flew on instruments through bad weather to rough landing zones between two jagged peaks to deliver twenty-four mules and twelve 75mm guns. On their return flights during August, they brought out more than two thousand persons, including wounded partisans and women and children.

In some ways, the demands on aircrews flying into northern Italy and the Balkans were more severe than those faced by the Carpetbaggers. Missions tended to be longer. The bombers, especially when they were flying out of North Africa, flew to targets as much as 600 or 700 miles distant, compared with 300 miles or fewer on most Carpetbagger flights. The C-47s operating out of

Brindisi routinely flew to targets 300 miles away and, on occasion, 450 miles away. Navigation was also somewhat more demanding because of long over-water segments and the lack of navigation aids. At times, however, the pilots found they could home in on enemy radio stations, especially in Belgrade.

The danger from antiaircraft fire and night fighters was generally less than in most of the area covered by the Carpetbaggers, although both fighters and flak were a constant worry.

On the night of 8–9 August, for example, 2d Lt. Sam O. Painter, a C-47 pilot, was attacked by a night fighter while he was in the pattern for his third approach to the drop zone. Painter completed his drop and then turned to face the fighter head-on. The startled enemy pilot blinked first in this aerial game of chicken and turned away. Painter escaped in the dark.

The rugged terrain in much of the Balkans was usually much more of a worry than the enemy. On most drops, the pilots flew at about six hundred feet, and, often, this meant flying three to five thousand feet below surrounding peaks and ridges. If a plane arrived at the designated drop zone and the crew did not see the expected signal lights down below, they could "stooge around" for as long as an hour, waiting for the lights—and dodging the rocks and trees the whole time.

On the night of 20–21 June 1944, while circling near a drop zone, Capt. Robert H. Snyder, operations officer of the 28th Troop Carrier Squadron, was confronted by a cliff rising out of the darkness. He banked sharply, stalled, and crashed with the loss of the entire crew.

Although the primary goal of the air operations was to keep the resistance fighters supplied so they could continue to battle the Germans, thousands of persons were evacuated to Italy by the troop carriers. In the year from 1 April 1944 to 30 April 1945, an estimated nineteen thousand persons were flown out of the Balkans—almost ninety-three hundred of them by the Americans in a six-month period in mid-1944.

One of the most dramatic—and important—evacuation efforts occurred in early June 1944.

At 4:30 A.M. on 25 May, German dive bombers hit Tito's head-quarters at Drvar, a village surrounded by three-thousand-foot mountains in western Yugoslavia. Two battalions of Germans swooped down on the area by parachute and glider. But Tito, sus-picious because of increased air activity in the days immediately before the attack, had pulled part of his staff back into a moun-tain ravine. The British and Russian military missions had their own camps in nearby ravines, and a small American meteorolog-ical team was also located there.

Tito's thousand-man force resisted the initial attack. But, on the afternoon of the day after the initial assault, a German armored column and additional infantry joined in. Along with the British, Russians, and Americans, Tito's headquarters party fled the area just before they were surrounded and escaped to a nearby town. On 3 June, a BATS team prepared an emergency landing strip. At ten o'clock that night, a Russian C-47 from a base in Italy picked up Tito and a group of key officers and flew them to Italy. On the next two nights, the Americans evacuated the rest of Tito's staff and the members of the foreign missions, saving them from almost certain capture.

While the troop carriers were flying their supply and evacua-tion missions, the heavy bombers concentrated on drops to more distant targets, mostly in south-central Yugoslavia and, later, in northern Italy.

In December 1944, the bomber force was augmented by the arrival in Brindisi of the Carpetbaggers' 859th Squadron from England.

Relations between the newcomers and the 885th Bomb Squadron—and especially its commander, Colonel MacCloskey—were strained. Al L. Sharps, a tail gunner on one of the B-24s sent down from England to help out, later gave this humorous account of their relationship:

"We did the job the 885th BS couldn't or wouldn't do. The 885th BS flew, to the best of my knowledge, into soft Greek and Italian targets or on milk runs over southern France or the *western* slope of Austria.

"Which gave the 859th BS plenty of room—the eastern slopes of Austria, Yugoslavia, Albania, the rough box canyons of the Alps, Moravia, Montenegro, etcetera.

"I don't think we should be overly concerned about Mac-Closkey's dislike of the 859th BS. We did sort of ruin his claim to being the inventor of Carpetbagging. We also terrified him. For on his one visit to the 859th BS area, he reamed out the guard at the entrance and told him to shoot at the next person who entered the area who failed to stop upon challenge. He then entered the officers' section of our just-finished hard-pine privy.

"The next person who entered the area was an old Italian grandmother, who knew not a single word of English, bringing back a basket of clean laundry. The challenge was made, she ran, he fired. The bullet passed diagonally between MacCloskey's open knees, shattering a pine knot, so that a goodly number of splinters were imbedded in the colonel's right inner thigh. The medic happily reported that blood had been drawn although there was some regret that the barrel of the .45 had not been a trifling to the right in its aim."

From the latter part of 1944 on, the Americans, including the special operations bombers, provided increasing amounts of aid to the Italian partisans harassing the Germans in northern Italy. The first drop to the Italians by the Americans, flying out of North Africa, did not occur until the night of 9–10 September. But in the next two weeks, they completed thirty-six sorties into Italy's Po Valley.

From November 1944 until the end of the war, Americans, flying both heavy bombers and C-47s, delivered virtually all the supplies reaching the Italian partisans by air. In the final months of the war in 1945, the C-47s dropped more than 1,800 tons of supplies to the Italians, and the bombers dropped another 1,260 tons.

With the Germans in retreat and with their defenses deteriorating, most of these missions were flown in the daytime. The supply planes normally picked up an escort of four American P-47 or British Spitfire fighters, but they encountered little or no opposition except for occasional bursts of flak.

Remarkably, considering that many missions were flown at night and in bad weather through rugged, poorly marked terrain, the Americans lost only ten C-47s and two B-24s in their operations out of North Africa and Italy.

While, in the early months of 1945, the Americans flying out of Italy put much of their effort into aiding the partisans in northern Italy, the Carpetbaggers flying out of England and new bases in France spent the last few months of the war flying daring missions into Germany itself.

CHAPTER 11
The Final Days

Early in 1945, with the arena of the war rapidly shrinking down to Germany itself, the Carpetbaggers were called upon for renewed missions over the Continent to insert agents into the enemy's homeland. Colonel Hudson H. Upham, a nonflier newly named as commander of the 492d Bombardment Group, objected. It was too dangerous, he argued, to send his B-24s, alone at night, on such perilous missions.

But the Office of Strategic Services was desperate to place as many agents as possible into Germany to scope out the extent and disposition of the Nazi forces as they drew back for a last-ditch defense of the homeland.

Particularly urgent was the answer to one question: was it true, as rumored, that the enemy was concentrating in an Alpine redoubt in southern Germany? If that were the case, Patton would have to swing south instead of moving on toward Berlin. The Americans could expect another ferocious battle, perhaps rivaling in intensity the bloody Battle of the Bulge they had just experienced.

Upham was overruled. The Carpetbaggers were ordered to penetrate into the heart of Germany, flying both from the Harrington air base in England and from new bases near Dijon and Lyon in central France.

Upham's fears of heavy losses were not borne out, for several reasons. A major reason was the decision by the Swiss, referred to in Chapter Nine, to permit the Carpetbaggers to fly over their territory. This allowed the B-24s to drop agents in Bavaria, where the redoubt, if it existed, would be located. They were thus spared exposure to the flak and night fighters they would have encountered on the longer route over Germany.

Flying from bases in France, the B-24s carried out the important mission of dropping agents into Bavaria. If the Germans were preparing to fight to the last man in that mountainous terrain, it would have been obvious by the movement of thousands of soldiers and long lines of equipment on the roads. The agents flashed back the word: the rumor about the enemy gathering in the redoubt was false. There would be no final bloody battle in the Alps.

A second major reason the Carpetbaggers were able to operate over Germany with relative impunity was that they were issued two new types of aircraft which could outrun and outmaneuver German fighters: the new American A-26 and the British Mosquito.

The assignment of the A-26 Invader was the beginning of a long and close association between the special operators and this sleek, high-speed twin-engine light bomber. Built by Douglas Aircraft, the plane was just coming into service at the end of World War II when the Carpetbaggers were assigned several of the planes for their special missions.

(The Douglas A-26 Invader is sometimes confused with the Martin B-26 Marauder, which also saw service during World War II. The confusion is compounded by the fact that the Invader was known as the B-26 for a long period after the war until the designation was changed back to A-26 during the Vietnam War.)

Carpetbagger crews completed their training to fly the A-26 in April of 1945 and were delighted with its performance: close to four hundred miles an hour, twice as fast as a lumbering B-24. Ross D. White, one of the A-26 pilots, recalled an incident when he stopped at an American night-fighter base:

"I had a mission to go and drop two agents in northern Germany near Kiel but had to pick them up at a United States night-fighter base in Germany. Some of the fighter pilots there saw this black A-26 parked on the ramp and became curious. They waited around operations until I came to take off. They asked me where I was going, but I could not tell them where I was going or what I was doing. They said they were going on a night mission and would escort me. I told them, 'No.' They said that since they were flying the radar-equipped P-61 Black Widow night fighter, I didn't have a choice. That airplane was fast, but the A-26 I was us-ing, all stripped down, was faster. I said they would never be able to keep up. They all thought that was nonsense.

"I took off, turned on course, finished my mission, and re-turned to land at the fighter base for fuel, where I again met some of the pilots. They said they had lost me after my first turn out of traffic and were amazed at the speed of the A-26. Because they took off with some of them ahead of me and some behind me, they were sure they could keep in touch, with their radar. A cou-ple of them said they saw me once on their radar but could not keep up.

"Incidentally, the two agents were Germans who had surren-dered in North Africa. I saw one of them after the war in Paris, and he said that when I pulled the trap door on him, he thought he had bought the farm."

White was referring to the unique system used for dropping Joes from the A-26. Because the plane was so small, it had little room for passengers and no space for a Joe hole like that installed in the B-24. Instead, plywood platforms were placed in the bomb bay, and two Joes lay on the plywood. When the time came for them to drop, the pilot gave them a brief warning and then sim-ply pulled the salvo switch. They were dropped like two bombs. The drop was usually made from an altitude of two to four hun-dred feet—just enough room for the static line to open their chutes before they landed. The Joes hated it.

Despite his reluctance to send the B-24s into Germany, Colonel Upham acceded to the request of the OSS to speed up the in-troduction of the A-26, and that may have contributed to the tragic outcome of the first flight.

Fish and others in the unit felt that the crews had not had enough time to familiarize themselves with this quite different aircraft before they were sent into combat.

"I think Colonel Upham knew we were not fully trained for that mission. He tried to compensate by using highly trained staff officers as some of the crew members," Fish later wrote. "Had I been at Harrington, I feel that I could have reasoned with Colonel Upham and have convinced him that we should not attempt that mission until we were fully qualified with a regular crew. On other occasions, he had respected my Carpetbagger experience and had listened to me on operational matters. This time, I was not there."

The first flight, in mid-March of 1945, was manned by a four-man crew of volunteers, all of them highly experienced Carpetbaggers. They were Lt. Oliver H. Emmel, pilot; Maj. John W. Walsh, navigator; Major Tresemer, bombardier; and SSgt. Frederick J. Brunner, gunner. Their assignment was to deliver their Joe to the Dümmer Lake area, north of Osnabrück, in western Germany.

The plane crashed that night not far from its destination, killing the crew members and the agent they were to drop. Exactly what happened will never be known. But Fish has a theory:

"In my opinion, they probably flew too near the ground, something or somebody malfunctioned, and they had no chance to recover before they struck the ground. . . .

"Tresemer had been my navigator on my crew from the time he graduated from navigation school. I trained him to be a crew member, and he was one of the best. I knew him well. He cross-trained as a bombardier after we arrived in England. . . . On the night of this A-26 mission, he did not function as a professional bombardier even though he was carried on the crew roster as a bombardier. On this flight, he functioned as a pilotage navigator. [Pilotage is the most basic form of navigation: looking at the ground as it passes below and comparing what is seen to a map.]

"On low level flights, when he functioned as a pilotage navigator, he liked to have the aircraft right down in the treetops, where he could clearly see positive details of the earth's surface.

On such missions, he repeatedly called for his pilot to fly lower so he could see better.

"When I piloted for him at night, I ignored his requests to fly lower whenever we were within three hundred feet of the ground. Oliver H. Emmel, who was the pilot on that fatal flight, was highly qualified as a pilot, but he had not previously flown combat with Tresemer. He had no way of knowing Tresemer's idiosyncrasy about altitude. There is a distinct possibility that he allowed Tresemer to induce him to fly too low."

The missions the Carpetbagger crews flew with their other new plane—the Mosquito—were at the opposite extreme from the low-level A-26 missions. The British-made Mosquito was a very light twin-engine plane made of plywood. Because it was so light, it could fly both very high and very fast. The Mosquitos were a key link in a unique system used by spies inside Germany to transmit reports back to their handlers. They used what was called the Joan-Eleanor system.

The agent broadcast his message from a device that directed it upward in a very narrow cone. In one instance, a spy continued transmitting from a church steeple while a German direction-finding van rolled by down below, oblivious to his presence.

The other end of the system was a receiver in the Mosquito, flying at forty thousand feet. At that altitude, the signal spread out into a circle with a diameter of about sixty miles, so the pilot could simply circle in the proper area while the message was recorded on a wire recorder. Upon the plane's return to Harrington, the recording wire was rushed to London by motorcycle for analysis by intelligence experts.

During the period in the spring of 1945 when these missions were conducted over Berlin and other German cities, it was daylight around the clock at the extreme altitudes flown by the Mosquitos. That meant they did not have the protection of darkness. But they were above the range of antiaircraft fire. Fighter planes that tried to reach them stalled out and began to spin toward earth until they reached thicker air.

Even down low, the Mosquitos were more than a match for fighters because of their high speed.

On one occasion, a Mosquito pilot on his way home from Germany deliberately refrained from turning on the signal that would identify him to Allied air defenses. He listened on his radio as the American Black Widow night fighters were scrambled. He heard their radar intercept operator tell the fighters: "The bogy is pulling away from you. He is very fast. He is getting away!" As the Mosquito pilot pulled away, he radioed: "Call your dogs off. This is a 'friendly' en route to England."

By the end of World War II, the Army Air Forces had built a formidable special operations capability—not only in specialized equipment like the night-flying B-24, the A-26, and the Mosquito but also in the knowledge of thousands of aircrew members with wartime experience in secret operations in the enemy's backyard. Like the rest of the United States military, much of this capability simply vanished in the rush to demobilize in the months immediately after the war ended.

PART 3
Korea and Beyond

CHAPTER 12
Drawdown and Rebuilding

Within weeks after the Japanese surrender on 14 August 1945 ended World War II, millions of American servicemen began streaming home, having fulfilled their obligation to serve for "the duration plus six months."

The result was a drastic shrinkage of the American military, from a wartime peak of nearly 12 million men under arms. Within five years, what was left was an under-strength, poorly equipped force of 1.5 million.

For most of the military, the shrinkage was just that—shrinkage. The basic structure remained—Army divisions, Air Force wings, Navy carrier battle groups. It was all just very much smaller.

But the formidable special operations capability the Army Air Forces had created during World War II did not shrink. It simply disappeared. Gone were most of the Carpetbaggers and Air Commandos along with their specialized equipment and their institutional memory of how to use air power to support those operating on the ground behind enemy lines—whether resistance fighters, saboteurs, or intelligence agents.

Thus, when North Korea launched its surprise attack across the line that had partitioned Korea into a northern area associated with the Soviet Union and China and a southern area associated with the United States and the West, the South Koreans and their American allies were sent reeling. The attack occurred on 25 June 1950. Three days later, Seoul, the capital of South Korea, fell. The defenders were quickly driven back into a tiny perimeter near the southern port of Pusan.

The United States frantically fed in poorly trained garrison troops from Japan to maintain a foothold on the Korean peninsula until reinforcements arrived from the United States and other members of the United Nations.

As the Cold War intensified in the late 1940s, the Pentagon had foreseen the need for an operation similar to the Carpetbaggers and had begun to put it together. But it was not even formally created until months after the North Korean invasion. This force, which later played a part in the Korean War, was the innocuously named Air Resupply and Communications Service. Its operations are described in Chapter Thirteen.

As far as the Air Force, which had become a separate service after World War II, was concerned, special operations in Korea was a total vacuum.

Into this vacuum stepped a young Air Force captain named Henry "Heinie" Aderholt. He arrived in South Korea on the first of August 1950 as commander of Detachment 2 of the 21st Troop Carrier Squadron, which was part of the 315th Air Division.

Aderholt set up shop at Taegu, a city in southern Korea. The enemy was just the other side of the hills to the north. Aderholt's pilots and planes came on temporary duty from the troop carrier squadron, based at first in southern Japan and then at a field near Tokyo. Some days, they flew their C-47s over from Japan, performed their missions, and flew back. On other nights, they remained in Korea and slept in their planes or on the ground. Their assignments ranged from flying ammunition to hard-pressed frontline units to dropping agents far behind enemy lines.

"I was taking all comers," Aderholt recalls. "If they wanted to do something, we did it."

Sitting in his office in Fort Walton Beach, Flordia, where he operates a shop dealing in oriental goods, Aderholt brings out a bound ledger of the type used by bookkeepers. Opening the aging pages, he shows the simple record-keeping system used by Det 2 to keep track of its operations. Whether consciously or not, Aderholt was carrying on the tradition from the original air commandos in Burma of doing their job with little or no paperwork.

"We had the aircraft number, the scheduled takeoff time, the actual takeoff time, and the arrival time back at base. Later, we showed the pilots who flew the missions and who we flew them for," he explains. "We flew mostly at night, every night. This is the only record. When a book got through, we threw it away. There is no record of this anywhere in the world but right here. I just happened to bring these home with me. This is the only record. That's how operations can run very well if you don't have too much bureaucracy. That's what kills special operations."

On 15 September, the Allies landed behind the enemy lines at Inch'on and quickly retook Seoul. Aderholt moved his operation to Seoul. From there, they flew a variety of special operations missions, even venturing into neighboring China. One of their major tasks was to make up for the lack of preparation before the war began. Military planning normally provides for "stay-behind assets" to be available in the event of an invasion. Their job is to remain in enemy-occupied territory to carry out sabotage and, most important, report on the location and strength of enemy forces.

In Korea, there were few if any stay-behind assets.

The solution to this problem was Operation Aviary, in which agents—code-named Rabbits—landed by parachute behind enemy lines. Some of them were young women, including a group of actresses and performers recruited by Madam Rhee, wife of Syngman Rhee, the South Korean president.

"The agents were furnished by the Koreans," Aderholt recalls. "We had hundreds of them. Madam Rhee furnished all the women. They had all their movie stars and everybody, the best looking girls. We put them out over enemy territory in the winter of '50–'51 when the outside air temperature was forty to fifty degrees below zero. They would go out in cotton-padded suit and shoes. They didn't weigh enough to get to the ground, you would think."

The typical female agent carried neither weapons nor a radio. She was instructed to mingle with the enemy troops and travel as far as possible toward the front lines. Then she would permit herself to be captured by the Allies. Once in a prisoner-of-war camp, she identified herself with a special signal. She was then quickly released to make her report on what she had seen behind enemy lines.

Many of the agents were dropped after 26 October 1950, when the Chinese entered the war by marching three hundred thousand troops across the border into North Korea and sending the United Nations troops fleeing south. The rout was so rapid that the retreating Americans, who made up the bulk of the United Nations force, didn't know where the enemy was—if they were not in deadly contact.

Aderholt got a call from Tokyo.

"They said they had lost contact with the Chinese army and the gooks, the North Koreans, and they would like to know if I had any way to find them," Aderholt says.

"We didn't have any radios that would work. We still had the hand-crank radios from World War II.

"I had been in World War II. Remember the invasion stripes on all the airplanes? So our own people wouldn't shoot 'em down?

"We put layers of agents along the peninsula—thirty miles ahead, forty miles ahead. We'd parachute them at night. They had smoke grenades, yellow, green, and red. We'd fly up there every morning and every afternoon in daylight so they could see us, see the stripes on the planes.

"They'd pop their smoke to tell us where the enemy was. He hadn't passed here. Or the Koreans had passed, or the Chinese had passed."

With intelligence provided by this makeshift reporting method, the defenders were able to draw a rough outline of the disposition of the enemy's forces and update it as they moved south.

Altogether, about a thousand "Rabbits," both men and women, were parachuted behind the enemy lines between September 1950 and June 1951.

These intelligence-gathering missions were carried out for the military's Far East Command. Aderholt's outfit also flew many special missions for the Central Intelligence Agency, continuing the strong link the special operators had forged with the fledgling intelligence operation of the OSS during World War II—a shadow relationship that was to continue for many years in the future.

"We had a lot of flights that went six hours, seven hours," Aderholt recalls. "We'd go from Pusan [on the southern tip of South Korea] all the way up to the Choisin Reservoir up on the Yalu [River], on the Manchurian border. These were mostly for the CIA. The Far East Command was more interested in where the troops were.

"Anybody walked in and said they wanted to make a drop into China, we said, 'When?' They said, 'Tonight,' and we loaded them up and took them there. We didn't tell anybody. We just did it. And this is the only record that it ever happened."

Aderholt's Det 2 also operated a daily service to a guerrilla camp on Paengnyong Do, an island off the west coast of Korea just south of the present demarcation line between the two halves of the country. The pilots landed on the beach at low tide, unloaded their cargo, and took off again before the tide came in.

"I took my turn like everybody else. I flew mostly drop missions," Aderholt says.

"We had volunteers [from the troop carrier squadron] to stay for thirty days. Some I ran off before thirty days. Some didn't volunteer to come back. I had a few mainstays that were good."

Why didn't pilots volunteer to remain?

"They were scared. You take your choice of being in Tokyo or up there living in a tent and flying six-, seven-hour missions up to China at night."

Despite the dangers of flying at night at low altitude over the rugged Korean landscape, Aderholt's outfit lost only two airplanes during the entire operation.

When Aderholt left Korea, he went to work for the CIA. He was to surface again in Air Force uniform in the early days of the war in Southeast Asia.

Although Aderholt had served as a pilot in World War II, Korea was his first special operations war.

A few others can claim to have flown as air commandos in three wars. One of them is Lt. Col. Robert A. Madden. In World War II, he was a P-51 fighter pilot flying with the 1st Air Commando Group in the China-Burma-India theater in the final months of World War II. Recalled as a National Guard pilot in 1951, he volunteered in 1952 to join a unit in Korea flying what by then was known as the F-51. But instead, he was assigned to the 6147th Tactical Control Group and became a "Mosquito." His job was to fly a single-engine T-6 trainer and act as a forward air controller and artillery spotter for the Army's 25th Infantry Division.

Although there was no air commando or special operations designation in the Korean War, Madden had no doubt that his assignment in Korea fell within that category.

"I am convinced that few aviation units have flown a more vulnerable mission and few were less recognized, publicized, and remembered than the Mosquito organization," he later wrote in an account of his experiences in that war. When he mentions his service as a Mosquito, some of his listeners tend to think of the twin-engine Mosquito light bomber flown in World War II; others assume he sprayed for insects; most just give him a puzzled look.

Madden's service as a Mosquito ended abruptly on his twentieth mission when he stumbled on a carefully camouflaged enemy supply depot that the 25th Division had been eagerly seeking for weeks.

Flying well behind enemy lines, Madden, with Lt. Ralph Olivette, an Army officer, as spotter in the rear seat, had almost finished his day's mission. Then, circling over a broad valley, he looked off toward the south and saw a large opening at the base of a hill.

He rolled in toward what appeared to be the entrance to a cave or tunnel so his backseater could see it and record the coordinates.

Madden knew the risk they were taking: he had to fly below fifty feet in order to see the hole, and he knew the supply center would be heavily defended.

As he dove toward the entrance to the tunnel, squeezing all the speed he could out of his engine, he rotated the control stick in a circle, jinking through a blizzard of tracer bullets, seeming to come from all directions.

"We lasted longer than I originally thought would be possible, considering the amount of fire we were drawing," Madden recalls.

"Thinking we might be able to get out of there, I began gaining a little altitude—up to three or four hundred feet. At that point, I heard a very ugly *ping*—the kind of *ping* you hate to hear on a combat mission. . . . I looked to the right. The right wing had ten to fifteen holes, and fuel was pouring from three or four holes in the right fuel tank.

"On the left side, the fuel tank had not been hit, and I remember thinking that we had enough fuel in that tank to make it back to friendlier forces. Then I looked down and saw the ugliest little blue and green and orange flame that I had ever seen.

"We had taken a hit that nicked a fuel line to the fuel selector valve in the front cockpit, and apparently a spark had ignited the fuel. Yelling over the intercom that we were on fire and for Ralph to get the fire extinguisher, I stomped at the fire, but it only seemed to grow and spread.

"After what seemed to be an eternity, I called Ralph to hand me the extinguisher. He replied that he couldn't get it out of the rack—that he couldn't break the safety wire.

"By this time, the flames were above my knees, my clothes were on fire, and the skin on the back of my right hand had split wide open from the heat. Our cause was now hopeless, so I climbed as rapidly as I could, getting up to twelve or fifteen hundred feet. I yelled to Ralph to bail out. He did, and when I saw him leave the plane, I opened my canopy. This sucked the flames—now almost to my face—outside, which immediately caught the gas streaming from the right wing. The plane was one big fireball at this point."

Madden and Olivette both reached the ground alive, but injured. Madden was badly burned, and Olivette broke his ankle and his nose. Both men were quickly captured. Madden later went on to fly in his third war as an air commando. He put in two tours of duty in Vietnam, including service as commander of the 1st Air Commando Squadron at Pleiku.

Shortly after his capture in Korea, Madden had the unpleasant experience of being near the target of a bombing raid by what, from the sounds of their engines, he concluded were American B-26 bombers.

Ironically, another veteran air commando who had served in World War II and would go on to serve in Vietnam could have been at the controls of one of those bombers.

Richard Snyder, one of the enlisted men who flew the single-engine liaison planes during the Burma operation (see Chapter Four) remained in the Air Force after World War II and earned his wings as a commissioned pilot.

Snyder volunteered for service in Korea. He ferried a B-26 from California to Japan and then flew fifty-five missions in Korea—all at night. In Korea, he was a member of the 452d Bombardment Group. Although there weren't any units designated as air commandos, Snyder was doing exactly what other pilots flying the same plane did later in the war in Southeast Asia.

"We were shooting up trains, trucks, anything we could see at night," he says. "We accidentally hit a bomb dump one night. That blew sky high. When we got back to K-9 [the designation for their airfield], there was a guy from headquarters in Japan who wanted to talk to me on the phone.

"He said, 'How did you find that dump at night? We've been looking for it for months.'

"I said, 'We saw some trucks down there, and we figured, where they were last seen turning off their lights, they had to be going into something. It was a big lie. What we were doing was we were trying to hit the trucks, and the navigator missed them, and we hit the bomb dump. So when it went off, I dropped all the bombs on it.'"

After dropping his bombs, Snyder made three strafing runs on the target, and, to his surprise, there was no return fire. But on the fourth pass, they had him lined up and hit him with everything they had. They knocked off his radio antenna and hit the plane in the tail but failed to down the plane.

His navigator-bombardier asked if they had any ammunition left and told Snyder: "They won't give us a medal if we've got any ammo left."

By that time, the plane was in a steep climb, away from the target and the North Korean guns.

"I held the damn trigger down, and I fired off about a hundred rounds of .50-caliber straight up in the air," Snyder says. "And I said, 'Now we're out of ammo!' We went back home. I wasn't about to go over that sucker one more time."

While Aderholt, Madden, Snyder, and others were carrying on the special operations tradition in Korea, the Air Force had underway a far more ambitious worldwide effort patterned on the Carpetbaggers of World War II.

Chapter 13
Rebirth and Decline

In the winter of 1950–51, Colonel Bob Fish, who had commanded the Carpetbaggers a few years earlier, was teaching at the Air University at Maxwell Air Force Base, Alabama, and looking forward to a new assignment in the Strategic Air Command. When an officer from the Pentagon dropped by and asked if he would like to become involved in a new, bigger, Carpetbagger-like operation, he had no hesitation in turning down the proposal. To him, it looked like a dead-end job.

A few days later, he was called to report to the university commandant. Fish tells what happened next:

"He said the chief of staff wanted to talk to me. He rang up the Pentagon, handed me the phone.

"I said, 'Colonel Fish.'

"The other guy said, 'This is Vandenberg [Gen. Hoyt S. Vandenberg, chief of staff of the Air Force]. Colonel, I understand you don't want to work for me.'

"I gulped a couple of times, and I said, 'General, that's not the way I'd put it. . . .'

"I went to the Pentagon, and we established a little headquarters on Wisconsin Avenue in Washington."

Fish, who had been present at the creation of the Carpetbaggers and stayed with them until the war ended, was thus in at the creation of the Air Resupply and Communications Service, or ARCS. And, as it turned out, he was there when it pretty much came apart a few years later.

What he found when he arrived in Washington was a very ambitious and very rapidly growing organization. It was designed to do what the Carpetbaggers had done during World War II, but on a much bigger and broader scale.

"There was a small group—a clique, you could call it—in the Pentagon at the time that was trying to grab off a great big mission that didn't really belong to the Air Force," Fish says. "They figured, if they could swing it, it would mean promotions for them and all that kind of good stuff. They really hadn't thought the thing through very well, because what they did was they combined, under the Air Force program, all the elements of the resistance movement of World War II. That took part of the Voice of America, part of the CIA's mission, and brought it into the Air Force.

The plan was to create six ARCS wings, with about six thousand persons in each wing. They were to be prepared to drop propaganda and put agents in place anywhere in the world.

Although ARCS never reached its full size of six wings, it did grow into a worldwide operation with three wings stationed at Clark Air Force Base in the Philippines and later at Kadena Air Force Base in Okinawa; Molesworth and later Alconbury, England; and Wheelus Air Force Base, Libya. The wings were equipped with four-engine, propeller-driven B-29 bombers, the same type that had carried out the massive bombing campaign against Japan in World War II. They were modified by stripping out all the guns except for a "stinger" in the tail and adding a Joe hole for dropping agents. ARCS also had C-119 and C-54 cargo planes, SA-16 amphibious planes, and, later, helicopters.

The ARCS organization was established on 23 February 1951—seven months after the Korean War began—and the first wing, the 580th ARC Wing, was activated at Mountain Home Air Force Base, Idaho, two months later. In announcing the activation of the wing, the Air Force described the new unit's mission: "These wings will have two major wartime missions. One, to prepare, reproduce, and disseminate psychological warfare materials as directed by the theater commander; and, two, the aerial resupply of military units."

That latter phrase probably didn't mean much to most of those who read the announcement. But for those capable of reading between the lines, it was a succinct statement of the kind of things Air Force special operators do—supporting guerrilla and resistance forces operating well behind enemy lines. But, in the context of the Cold War, it also meant operations across the borders of countries with which the United States was not at war—although not quite at peace either.

The focus was on the global confrontation with the Soviet Union. But as soon as the first ARCS wing had completed its training, it joined the hot war in Korea.

While the bulk of the wing operated out of the Philippines, one special unit was stationed in Korea. It was a helicopter unit that carried out secret operations—mostly at CIA direction—behind enemy lines. Except for the brief use of a primitive helicopter in Burma in 1944, it was the first use of helicopters by Air Force special operations—a pioneering operation that foreshadowed the way the helicopter later became one of the most important tools used by the special operators.

Robert F. Sullivan, a retired major who lives in South Hadley, Massachusetts, was one of the six ARCS helicopter pilots attached to the 58th Air Rescue Group at Seoul. He recalled his experiences in Korea in a memoir written for the *ARC Light,* the newsletter of the Air Resupply and Communications Association, in January 1995:

"We had a strange mission, or perhaps I should say all sorts of strange missions. Our primary mission of course was PsyWar, although to be honest I do not think any of us at the time thought of what we were doing as waging psychological warfare. We certainly were aware we were dealing with some pretty strange people, but I don't think I personally ever equated putting spooks ashore with PsyWar as such."

The original unit was made up of four helicopters, six pilots, one noncommissioned officer, and a dozen enlisted men fresh out of tech school.

"We pilots arrived in Korea on 5 October 1952. We asked where the 581st [the unit to which they belonged] was, and people looked at us and said, '581st what? There's no such outfit in Korea!' Now, that's the Fifth Air Force talking! Our new bosses. I think everyone was underwhelmed by that answer!

"We had no helicopters, no tools, no people, no housing, no supplies, no weapons, and without Third Air Rescue's generosity, no place to even sleep or eat."

Within a few days, the men organized themselves into something like a military unit and watched as Korean workers installed landing pads for their helicopters. But they still had no choppers.

"No one knew where the helicopters were," Sullivan says. "Someone at Fifth Air Force remembered something about helicopters in crates over at Kisarazu [Japan] and got on the phone. There they were, four brand-new H-19As right out of the factory.

"We put our first 'people' ashore in North Korea on, I think, 27 December 1952. We flew off Ch'o Do [an island off the west coast of North Korea] and put these folks in well above Chinnampo on the mud flats. [Chinnampo is about seventy-five miles north of the demilitarized zone, not far from the North Korean capital of P'yongyang.] We flew north, angling slightly away from the beach until we were well off shore, then turned west and finally southeast and went back to Ch'o Do.

"This route was flown right down on the water, without benefit of radar, radar altimeters, or anything else, except for an altimeter, setting at Ch'o Do and the M-1 eyeball. I personally dragged my nose gear in the water on one of the missions, causing a nose down-pitching motion, which of course caused major heart palpitations, and an extremely tight grip on the seat cushion!

"Joe Barrett and Frank Fabijan picked a Marine major named [Dave] Cleeland off the ice on the Haiju Reservoir in a big daylight shoot-out. Frank Westerman and Larry Barrett went inland and grabbed a chap named Cottrell, who was in deep, serious trouble at the time: another shoot-out. Don Crabb and I pulled [Air Force Capt.] Joe McConnell out of the water north of Ch'o Do after he shot down his eighth MiG and was downed in turn."

Many of these operations were done in daylight, in support of the air rescue unit, rather than as part of the unit's real mission of delivering agents behind enemy lines.

On one mission, Sullivan and Frank Westerman, the unit commander, flew deep into enemy territory in a vain attempt to locate an American reportedly attempting to avoid capture near the city of Antung. The crew was told that this mission was the deepest helicopter penetration of enemy territory during the war.

"That one happened to be our own mission," Sullivan says. "One of air rescue's SA-16 crews flew navigation for us on that mission at about a hundred feet off the water and then stayed up there with us until we came back out offshore. Man, that crew was good!"

Sullivan's own account understates the difficulty and danger of the mission. He and Westerman took off from Ch'o Do before dawn and flew just above the waves for two hours. At dawn, they dashed inland toward the position where radio signals indicated an American flier was awaiting rescue. Antung, a major Chinese fighter base, was only ten minutes' flying time away.

As they came into the valley where the pilot was believed to be, hundreds of guns opened up. Quickly realizing they had been lured into a trap, they turned and fled successfully back out to sea. For their attempt, Westerman and Sullivan were awarded the Silver Star and Distinguished Flying Cross.

"All in all, we—six of us—put roughly one thousand hours on four H-19s," Sullivan continues. "We did both the ARCS mission and the air rescue mission, having never refused a single one. We earned a bunch of decorations, took our share of battle damage, yet never, as long as combat missions were flown in that theater, had an accident, a combat loss, or a fatality. Not too shabby for a bunch of beginners, huh?"

A major assignment for the ARCS unit was dropping propaganda leaflets over enemy territory. Some of the leaflets warned civilians of bombing raids; others urged enemy soldiers to defect; still others were calculated to undermine enemy morale.

The wing was capable of producing and distributing an amazing volume of leaflets: as many as 4 million five-inch by seven-inch leaflets a day, printed in two colors on both sides of the sheet.

It was on a leaflet-dropping mission near the Chinese border that the 581st Wing suffered one of its most serious losses, one that also focused unwanted attention on what was supposed to be a very secret operation.

On the night of 12 January 1953, a B-29 piloted by Col. John K. Arnold, commander of the 581st Wing, was assigned to drop leaflets—some of them warning of imminent B-29 bombing attacks—over five North Korean towns. As the plane approached the last target, the village of Ch'olson, it was suddenly illuminated by searchlights. Seconds later, it was attacked by a MiG-15 fighter plane. The right inboard engine burst into flames.

For these special missions, the plane had been stripped of all its guns except for one gun position in the tail. The tail gunner fought back as two more MiGs joined the attack, but he was badly outgunned. Two more engines were hit. With the plane fatally crippled, Arnold rang the bail-out alarm. Eleven members of the fourteen-man crew survived the crash. They were quickly captured and moved across the border into China, where they were accused of espionage.

Arnold and the other members of his crew remained in captivity until their release on 3 August 1955—the last American prisoners of the war to be released by the Chinese.

As the Korean War wound down and the United States moved into its traditional postwar downsizing, it became obvious to leaders of ARCS that they had better come up with an important peacetime mission or they would be out of business. The dilemma was that ARCS had no peacetime mission beyond training. Once crews were trained, there was little or nothing for them to do.

Brigadier General Monro MacCloskey, who was the controversial commander of special operations forces operating out of Italy in World War II, became commander of ARCS on 15 September 1952 and immediately set about finding a peacetime mission for his command.

Early in 1953, he organized Operation Think. The object was to stimulate everyone in ARCS to think up jobs the unit could do in peacetime.

Suggestions poured in. Most focused on ways to "create fear, panic, and general unrest among enemy groups" in the Soviet Bloc. Red Fratricide was a plan to spread discrediting information about communist military leaders and thus undermine confidence in their leadership. Red Finesse was a proposal to target the control elite of the Communist hierarchy for propaganda attacks. This Week was a plan to encourage Soviet Bloc aircrews to defect with their airplanes.

Of nearly a hundred suggestions, thirty were considered promising enough to be sent on to the United States Information Agency and other government organizations for consideration.

While a few of the proposals were adopted—the suggestion to encourage defections by aircrews became an operation with the code name of Gretna Green—ARCS was told to concentrate on projects that could be done by the Air Force alone, and then came the event that MacCloskey and others had feared: ARCS itself was put on the budget chopping block as the perceived threat of war with the Soviet Union declined and the Eisenhower administration looked for ways to cut spending.

Fish recalls being assigned to sort out the functions that ARCS had tried to bring under its umbrella:

"I was called back to the Pentagon on short notice to complete the downsizing of this program. I was sent to Wiesbaden to look at the whole program and assign parts to an appropriate government entity. We had the Army, Navy, Air Force, State Department, CIA, FBI, the Voice of America on the committee. We spent three weeks sorting it out. When it was done, the Air Force had the flying end left. That was it. By the 1960s, it was all gone."

During the latter part of the 1950s, the ARCS wings shrank to group size and then down to squadrons, but they continued with their basic Air Force special operations for a number of years.

Units operating out of England and Libya dropped agents in Albania and other Balkan countries as the CIA sought to influence events in those areas.

In the late 1950s, the ARCS amphibious SA-16s stood by to rescue U-2 pilots if they crashed. The lightweight U-2 planes, flying so high they could not be reached by Soviet fighters or antiaircraft rockets, flew back and forth over the Soviet Union, photographing air bases and missile sites. On two occasions, U-2 pilots were rescued by the SA-16s after landing in the water, once in the Black Sea, on another occasion, in the Caspian Sea. The U-2 program over the USSR came to an end after a U-2 flown by Francis Gary Powers was finally hit by a surface-to-air missile on 1 May 1960.

As early as 1953, ARCS crews in the Far East were called upon to support the French in their losing battle against the Vietminh in Vietnam.

Some of the early flights, carrying supplies from the Philippines to the French in Hanoi, were considered something of a junket. On one occasion, twelve members of the organization went along on what seemed like a sightseeing trip in a C-119. They were supposed to land, unload their cargo of aircraft engines, and return home the next day. But their plane had a malfunction, and they were stranded in Hanoi long enough to survive an attack on the airfield where they had landed.

Later, the ARCS unit at Clark Air Force Base in the Philippines became both a training center for civilian pilots flying for Civil Air Transport, a company operated by the CIA, and the source of fresh aircraft for the French. Planes flown in from Japan entered a hangar with American markings and emerged with French markings. ARCS crews then flew them to Hanoi and picked up war-weary planes, which they flew back to the Philippines.

By the late 1950s, the Air Force ability to carry out a significant special operations mission had been allowed to wither almost completely away. It was time for another rebirth.

PART 4
The Longest War

CHAPTER 14
They Called It Jungle Jim

I n the spring and summer of 1961, Air Force crew members in various parts of the world received mysterious, disturbing orders: "Report to the base commander."
There was a note of urgency about the orders. One pilot returned from a flight one evening and was told to report at eight o'clock the next morning—a Sunday.

Richard Secord, then a captain, recalls returning from a test flight in a jet fighter and being ordered to report to a major general. Since leaving West Point, he had never even met a general officer. He figured something very big, or very strange, must be going on.

The first reaction, of course, was an anxious review of the last few weeks: "What have I done wrong?"

When the men reported, they were greeted cordially. It soon became apparent that they were not there for a chewing out. Then came the questions:

"Would you like an interesting flight assignment in World War II aircraft?

"Would you like to fly these aircraft in foreign countries?

"Would you be willing to fly them in civilian clothes?

"Would you fly them in hostile-fire situations?"

A single negative answer was enough to end the interview.

Those who passed this simple test were then subjected to a more intrusive two-day series of psychological tests. As many as 40 percent of some groups of volunteers washed out. One officer figured the goal of the exercise was to pick the crazy ones for this mystery assignment.

For many of those chosen, the next stop was the Air Force Survival School at Stead Air Force Base, Nevada. It was a grueling three-week course designed to teach the fliers how to survive off the land in hostile territory and how to behave if they were captured.

From there, they went to the Florida panhandle and checked in at one of a series of long wooden one-story buildings at auxiliary field No. 9 at Eglin Air Force Base. That field, one of a number of satellite fields in the swampy tidelands surrounding the main Eglin compound, is now Hurlburt Field, home of the Air Force Special Operations Command.

When the men arrived, they learned that they were members of something code-named Jungle Jim. More formally, it was known as the 4400th Combat Crew Training Squadron. It was divided into three sections, and each section was assigned to one of the long wooden buildings: C-47 crews in one building, B-26 crews in another, and T-28 crews in a third.

The 4400th Squadron was created by Gen. Curtis LeMay, the Air Force chief of staff, on 14 April 1961.

Creation of the Jungle Jim operation marked the reluctant recognition by the conventional Air Force of the new world of counterinsurgency or brushfire warfare—what the Communists called wars of national liberation. It also formally recognized what the Air Force, or at least some of its members, had already been doing for several years, usually in close cooperation with the CIA.

Even though Air Force thinking and doctrine had been dominated by bomber generals such as LeMay, who had led strikes against Japan in World War II and then built the Strategic Air Command into a formidable weapon designed to destroy the Soviet Union, a fringe group of Air Force officers had been doing some strange and secret things in various parts of the world.

In Operation Haik, in 1958, the CIA set up a small air unit to provide air support to rebels against the Indonesian government headed by President Achmed Sukarno. The original plan had been to train Indonesians to fly the planes, but they lacked experience. Instead, the CIA relied on a combination of former United States Air Force pilots plus several Poles and Hungarians who had been flying B-26s on reconnaissance missions in Europe.

On 28 May 1958, Allen Pope, one of the Americans, was shot down as he attempted to attack a convoy of government ships moving in for a landing on the island of Morotai.

The Indonesians imprisoned Pope and threatened to execute him. There was well-based fear in Washington that the threat would be carried out.

A CIA crew was secretly trained in the Philippines to snatch Pope from his prison compound. The rescue of Pope would be the first operational test of an ingenious device called the Fulton Recovery System, for its inventor, Robert Fulton.

In the Fulton "sky hook" system, a package is dropped to a man on the ground. It consists of a pair of coveralls with a parachute harness sewn in, a balloon and tank of gas, and a long nylon cord.

The plan was this: agents in Indonesia would smuggle a pair of the special coveralls to Pope. Working outside the prison at night, they would inflate the balloon and release it to lift the nylon line high in the air. When the balloon was in position, they would throw the nylon line over the wall. Pope would grab the end of the line and attach it to his harness. A plane would then swoop down and snag the line with a boom fastened out in front of its nose. When the line became taut, Pope would suddenly rise straight up and disappear into the darkness. The plane crew would reel him in and fly away. There would be one less prisoner at the body count the next morning.

Plans for the rescue attempt were dropped in 1961 after the pilot carefully trained for the pickup mission was killed while dropping supplies in Laos. Perhaps fortunately for Pope, the United States government found a more conventional way to spare him from execution, and he was released in 1962 after the United States paid a hefty ransom in the form of four of the new C-130 transport planes—the first of the planes delivered to a foreign country.

Purists may argue that Operation Haik was not truly in the Air

Force special operations, or air commando, tradition. But the planes were former Air Force planes, and some of those involved were either on active duty or only temporarily out of Air Force uniform to lend their expertise to the CIA. One of these was the ubiquitous Heinie Aderholt, who seemed somehow to be present whenever something a little out of the ordinary needed doing.

In the late 1950s, Aderholt became commander of an outfit known as Detachment 2, 1045th Observation, Evaluation and Training Group, based at Kadena Air Base in Okinawa. What they did was very secret.

Behind that dull-sounding bureaucratic mouthful, Aderholt and his small team masterminded an operation to support Tibetan resistance to the Chinese, who had taken over the country and eventually drove out Tibet's spiritual leader, the Dalai Lama.

Their plan was an ambitious one: Tibetans were smuggled out of their country, trained high in the Rockies at Camp Hale, near Leadville, Colorado, parachuted back into their homeland, and then supplied by air. It was all very reminiscent of what the Carpetbaggers did during World War II, supporting resistance fighters behind the German lines. The problem in Tibet, of course, is the extreme altitude—so high that the "lowlands" lie at thirteen thousand feet. The only plane Det 2 had available when it started out was a four-engine propeller-driven C-118—a military version of the DC-6 airliner. The plane could carry only a small cargo as it struggled over the Tibetan peaks. If one of its engines quit, the plane would go down.

To remedy this situation, the Air Force agreed to provide several of its new long-range C-130 planes to carry out the Tibetan supply missions.

Under the supervision of Aderholt and his team, the planes were flown to Takhli, Thailand. There, the United States markings were painted over and the Air Force crews turned the planes over, to civilian crews employed by Civil Air Transport—one of several companies used by the CIA to disguise its operations.

The contract crews were paid $350 for a routine flight and $500 if unusual hazards were involved. They earned their money.

The crews flew at night. Like Carpetbagger crews, they preferred some moonlight to make their navigation easier. But unlike the World War II aviators, flying over the carefully mapped terrain of western Europe, the CAT crews flew with few navigation aids over rugged terrain that was either not charted or, perhaps even more dangerous, inaccurately charted. Some of their maps came in sections. Too often, they found the route of a river or road offset by several miles at the juncture between one map section and the next.

The Tibetans caused severe problems for the Chinese invaders, although they could not force them out of their land. Perhaps their most important achievement was to set up the clandestine air drops of supplies that sustained the Dalai Lama and his entourage on their escape overland from Tibet to India in 1959.

At the same time as the Tibetan airlift, Aderholt was also involved in the first CIA-organized aid to Vang Pao, the charismatic leader of the Hmong hill people in central Laos. (Although records of the time often refer to Vang Pao's people as the Meo, that name was actually derived from a term of derision used by the Chinese.) For years thereafter, Vang Pao and his people carried on a fierce resistance to the North Vietnamese and the Pathet Lao—a force supported by the North Vietnamese. In this, they were closely allied with the CIA and generations of air commandos.

"About December 1960, we made the first drop to Vang Pao at Padong," Aderholt recalls. Padong is a settlement in central Laos near Vang Pao's longtime headquarters at Long Chieng.

A few months later, Aderholt's outfit, working as the liaison between the CIA and the Air Force, drew up plans for a very secret unit, known as Project Mill Pond, to fly B-26 bombers in "armed reconnaissance" missions over Laos. *Armed reconnaissance* was one of the first of the euphemisms that became common as the war in Southeast Asia grew. The object was not simply to fly reconnaissance missions, with guns for protection. Rather, the emphasis was on the word *armed*. The job of the Mill Pond pilots was not only to do reconnaissance but also to strafe and drop bombs.

Records are still classified or incomplete. But some sixteen or so aging B-26s were gathered up, most of them from the aircraft graveyard maintained by the Air Force near Tucson, Arizona. The planes were flown to Okinawa.

Meanwhile, eighteen Air Force pilots were selected and sent to Eglin for a brief familiarization with the B-26. They were then discharged from the Air Force and handed first-class tickets to Bangkok. From Bangkok, they were flown to the royal Thai air base at Takhli. After a few days there, they flew to Okinawa in an Air Force transport to pick up their B-26s. All identifying markings had been removed from the planes, and the flight down to Takhli was made in radio silence.

In Laos, in the spring of 1961, the Pathet Lao was making significant headway against forces trying to defend the capital of Vientiane. The Mill Pond pilots—by now sporting commissions in the Royal Lao Air Force—were ordered in early April to prepare for a four-pronged strike against Pathet Lao forces in the Plaine des Jarres in mid-Laos.

The attack was called off, but the crews remained on alert and began flying reconnaissance missions over Laos, many of them along the road and trail network through eastern Laos that later became famous as the Ho Chi Minh Trail used by the North Vietnamese to supply their forces in South Vietnam.

On several occasions, planes were hit by antiaircraft fire, but none of them was shot down.

In May, the reconnaissance flights were called off after President John F. Kennedy and Soviet Premier Nikita Khrushchev reached agreement to avoid a confrontation between the two powers in remote Laos.

Several months later, in August, U. Alexis Johnson, the United States ambassador to Thailand, learned belatedly about Mill Pond and the fact that American-piloted planes were standing by in "his" country to carry out attacks on neighboring Laos. He was not happy.

"When the ambassador found out we had all those munitions, he ran us out of there," Aderholt says. By the end of August, the planes and pilots were gone and Mill Pond had reached the end of its shadowy existence.

Although Aderholt dates his tour of duty as commander of

Det 2 in Asia from 1960 to 1962, he was back in the States for a while in early 1961, working with the CIA to prepare for the Bay of Pigs invasion of Cuba.

One of his major assignments was to find a remote landing field on the Nicaraguan coast and obtain permission from the Nicaraguan government to use it as a base for B-26 bombers flying in support of the invasion force. The base chosen was at Puerto Cabezas—a field code-named Happy Valley. It was the closest they could get, but it was still a long flight—590 miles—from the Bay of Pigs on Cuba's south coast.

Following the same pattern as in Mill Pond, about twenty B-26 bombers were taken from the aircraft graveyard near Tucson and spruced up as the "air force" for the invasion. One reason for choosing the B-26 for the mission was that the twin-engine plane had the range to make the long flight to Cuba, spend some time in bombing and strafing attacks, and then make it back to Nicaragua. Another reason for the choice of the B-26s was that Fidel Castro had several of the same kind of planes in his air force—although fewer than the number available to the invaders. The invaders' planes were painted so they appeared to be part of Castro's air force.

Aderholt also was instrumental in recruiting a team of volunteers from the Alabama Air National Guard, who had until shortly before been equipped with B-26s. They set up shop to train the Cubans and maintain the planes at a secret CIA field—code-named Rayo Base—at Retalhuleu, Guatemala.

The goal of the CIA-planned operation was to land a force of Cuban refugees who, with help from a popular uprising, hoped to overthrow Castro. The whole operation was carefully—but, as it turned out, unsuccessfully—planned to appear to be carried out spontaneously by anti-Castro Cubans without links to the United States.

In truth, the CIA was heavily involved, and, on the day of the invasion, the landing parties had limited support from the United States Navy.

The first phase of the actual operation was an air attack on 15 April 1961 against three Cuban airfields by B-26s flown by Cubans out of the Happy Valley airstrip in Nicaragua. The goal was to knock out Castro's ability to respond to the landing two days later. One of the invaders' B-26s was shot down that day.

That first phase of the operation had been curtailed to keep it from appearing too much like an overt United States attack. The result was that, when the day of the invasion came, Castro still had an air force capable of causing plenty of trouble. Several landing craft were destroyed or badly damaged, and three more B-26s were shot down over the invasion beaches.

Before the operation, the National Guard pilots serving as advisers to the Cubans were specifically ordered, by name, not to become involved in the conflict. However, on 19 April, the third day of the invasion, with the force on the beach in serious trouble and Castro's reinforcements on the way, that order was rescinded. Before the day was over, two more B-26s were shot down and four Americans were dead. They were Riley Shamburger and his navigator, Wade Gray, and Thomas W. Ray and his navigator, Leo Baker.

While the National Guardsmen were permitted to fly, United States Navy fighters flying high over the beachhead were under strict orders not to become involved in the fighting. They had to watch helplessly as the B-26s were shot down.

By coincidence, the Jungle Jim squadron in Florida had been created on 14 April, just one day before the initial air strike that paved the way for the Bay of Pigs invasion. Thus, when the aircrews received their mysterious orders to report to Eglin auxiliary field No. 9, several of them assumed, from the strange questions they had been asked, that they were being prepared to go back to Cuba and do it right the next time.

Actually, the charter for Jungle Jim was much broader. Its job was to provide planes and crews to go anywhere in the world they were needed to provide close air support for American and allied forces fighting behind enemy lines and to help friendly developing nations deal with guerrilla uprisings.

The creation of Jungle Jim was part of the major expansion in the nation's counterinsurgency or irregular warfare forces that resulted from prodding by President Kennedy, who had taken office in January. In that same period, the Navy organized its first two SEAL teams, and the Army's Special Forces, the Green Berets, embarked on a major expansion program.

It was only after the Army proposed that it set up its own little air force to support the Green Berets that the United States Air Force decided it had better get into this new game in a serious way—much as it would rather have focused its time, money, and attention on fast fighters, high-flying bombers, and the new intercontinental missiles.

The force assembled in Florida was just the opposite of the way the Air Force liked to think of itself. The planes were old. Not only were they based on 1930s technology, but they all had many hours in their log books. And they all had big fans out in front. There wasn't a jet engine to be seen or heard.

One leader of the unit described himself as the "commander of the only flying museum in the free world."

The planes were all capable of flying from short, rough fields. They were all relatively easy to maintain. And, with their gray paint and lack of markings, they could slip in and out of many strange places in the world without attracting much attention.

As bombers, there were eight B-26s—from the same graveyard that had supplied the planes for Mill Pond and the Bay of Pigs.

For cargo, there were sixteen C-47s—the same twin-engine plane that had first flown as the DC-3 airliner in the mid-1930s and served on every front in World War II.

And as all-purpose fighters, there were eight T-6 Trojan trainers that could be used as light bombers or in close air support of troops on the ground. The T-6 was a beefed-up version of the plane that had served the Mosquitos of the Korean War a decade before. With the modifications, it had a bigger engine and could carry two .50-caliber machine guns, two five-hundred-pound bombs, and two rocket launchers. But its maximum weapon load was only fifteen hundred pounds.

The initial cadre of Jungle Jim consisted of 352 officers and men.

For the next six months, they did a lot of things that no one else in the Air Force did—at least not without being quickly court-martialed.

One of the C-47 pilots, Wade Everett, later recalled: "No one controlled the 4400th. We literally flew treetop level, cross-country flights all over the United States. We flew through ADIZs [air defense identification zones], control areas, restricted spaces, anywhere; and every time an agency tried to write up a violation, Ben King [Col. Benjamin H. King, the squadron commander] would laugh and tell them to call someone in the Pentagon, and that was the last heard of any violations."

Much of their training was at night. They practiced landing on short fields, guided only by men on the ground holding flashlights. Occasionally, one of those on the ground, fearing a plane was about to run him down in the dark, would flee—and forget to drop his flashlight. The pilot, of course, would follow the flashlight right across the field.

Only five months after their training began, the Jungle Jim crews were declared operationally ready. In September, the 4400th Squadron sent its first unit, Detachment 1, overseas. The destination wasn't, as some still suspected, Cuba. And it wasn't Vietnam either. Instead, two C-47s and their crews flew to the West African nation of Mali to provide peacetime training to the country's paratroops. The Americans found it a little strange to be sharing the field with Russian and Czech crews flying Russian planes for the national airline.

On 5 November 1961, Detachment 2 departed for its own overseas deployment. This time, the crews were embarked on a mission that would begin the longest and most demanding era in air commando history. Their destination: Vietnam.

CHAPTER 15
Leading the Way

As the crews of four C-47s approached the South Vietnamese air base at Bien Hoa in mid-February 1962, they received an unusual warning: "Tanks on the runway." It was a revealing indication of the kind of strange little war they were about to become involved in.

The C-47s left Florida early in February and hopscotched halfway around the world: to California, on to Honolulu, to Johnston Atoll, Wake Island, Guam, the Philippines, and finally, after two weeks and nearly seventy-five hours of flying, to Bien Hoa.

As the first C-47 landed, it was, indeed, greeted by a tank. The tank crew kept its cannon aimed at the cockpit until the nervous fliers established who they were and what they were doing there.

The day of their arrival, as it turned out, was the same day a group of rebellious South Vietnamese pilots picked to attack the presidential palace in Saigon.

The first members of Detachment 2 of the 4400th Combat Crew Training Squadron—the Jungle Jim outfit—had arrived at Bien Hoa in November of 1961 and started to learn their way around. The Vietnam detachment received a new code name: Farmgate. Over the next three months, the Farmgate force grew to include four C-47s, four B-26s, and eight AT-28s.

Accommodations at Bien Hoa in those early days were spartan.

The crews slept in tents set up on planks. "Air-conditioning" in the steamy weather was provided by a screen between the waist-high wall of the tent and the canvas roof. When the crews were sent to stand alert at other bases, such as Da Nang or Soc Trang, they often slept under the wings of their planes.

The Farmgate crews were, when they weren't flying, largely confined to Bien Hoa. One man would be assigned to drive into Saigon to pick up groceries and replenish the unit's liquor supply.

This was all part of the pretense that the Americans weren't there—or, if they were there, that they were simply there to advise the South Vietnamese. The Geneva accords of 1954, which had divided Vietnam into a Communist north and a south aligned with the United States, limited the foreign military advisers on each side to 585. The North Vietnamese in the country certainly exceeded that figure, and, by 1962, the number of Americans in country was also several times the limit—a fact apparent to, and reported by, the growing contingent of reporters attracted by the buildup in Southeast Asia.

Despite the fiction that they were "advisers," the Farmgate fliers almost immediately began flying combat missions. It was hard, dangerous work. They flew old planes with minimal navigation aids at night and in bad weather against increasingly sophisticated and deadly enemy air defenses, making up tactics on the wing.

One of the hazards was the requirement that the Americans always had to carry a Vietnamese along—to maintain the fiction that they were training the Vietnamese. Any unfortunate Vietnamese who happened to be nearby when a mission was scheduled found himself strapped into an airplane—often the first time he had ever been off the ground.

Richard Secord, then the junior captain among the Farmgate AT-28 pilots and later a major general, thought he was going to die one day because of his Vietnamese passenger.

As he rolled in and started down toward his target, he felt a sudden jolt on the controls. He thought the plane had been hit. Breaking off the attack, he pulled up, decided everything was okay, and rolled in again. Once more, he felt the strange pressure on the controls. His terrified passenger was pulling back on the stick as hard as he could.

Secord ordered him over the intercom to keep his hands off the controls.

Again, he pulled up, rolled in, and headed for the target. This time, he felt the stick jam forward. The dive steepened and the plane headed directly toward the ground. Secord inched the stick back with all his strength, overpowering the terrified Vietnamese. They pulled out just above the trees.

Frightened and furious, Secord pulled his .38-caliber Smith & Wesson pistol as soon as he leveled off and twisted around to point it at his backseater, ready to kill him. Just then, his passenger lost his lunch all over the cockpit and collapsed into a small bundle of miserable humanity. Secord couldn't bring himself to shoot such a pathetic creature.

In the early days, there was a very steep learning curve as the crews, coming from an Air Force attuned to high-tech warfare against a sophisticated foe, learned to fight a low-tech war with aging equipment against a foe that was poorly armed but clever and elusive.

At first, B-26 crews made the mistake of meeting with the Vietnamese forward air controller (FAC) in his little plane and circling the target area once or twice before attacking. By that time, it finally occurred to them, the Vietcong had had time to hear the planes and disperse. The new rule was to rendezvous some distance from the target. The FAC would then drop his smoke to mark the target, and the B-26 would roll in almost immediately.

It also took several months to realize how dangerous it was to load bombs and napalm canisters on the wings of the plane. Since all the wing mounts on the B-26 used the same release system, it was possible for a harried pilot to drop a bomb rather than napalm, or vice versa. Napalm was often dropped from as low as fifty feet—so low that pilots sometimes came home with mud and branches hanging from their planes. But a pilot who dropped a five-hundred-pound—or even a one-hundred-pound—bomb below about a thousand feet would probably be hit by the fragments and wouldn't come home at all.

The solution was to carry the napalm on the wings and the bombs in the double bomb bay. One technique that worked well was to start the attack with a strafing run at fifty to two hundred feet off the ground to make the enemy pull their heads down. That was followed by napalm, also dropped down low. Then came bombs, followed by rockets and more strafing.

The B-26 crews faced a special hazard. Unlike the T-28s, which flew in pairs, the B-26s flew singly. If one was lost, it might be hours before anyone knew.

"With only a few aircraft over there, we flew them single ship, and, consequently, when we lost a 26, we didn't know he was lost," Colonel Roy C. Dalton, one of the early Farmgate B-26 pilots, recalled. "If he was out on a photo mission, for example, he wasn't in contact with anybody?. . . I know that we were never able to confirm that we lost a B-26 until his fuel ran out and he became overdue. We had no radio contact with him, nobody else had any radio contact with him, except the fort that he was trying to defend.

Farmgate lost its first B-26 on the night of 4–5 November 1962 in one of the nighttime missions that had become almost routine—but were still extremely dangerous.

When reports of an outpost under attack came in that night, a B-26 and a C-47 flare ship were dispatched. A short time later, another 26 was sent to help out. The first 26 returned safely. But then came word from the crew of the C-47 that they had lost contact with the other B-26 and had seen a large fire on the ground.

When daylight came, the wreckage was found. The crew—two Americans and a Vietnamese—were dead. The Vietcong had already stripped the wreckage of anything valuable, but the bodies were recovered.

Just what happened was never determined. The plane may have been shot down. A single rifle bullet in the wrong place was enough to knock a plane out of the sky, although that is unlikely to have happened to a twin-engine B-26. As the air threat increased, the Vietcong kept pace, introducing 12mm and 14.5mm Soviet antiaircraft guns and, later, 23mm ZPU-23s capable of hurling an explosive shell as high as twenty thousand feet.

More likely in this case is that the plane simply flew into the ground. Every Farmgate pilot had stories to tell of times when he became disoriented in the dark and avoided crashing only by luck.

Flying night attack missions was so difficult and dangerous that the Vietnamese couldn't, or wouldn't, do it. This left these missions to the American B-26 and AT-28 pilots.

During most of the war, tiny outposts were scattered throughout South Vietnam. Almost every night, a number of these outposts came under attack.

In the early days of the war, they were often quickly overrun. Then the Vietnamese and Americans began flying C-47s equipped with flares. One group of pilots—the "Dirty Dozen"—flew with the Vietnamese. The Farmgate pilots flew their own planes, with at least one Vietnamese aboard. At first, a few flares were all it took to light up the battlefield and chase away the attackers. But the Vietcong knew the flares themselves couldn't hurt them and quickly adapted their tactics to take advantage of shadows and moments of darkness to penetrate the defenses.

The next step in this constantly escalating warfare was to add attack planes to bomb and strafe the troops exposed by the flares.

As soon as the first plane arrived, the defenders would ignite a "fire arrow" pointing in the direction of the attack. The fire arrows were sometimes made of electric lights. More often, they were flares or even little bonfires.

To avoid hitting the defenders, the attack pilots normally flew parallel to the defense line. But, sometimes, they flew over the outpost and dropped their bombs or strafed as they crossed the wall. On occasion the pilots boasted, they dropped napalm so close it splashed on the outpost walls. Actually, they tried to drop their ordnance at least fifty meters away—about the distance of a city block and a half.

Attacking in the light from the flares was a hellish challenge for the pilots.

If they flew below the flares, they were silhouetted against the light, a target for every enemy gun in the area. It didn't take long to change tactics and drop the flares off to the side so they would illuminate the battlefield but not make the planes such glaring targets.

On a bombing run, pilots were often blinded by the light of the flares and the reflections on their canopies. In the B-26, especially, the instruments were difficult to read. Often, the pilot concentrated on flying, and the navigator used a flashlight to watch the instruments. If he saw that they were getting too low, he gave the pilot a friendly tap on the shoulder.

As soon as a plane ended a bombing or strafing run, it nosed up out of the bright glare of the flares into the deep blackness of the night. With their pupils contracted by the light of the flares, pilots were almost literally blind as they maneuvered for the next attack. Even the most experienced pilots suffered from severe bouts of vertigo, unsure whether they were going up or down or whether they were right side up or upside down. And all of this was compounded by the difficulty of reading the instruments.

The Farmgate pilots were a picked crew, the best pilots in the Air Force. But in those early days, they were more like the barnstormers and mail pilots of the 1920s than the jet jockeys of the 1960s.

For newcomers to Vietnam, even finding one's way around in the daytime could be a challenge. Frank J. Gorski, Jr., then a captain, recalled his second combat mission as an AT-28 pilot in 1962. He and 1st Lt. Tom Shernak took off from Bien Hoa on a helicopter escort mission. They were then ordered to help out at an outpost under attack deep in the delta.

"We proceeded south and, shortly, I flew off my map into IV Corps [the southernmost of the four military districts into which the country was divided]," Gorski says. "We pressed on. I casually asked over the radio where we would be recovering. He [Shernak] said, 'Soc Trang.' Well, I had no idea where Soc Trang was. We went on down there, and Tom proceeded to get shot down. We had a regular old firefight going there, as I recall. He got hit by ground fire and bellied into a rice paddy. No problem. He got out all right. Nobody got hurt. We lost an airplane.

"But I remember circling my downed leader, wondering where and what to do next. My initial thought was to head east because I knew there was a coast out there someplace and then head north, which would get me back on my map. But I called rather blindly over the radio and said, 'Does anyone know where the nearest air patch is?'

"Some fellow—I didn't know who he was at the time—I turned my head and I saw him sitting out on my wing in another T-28. A big mustache, commando hat—looked like *Terry and the Pirates*. . . .

"So I said, 'Well, you look like a friendly old cuss, so I'll just hang on.'

"He said, 'We're going home to Soc Trang.'

"So I said, 'Thanks, I'll finally find out where this place is.'

"That was sort of my initiation into early combat in Vietnam."

Soc Trang, deep in the delta, soon became a home away from home for Gorski and the other pilots as they alternated between Bien Hoa and Soc Trang. One flight was on alert at Bien Hoa and one at Soc Trang while the other pilots took a day off.

"There were times when we were covering pretty much of III and IV Corps [roughly, the southern half of South Vietnam] with maybe three or four airplanes, trying to keep all the corners nailed down, which was obviously not quite working. But we did a good job, I think. It was probably the most interesting flying I have done in my career," Gorski says.

In July 1963, with the growth of the American involvement in Vietnam highly visible, General LeMay, the Air Force chief of staff, decided it was well known Farmgate was an American operation and removed the secret classification. Det 2 became the 1st Air Commando Squadron (Composite) of the 34th Tactical Group, although they continued to use the Farmgate name, at least unofficially.

The change in Vietnam coincided with a dramatic expansion of the Air Force counterinsurgency force.

In rapid order, the 4400th Combat Crew Training Squadron was replaced by a new Special Air Warfare Center at Eglin. A new officer specialty in counterinsurgency was established, and the call went out for volunteers. The original 350-man Jungle Jim squadron grew, by July 1963, to 3,000 men.

By that time, there were sometimes more pilots in Vietnam than there were planes or missions to fly.

"I think that the main problem with morale over there was that there sometimes wasn't enough to do in the way of flying—guys sitting around playing pinochle," recalled Roy H. Lynn, who went to Vietnam as a C-47 flare-ship pilot in the spring of 1963. Someone, however, was always coming up with new jobs for the air commandos.

In November 1961, they were given an assignment different from anything they had done before. Six C-123 transport planes were quickly modified into spray planes, and in January 1962, three of them arrived in Vietnam. That was the beginning of Project Ranch Hand. For the next decade, crews of air commandos flew their lumbering C-123 cargo planes at low levels over much of South Vietnam, the demilitarized zone, and parts of Laos, spraying chemicals to burn the leaves off the trees and wither food crops in enemy areas.

The spraying opened up large areas of the jungle-covered countryside, making it much more difficult for Vietcong and North Vietnamese units to move without being seen and attacked.

Each plane carried a thousand-gallon tank of herbicide—enough to spray a path more than eighty yards wide and as much as ten miles long. Flying in a four-ship formation, the Ranch Hand planes were thus able to defoliate a swath of jungle a fifth of a mile wide and ten miles long in one pass.

Between January 1961 and its last mission on 7 January 1971, Ranch Hand delivered 18.85 million gallons of herbicide. More than half of that—11.22 million gallons—was a chemical known as Agent Orange, from the color of the markings on the containers in which it was delivered. Although the United States contended that the chemical was not harmful to humans, evidence later developed that it caused health problems for Vietnamese and for American servicemen in the areas where it was sprayed, as well as for crew members of the spray planes.

At the time, the crew members worried more about the danger from enemy gunners than they did about the material spewing from the spray booms mounted under each wing and the tail. The missions were flown at 130 knots and as low as possible, making the twin-engine planes inviting targets for enemy gunners.

On 2 February 1962, a C-123 was lost on a training mission,

and its three-man crew was killed. Although the plane had probably not been shot down, from then on, the Ranch Hand planes were escorted by air commandos and later by jet fighters. Even with that protection, five more of the planes were lost in Ranch Hand operations. In only two of those instances did the crew members survive.

The Ranch Hand planes also had an escort of another kind. Air commandos in C-47s flew ahead of them, dropping leaflets to explain the defoliation program to villagers. This was only a small part of the psychological warfare efforts of the special operations crews. On some missions, flying in small U-10 utility planes, the pilots carried powerful loudspeakers that broadcast tape-recorded propaganda messages to the populace. The "bullshit bombers," as they sometimes called themselves, were probably shot at more than any other planes except for the Ranch Hand spray planes.

One of the most demanding and dangerous leaflet-delivery missions was performed by a unit of Combat Talon MC-130s stationed at Nah Trang, in South Vietnam, in the late 1960s. The unit was Detachment 1 of the 314th Tactical Airlift Wing, which later became the 15th Special Operations Squadron.

Their job was to drop propaganda leaflets over the major population centers of North Vietnam. Ronald Jones, now a retired colonel living in San Antonio, was one of the pilots in the unit whose emblem was, appropriately, a stray goose.

"It was strictly a single-ship operation," he explains. "We would file a flight plan for Da Nang. Then, going into Da Nang, we would cancel our instrument flight plan and go tactical."

Instead of landing at Da Nang, they would drop down to about five hundred feet off the water and head north. If the wind was blowing from the east, they would climb to altitude over the water offshore from Haiphong and drop their leaflets. The more challenging task came when the wind was blowing from the west.

"If the wind was out of the west, we would enter about five hundred feet and go inland and climb up, depending on how accurate the charts were. Many maps would just show big white areas: terrain data not available.

"We were outside the SAM [surface-to-air missile] rings. The thing we were primarily concerned about was fighters. We had a set procedure. If we were picked up by GCI [ground controlled intercept] radar, if we started getting painted by a height finder, we would get the hell out of there. That meant they had you in azimuth and elevation, and they could vector a fighter in on you without his ever having his radar on. We got nervous if we were painted by GCI radar. But if we got hits by a height finder, we were gone."

The slow, four-engine planes were unarmed and had no fighter escort. If a fighter came for them, their only chance was to dive for the ground and hope the fighter wouldn't follow.

One of the planes disappeared on a mission in 1966, and the assumption was that a fighter had shot it down. Fortunately for the Americans, the North Vietnamese seldom scrambled their fighters in response to a one-plane incursion.

Although their route was planned to avoid known missile sites, the possibility of being hit by a missile was always on the fliers' minds. The planes were equipped with electronic countermeasures to detect a SAM launch and prevent the missile from locking on to their plane.

"We tried never to put ourselves into a position, at high or low altitude, where we would be doing battle with a SAM," Jones says. "That would be going into a fight unarmed. We were strictly unarmed. We relied on our ECM equipment [electronic countermeasures], and we had people watching. The loadmaster, with the ramp and door open, could see a missile coming. We were always watching."

Depending on the strength and direction of the wind, the crew would take up position sixty or seventy miles west of the city targeted for the leaflet drop at an altitude of up to about twenty thousand feet and then fly straight and level during the drop.

"Our average drop leg was nine to ten minutes," Jones says. "It was the longest nine minutes in the world. There is nothing more exhilarating than sitting up at twenty thousand feet at 150 knots with your ramp and doors open, looking out at the lights of Hanoi.

"As soon as you reached your altitude, you kicked out the first bundle and then you had a specific interval, normally about every fifteen seconds, you would kick a bundle. In a ten-minute drop leg, you would have about forty bundles. Then you would immediately go back down to low level and get out."

The bundles of leaflets were rigged to pop open after leaving the plane. Tens of thousands of leaflets would spread out in a big paper cloud, to flutter down many miles away.

The leaflets were cleverly designed to attack both North Vietnam's morale and its economy. The propaganda message was printed on a tab attached to a skillfully counterfeited piece of North Vietnamese currency. The assumption was that those who found the leaflets might or might not pay any attention to the propaganda message, but they would certainly pocket and spend the money.

Jones says the money-bombing strategy was so successful that the North Vietnamese demanded, during peace talks in 1969, that the campaign be stopped before an agreement could be reached. The dropping of the currency leaflets stopped about that time.

On some missions, the planes also dropped tiny radios packed in a little styrofoam case. The radios were preset to the frequency of a station in the south broadcasting propaganda messages.

The Stray Goose unit flew over the north once or twice a month. When they were not dropping leaflets, they flew a number of missions delivering Special Forces soldiers to enemy-controlled areas in operations reminiscent of the Carpetbagger agent-delivery flights in World War II.

And some of the flying was, as Jones puts it, "just general trash hauling."

Other air commandos were involved in flying C-123s in Project Mule Train, in which they carried troops and an amazing variety of cargo all over South Vietnam. One of their unusual assignments was to deliver fresh meat on the hoof—live cows, pigs, chickens, and ducks—to remote outposts. If they could land, they did. If not, they delivered their live cargo by parachute.

In one instance, three C-123s teamed up to reposition two 105mm and two 155mm howitzers into a firebase that could not be reached by road. In nine flights, they landed and took off from a narrow steel-mesh airstrip, delivering a total of one hundred thousand pounds of guns, ammunition, and troops.

In all their combat missions, the air commandos relied heavily on forward air controllers (FACs) of various kinds to guide them to the target. In the early days, many of the FACs were Vietnamese. Often, the aircrews and the FACs had difficulty understanding one another. Even when the plane carried an English-speaking Vietnamese, there was a time delay in relaying information between the ground or airborne controller and the plane. As the American buildup continued, the Farmgate crews were delighted whenever they heard an American voice guiding their attack.

Airborne forward air controllers were not all air commandos. But a number of air commandos served as FACs, and they were responsible for some of the most impressive chapters in the story of special operations during the Vietnam War.

On 5 March 1966, two defectors walked into a remote outpost in the A Shau Valley about twenty miles southwest of the city of Hue and only about two and a half miles from the Laotian border. The outpost, manned by 10 American Special Forces soldiers and 210 Vietnamese irregular troops, had been established to monitor enemy forces moving from Laos through the valley into position to attack South Vietnamese cities.

The defectors reported that a North Vietnamese army division, plus two battalions, was in the area, in a position to overrun the outpost and keep on coming.

American commanders, eager to draw the enemy into a battle where they could be hammered by United States firepower, reinforced the little compound with seven more Green Berets, 149 Chinese Nung troops, and nine interpreters. They became the bait in the trap.

At 2 A.M. on 9 March, the enemy struck, destroying the camp's supply depot and inflicting some casualties. By mid-morning, the post was in danger of being overrun. Low-lying clouds made close air support almost impossible.

In a desperate effort to hold off the attackers, an AC-47 gunship (see Chapter Sixteen for an account of the development of the gunship) flew, at treetop level, under the clouds that covered the area. On its second firing pass, the plane's right engine was torn from the wing by machine-gun fire. As Capt. Willard M. Collins and his copilot, 1st Lt. Delbert R. Peterson, fought for control, the other engine was hit, and they crashed into a hillside five miles from the camp, well outside the defense perimeter.

The six-man crew survived the crash, although one gunner broke both legs. Enemy troops quickly moved in. The crew fought off the first attack, but on the second assault, both Collins and the wounded gunner were killed.

As a rescue helicopter moved in to pick up the survivors, Peterson, armed only with an M16 rifle and a .38-caliber pistol, charged the enemy. He bought enough time for the chopper to scoop up the other three crew members and take off under heavy enemy fire, but Peterson was left behind, listed as missing in action.

Overhead, Maj. Bernard F. Fisher led a flight of two A-1E fighter-bombers from the 1st Air Commando Squadron base at Pleiku. He and his wingman worked their way back and forth, strafing the enemy. They destroyed the wrecked AC-47 and provided protection for two C-123s as they dropped medical supplies and ammunition to the defenders.

At 2 A.M. the next day, the enemy resumed its assault with a barrage of mortar shells, followed by a human-wave attack that broke through the perimeter wire.

When Fisher and his wingman returned a little after 11 A.M. that morning, they could see that the enemy held the south wall and half of the east wall of the triangular fort. The defenders were pushed back against the north wall, calling for napalm and strafing attacks on the south and east walls of their own fort.

Fisher was joined by another two-plane flight of A-1Es from a fighter squadron based at Qui Nhon. It was led by Maj. Dafford W. Myers. The four planes set up a strafing pattern over the enemy positions. But Myers's wingman was hit almost immediately and had to leave because one of the bullets had shattered his canopy, making it difficult to see.

Then, on his third pass over the fort at about eight hundred feet, Myers was hit by at least three .50-caliber bullets. The cockpit filled with smoke. Oil on the windscreen blocked his view. With radioed guidance from Fisher, Myers made a wheels-up crash landing on the steel-mesh runway, which was outside the fort perimeter.

When he hit, his belly tank exploded, and the flaming wreckage skidded two hundred yards before veering off into an embankment. Myers, who was not badly hurt, jumped out of the plane and ran for a weed-covered ditch.

Fisher's first thought was to call for a rescue helicopter. But the chopper would take too long to get there and probably had little chance of landing, picking up Myers, and getting away without being shot down. The only way to save Myers from death or capture was for Fisher to land and try to get him out of there.

Fisher made one attempt to land from the north end of the runway, but there was too much smoke. So he swung around and came in from the other end. The twenty-three-hundred-foot runway was so short and in such poor condition that planes like the one flown by Fisher were not supposed to land there, even under the best of conditions. His landing was under the worst of conditions. As he rolled down the runway, he had to dodge mortar holes, old oilcans, and pieces of Myers's plane. At the end of the runway, he spun around and taxied back the way he had come at full speed, looking for Myers as he went.

He spotted Myers waving from the ditch near the wreckage of his plane. Fisher assumed Myers was hurt. So as soon as he stopped, he began to unbuckle himself to go to Myers's aid. But Myers, with a full surge of adrenaline, dashed from his hiding place with a stream of bullets following him and clambered up into the plane. Fisher reached back and pulled Myers into the cockpit headfirst.

The first words from the grateful Myers were: "You dumb SOB, now neither of us will get out of here."

But Fisher pushed the throttle full forward, and they did get out, flying at treetop level until they gained enough airspeed to climb up through the overcast, away from the enemy guns. Myers later explained that he could see the enemy troops had set a trap for anyone trying to rescue him, and he would have warned them away if he had had any way to communicate.

Fisher became one of five air commandos to receive the Medal of Honor during the war in Southeast Asia.

Fisher's heroic rescue of Myers came two years after a severe crisis involving both equipment and the morale of air commando crew members.

Beginning in 1963, there was a series of crashes of B-26s and AT-28s that had little or nothing to do with enemy actions. The old planes were simply coming apart, the result of age and the strains of operating fully loaded off rough, bumpy airfields; maximum-performance takeoffs to get above enemy ground fire; and daily dive-bombing missions. To compound the problem, it was not until months after they had begun combat operations in Vietnam that the B-26s were fitted with meters to tell the pilots how much stress they were putting on their wings when pulling out of dive-bombing runs.

One B-26 lost a wing on 16 August 1963. Another crashed a few days later, with the loss of two American and one Vietnamese crew members. That crash was blamed on enemy fire.

Crew members grumbled about "flying garbage cans," but the danger from continuing to fly the aging planes received little attention until early in 1964, when two incidents brought the issue into public view.

On 11 February 1964, the Air Force arranged an air-power demonstration at Hurlburt and invited the press. During the show, a B-26 lost its left wing and crashed, killing the two crew members.

In May, *U.S.News & World Report* magazine printed a series of letters written by Capt. Edwin G. Shank, an air commando AT-28 pilot who had been stationed at Soc Trang since November of the prior year. He told of crashes of both B-26s and AT-28s and complained that the World War II aircraft "have been through so many wars and dogfights that they are coming apart."

Adding strength to Shank's message was the fact that his letters were printed after his death on 24 March 1964. He and another AT-28 pilot were both killed on the same day in separate accidents when the wings tore off their planes.

The secretary of the Air Force was called to testify before alarmed congressmen. He explained that the planes had undergone intensive rebuilding and testing to be sure that they were safe. However, both the B-26s and AT-28s were taken out of service by the air commandos.

They were replaced by a plane that was to become one of the most reliable workhorses of the conflict: a Korean War–era Navy plane called the Douglas Skyraider. The single-seat Navy version was known as the AD-6, the two-seat model as the AD-5. The Air Force overhauled 150 of the planes at a cost of $123,000 apiece and rechristened the single-seat plane the A-1H and the two-seat model the A-1E. These modified planes were hurried to Vietnam beginning in May 1964 to replace both the AT-28s and the B-26s. It was this kind of plane that Fisher and Myers were flying at A Shau in 1966.

The propeller-driven A-1 was an almost ideal weapon for the work of the air commandos. It had a big twenty-seven-hundred-horsepower engine, a top speed of 350 miles an hour, and a range of twenty-five hundred miles, and it could remain aloft for as long as nine hours, loitering over a threatened outpost waiting for the enemy to make a move. Most important to the pilots, it was a rugged machine, capable of taking a battering from enemy guns and still bringing its pilot back in one piece.

The A-1 quickly picked up the nickname of the Spad—a World War I fighter. It was also known, from its call sign, as Sandy.

While a variety of planes were used by forward air controllers during the course of the war, three planes saw primary service in that role. First came the Cessna O-1 Bird Dog, a plane first flown by the Army in 1950 and not much different in appearance from the small planes flown in the Burma operation of 1944. It was replaced by the Cessna O-2, an unusual craft with one propeller in the front and the other in the rear of the fuselage. The most effective forward air control aircraft was the OV-10 Bronco, introduced in 1968. It had two engines, carried a pilot and observer, and was armed with four machine guns, with room to carry bombs or marker rockets.

The air commandos also flew another unusual plane, a converted jet trainer known as the A-37 Dragonfly.

Because it was derived from a trainer, the pilots of the powerful F-100, F-4, and F-105 fighter-bombers looked down on the Dragonfly and didn't consider it a serious warplane. They had a derisive name for it—the Tweetybird—because of the high-pitched sound made by its engines. For the air commandos, however, it was an almost ideal plane: light, maneuverable, easy to maintain, and a real workhorse, providing quick reaction to reports of enemy movement or troops in trouble on the ground.

As the United States adapted old planes to fight this new kind of warfare, the most dramatic success story involved one of the oldest planes in the conflict, the C-47, the same plane that had served the Air Commandos and the Carpetbaggers so well in World War II and their successors in Korea.

CHAPTER 16
Death from the Sky

The C-47 flare ships had been flying for three years when a small outpost in the delta came under attack and called for help. Although the troops on the ground didn't realize it, they were about to help make history. Responding to their call for help was a new kind of weapon—the gunship.

The defenders were well prepared. They had a large wooden arrow mounted on a swivel with flare pots along the head and shaft. When they heard the sound of the C-47 engines approaching, they swung the arrow in the direction of the attack and lit flares to indicate the distance, with each flare pot indicating one hundred meters.

Normally, the C-47 would drop flares, providing enough light for fighter-bombers to see the men attacking the outpost. But, on this night, the situation was different.

An official Air Force history gives this dramatic account of what happened next:

"Since the gunship was flying blacked out, it could not be seen from the ground. All that could be heard was the drone of its engines—and then a terrible roar as a tongue of fire seemed to burst from the heavens and lick along the ground. Then only the drone of the engines again. As the defenders shifted their arrow to the next target, there was another roar and the tongue of flame again seared its way through the enemy ranks. Still a third burst and the Vietcong fled in terror.

"Never having seen an FC-47 [the designation was soon changed to AC-47] before, the defenders inside the fort were filled with the same fear and awe as the enemy. What was this dreaded monster that breathed fire and destruction upon its foes? They began to gesture wildly toward the sky and scream, *'Rahng, Rahng,'* Dragon, Dragon. Thus was born Puff, the Magic Dragon, the first of a family of USAF fixed-wing gunships."

The Air Force fixed-wing gunship—as distinguished from the Army's helicopter gunship—was one of the most innovative and important new weapons to be introduced during the Vietnam War and certainly the most important in the history of Air Force special operations.

Ironically, this new weapon system began with one of the oldest pieces of machinery still flying—the twin-engine C-47. When the civilian version of the plane first flew on 18 December 1935, it was a technological marvel. But by the time it underwent conversion to the gunship configuration, three decades had passed and the airlines had long since consigned their DC-3s to the junk heap or sold them off to third-world airlines.

Actually, the idea of a fixed-wing gunship was even older than the plane itself, but no one had previously moved the idea from the back-of-the-envelope sketch to the battlefield.

The concept is simple. If a pilot flies in a circle—in what is called a pylon turn—he can keep the tip of his wing pointed at a specific spot on the ground. If a gun is fired along that same line, the bullets will hit the spot on the ground. In 1926 and 1927, 1st Lt. Fred Nelson mounted a .30-caliber machine gun on a World War I–era DH-4 bomber and, using an aiming device fastened to a wing strut, fired accurately at a target on the ground.

The advantages of such a system are obvious. In a fighter-bomber, the pilot makes a strafing run over a target on the ground and must then circle around and come back to make another attack. Since he is passing over the target, most of his bullets fall short or long, and even if he is very skilled, only a few hit the target. But if the pilot of a circling gunship fires accurately, all his bullets hit the target.

The concept was resurrected during World War II but did not get beyond limited experiments.

One of those who pushed the concept toward the end of World War II was a lieutenant in the coast artillery named Gilmour Craig MacDonald. In 1961, by then a lieutenant colonel in the Air Force, he resurrected his idea for use in the low-intensity, counterinsurgency type of warfare that was then commanding the attention of President Kennedy and of many in the military.

But it was not until late 1962 that his idea was picked up by Ralph E. Flexman of the Bell Aerosystems Company, who did some tests and pushed the concept within the Air Force.

For a year and a half, a small group of dedicated Air Force officers experimented with the gunship concept. A series of review boards scoffed at the idea and even turned down requests for funds for testing. Several tests were carried out anyway, camouflaged as parts of other test programs. The project, at this time, had the unfortunate name of Tailchaser, accurately reflecting the view of the critics.

In the summer of 1964, a fighter pilot named Ronald W. Terry came across a report on Project Tailchaser and became intrigued by the concept. He had just returned from a trip to Vietnam, where he had spent almost six weeks touring bases in the country, under assignment from the Air Force Systems Command, trying to learn what kind of equipment and tactics were needed in this new kind of warfare. The gunship seemed to him an ideal way to protect isolated hamlets and outposts, operating as a kind of policeman on the beat to move in at the first sign of trouble. Terry volunteered as project pilot for Tailchaser.

An Air Force history of the project summed up the importance of Terry's involvement this way: "His personality projected a subtle blending of tact and tenacity, self-confidence and openness, intelligence and common sense, and, most significant for the progress of the gunship, an uncommonly convincing salesmanship."

In September 1964, three rapid-firing miniguns were installed in a C-47 for a test. This combined one of the oldest items in the

Air Force inventory with one of the newest. The brand-new electrically driven minigun had six barrels mounted so they rotated about a central axis, rapidly coming into firing position and then moving on. With its six barrels, the Gatling gun—named for Richard Jordan Gatling, who developed a crank-operated predecessor of the machine gun that was used in the Civil War—was capable of firing at the rate of six thousand rounds of 7.62mm bullets a minute, although the gun was fired for only a few seconds at a time. Each 7.62mm projectile is tiny—the same size as the standard NATO cartridge fired by the M14 rifle—and not powerful enough to knock out a hard target, such as a tank. But, rained down on enemy soldiers attacking an outpost, the little bullets were devastating.

In 1964, the United States was still technically at peace despite its growing, toe-in-the-water involvement in Vietnam. And in peacetime, the military habitually makes decisions at a glacial speed, especially when they involve controversy, spending money, and innovation. It is a testament to Terry's ability as a salesman that he and a colleague, 1st Lt. Edwin Sasaki, managed to wangle an audience with General LeMay, the Air Force chief of staff, to argue for a chance to demonstrate what the gunship could do.

LeMay was briefed on 2 November 1964. The presentation by Terry and Sasaki must have been impressive. Many in the Air Force were bitterly opposed to the gunship concept. And even LeMay later expressed his own reservations: "It's not a very good platform, and you can't carry the load. You don't have the range, staying capacity, or anything else. They're too vulnerable both on the ground and in the air."

But LeMay was sufficiently impressed to give his approval to modify a C-47 as a gunship and test it in combat in Vietnam.

Exactly a month after the session with LeMay, Terry and a test team arrived in Vietnam. Miniguns were installed in two air commando flare ships. The first daytime combat mission was flown on 15 December. A week later, the gunship was called in to hit a building that a number of Vietcong had been seen running into. When ground forces checked the building, they found twenty-one bodies and reported that the building "looked like a sieve."

The first night mission was flown on 23–24 December. In quick succession, the plane fired a total of nine thousand rounds, driving attackers away from two outposts west of Can Tho, deep in the delta region.

On a typical mission, the gunship flew in a circle around the target at about three thousand feet. While the crew members in the cargo compartment prepared the guns, the pilot used a simple sight on his side window to tilt the plane so the guns were pointed at the target. When he pressed the trigger, a sheet of flame erupted from the side of the plane, and bullets rained down on the target. The slant range from the plane to the target was about a mile, putting the plane safely outside the range of the rifles and machine guns with which the Vietcong were normally equipped.

At first, the gunships were flown out of Bien Hoa, the original home in Vietnam of the air commandos. Later, they were based at Tan Son Nhut, Da Nang, Pleiku, Nha Trang, and Binh Thuy. The 1st Air Commando Squadron called its planes Puff the Magic Dragon, or, more often, just plain Puff, or the Dragonship. When the 4th Air Commando Squadron was set up and began flying the planes in late 1965, they adopted another call sign: Spooky. A third gunship unit, the 14th Air Commando Squadron (later known as the 3rd Air Commando Squadron), was added in the fall of 1967.

Colonel Charles A. Riley, who flew with the 4th Air Commando Squadron, recalled a typical night for a gunship crew in a memoir written for the *ACA Newsletter* in 1990.

While flying nighttime alert, his crew received an urgent call to help a fort under attack by a reinforced battalion of Vietcong troops. Riley describes the situation:

"The crew made repeated passes under heavy ground fire, destroying five heavy-mortar positions and a heavy machine gun that was giving us trouble, as well as the fort. Heavy casualties were inflicted upon the Vietcong battalion, which quickly withdrew.

"After landing to rearm and refuel at Binh Thuy, we again assumed airborne alert over the area. During the early morning hours, following another fire support mission, we were called by a downed Army helicopter pilot who was under heavy attack on the ground and in imminent danger of being overrun. We chased the bad guys off and stayed with the crew until daylight, when they were rescued. From dusk until dawn, we had flown all night for a total of over thirteen hours of combat flying."

Understandably, the gunship quickly became a favorite of the Americans and Vietnamese defending the vulnerable little outposts, often located in remote parts of the country.

Riley recalls meeting several young GIs in a restaurant in Saigon as the soldiers were preparing to return home after a year of combat near the Cambodian border.

"Roy [Capt. Roy White] and I were in civilian clothes, causing one of the GIs to ask where we worked. We replied that we were 'Spooky' pilots from the 4th Air Commando Squadron. This brought big smiles of recognition: 'You guys saved our asses more times than I can count. If it wasn't for you guys, I wouldn't be going home.' Whether we were actually 'those guys' or not I'm not sure, but it was nice to hear. . . . After finishing our meal, the waiter informed us that the GIs had paid our bill and left him a big tip."

The GIs' enthusiasm for the gunship was not shared by many among the Air Force brass.

General Walter C. Sweeney, Jr., head of the Tactical Air Command when the gunship was first introduced, was one of its most outspoken critics.

"This concept will place a highly vulnerable aircraft in a battlefield environment in which I believe the results will not compensate for the losses of Air Force personnel. . . ." he said. "We should continue to vigorously oppose the offensive . . . employment of all such highly vulnerable aircraft."

Heinie Aderholt got a strong dose of the opposition to the gunship while commanding a group of pilots at Hurlburt in the mid-1960s. He tells what happened:

"The Army requested we put on a demo of the gunships to show their capability. I said, 'We're going to knock the Army's eyes out. We're going to show them what this gunship will really do.' We were planning this big show. And I got called in by the commanding general.

"He said, 'I want you to downplay this operation.'

"I said, 'Why?'

"He said, 'The old man, Momyer [Gen. William W. Momyer, at that time commander of the Tactical Air Command], doesn't like the gunship, doesn't think it's good for the Air Force. And he doesn't want this show to go off as you planned this big deal.'

"I said, 'General, I only know how to put on but one kind of show.' I told my aides, 'It may get us fired, but let's put on a real show!' And we did.

"Another time, the general calls me in and says, 'I want you to find out how we can get Terry transferred to the special operations command.'

"I said, 'You mean Captain Terry up at Wright-Pat [the Air Force test center at Wright-Patterson Air Force Base near Dayton, Ohio]? Why?'

"He said, 'We want to get that son of a bitch under our thumb.' They didn't want the gunship. They were going to kill it. Wright-Pat was developing this thing. I told them, 'They're after Terry. Don't let them get him.'"

Terry himself seemed almost to thrive on the opposition. When his foes cut off funds, he used his own personal credit card to keep things moving. When other Air Force projects were encumbered by layers of bureaucracy and routinely coming in behind schedule and millions of dollars over the original cost estimates, Terry and his team did things faster than expected, under their cost estimates. And when a new system was ready to go to war, Terry himself flew the early combat missions to make sure the system was working right and to train air commando crews in its use.

Some of the criticism of the gunship, especially in the AC-47 version, was not only justified but acknowledged by Terry and its other supporters.

One disadvantage was that the C-47 is a low-wing monoplane. The position of the wing makes it hard for the pilot to see his target.

Another valid criticism was that the plane flies at only about 180 miles an hour, hundreds of miles an hour slower than jet fighters. For a sophisticated radar-directed antiaircraft gun, it is, if not quite a sitting duck, at least a very slow-flying one. Terry and the other developers of the concept knew this and tailored the plane for a mission in which it would not operate in areas where deadly AAA guns or even rockets were deployed.

This vulnerability was tragically demonstrated in early 1966, when gunships were assigned to attack trucks moving down the Ho Chi Minh Trail through Laos into South Vietnam.

In the first half of 1966, the 4th Air Commando Squadron lost four planes. The loss rate, projected over a full year, would have been an 80 percent loss of planes and a 61.5 percent loss of personnel. To make matters worse, two more gunships had been lost in the last two months of 1965.

"The mountainous and totally dark trail, usually covered by bad weather and mobile 37- and 57mm AAA guns, was a pretty hostile environment for an old, slow gooney bird," Riley recalls. "We were able to destroy a lot of trucks, but we lost four aircraft and over thirty aircrew members in a short time. These men are all listed KIA/MIA and are unaccounted for to this day. . . .

"Shortly after this period, when we lost nearly a third of the squadron, we were reassigned to the in-country war, where we belonged. We did lots of good work, and during the first eight months in-country, the 4th Air Commando Squadron crews flew fifteen hundred combat hours, logged 3,463 combat missions, fired 7 million rounds from its 7.62mm miniguns, successfully defended 450 forts and outposts, and accounted for over four thousand enemy personnel killed in action."

The return to Vietnam did not mean the gunships were immune from enemy fire. On the night of 24 February 1969, an AC-47 of the 3rd Air Commando Squadron was firing in support of ground troops near Long Binh when the plane's right wing was hit by what was later determined to be a shell from an enemy 82mm mortar. Although probably just a chance hit by a shell intended for the defenders, the lucky hit created chaos inside the plane.

When the shell hit, one crew member had his finger through the safety pin ring and was preparing to drop a 2-million-candle-power magnesium flare. He dropped the armed flare on the floor of the plane. It was set to go off in twenty seconds, burning at four thousand degrees Fahrenheit.

Airman First Class John L. Levitow, although severely injured by shrapnel from the mortar, picked up the flare, crawled to the open cargo hatch, and pushed the flare out just before it ignited.

Levitow won the Medal of Honor for his heroism. He was one of five air commandos to win the nation's highest award in Vietnam and the only enlisted member of the Air Force to be so honored.

At various times during the Vietnam conflict, the AC-47 carried three different sizes of guns. When not enough of the new miniguns were available, Terry found a batch of World War II–era .30-caliber machine guns that were about to be destroyed and arranged to have them installed in the gunships. Later, heavier .50-caliber machine guns were used. For some types of targets, the AC-47 was short of the needed firepower. And the basic plane was relatively small, limiting the weight of guns and ammunition it could carry. Almost as soon as the concept was proved in combat, attention focused on developing a bigger gunship with more powerful guns and with armament to protect the crew.

The obvious choice was the Lockheed C-130, a four-engine cargo plane that, by the time of the Vietnam War, had taken over the basic workhorse role filled by the C-47 in World War II and Korea.

Work on the new gunship coincided with an all-out push by the Pentagon to overcome one of the most serious problems United States forces had encountered in Vietnam: the enemy traveled and often fought at night, taking advantage of the darkness to move in and launch attacks. The original gunships also operated at night, but they couldn't bring their guns to play until the enemy had committed himself to an attack—and by that time, the defenders were already in serious trouble. One of the most important hoped-for attributes of a new gunship was the ability to see the enemy moving in the dark and hit him while he was getting ready to attack, not after he was already climbing the ramparts.

A partial answer to this problem was the appearance in Vietnam on 21 September 1967 of the first AC-130A gunship, a prototype of the plane that was later to become one of the most valued weapons in the Air Force special operations inventory.

The Gunship II, as it was called, was a dramatic advance over the original AC-47. It carried four 7.62mm miniguns plus four 20mm cannons capable of firing at the rate of twenty-five hundred high-explosive incendiary shells a minute. Probably even more important were the advanced sensors: a starlight scope, a kind of telescope that enhanced the faint light from the stars so the crew could see in the dark; a forward-looking infrared system, and a side-looking radar. The infrared system made it possible to detect the heat of a truck even after the driver had parked and turned off his engine.

Once the target had been spotted, it could be lighted up by two twenty-kilowatt xenon lamps. They were not only capable of giving off visible light but could also radiate infrared or ultraviolet light, making it possible to illuminate the target with a light the enemy could not see.

The sensors were all linked up to an automatic fire-control system that permitted the pilot to fire accurately without ever seeing the target with his eyes.

With its more powerful engines, the plane was also able to operate at altitudes of six to ten thousand feet—two or three times as high as the AC-47—providing greater protection from antiaircraft fire.

Despite the success of the earlier gunships in Vietnam and the urgent need for the ability to fight in the dark, the Gunship II project got something less than enthusiastic support from the brass. The plane assigned for the tests had already been in three major accidents. Its serial number was 54-1626. The crews called her "sick-two-six."

For the tests at Eglin and the introduction into combat, half the crew was made up of scientists, such as Lt. Col. James R. Krause, a master navigator and one of the Air Force's leading infrared experts, and gunship pioneers such as Terry.

Considering the amount of brand-new equipment carried by the plane, the time taken for its development and testing was amazingly brief. Modification of "sick-two-six" began on 1 April 1967, tests at Eglin began on 6 June, and the plane arrived in Vietnam ready for its introduction to combat on 21 September.

Even in its early, prototype version, the AC-130 seemed in many ways the ideal gunship, useful not only for defending outposts under attack but also for finding and destroying trucks moving down the Ho Chi Minh Trail.

But, at least partially because there were not enough C-130s in the Air Force inventory to serve as gunships and also to fill the plane's basic role as a carrier of troops and cargo, the decision was made to develop another plane—the older twin-engine C-119 Flying Boxcar—as an interim gunship.

The AC-119 was no match for the AC-130 and, some critics complained, was not even as good as the AC-47. Its major disadvantage was that it was seriously underpowered for carrying the gunship's heavy load of ammunition. If an engine failed on takeoff, it had a climb rate of only one hundred feet a minute. As one bemused pilot noted, a minute is a long time when there are tall trees at the end of the runway. Critics called it a "flying anachronism."

Perhaps reflecting the critical attitude toward the AC-119, it was originally given the call sign Creep. Furious crew members complained, and the designation was changed to Shadow and, later, to Stinger.

The AC-119G Shadow was first operational in December 1968. The AC-119K Stinger, which came into service about a year later, was a considerable improvement. To boost its takeoff power and the weight it could carry, it had two extra J-85 jet engines, which burned the same aviation gas as the plane's two conventional engines. This raised the gross takeoff weight from the Shadow's 64,000 pounds to 80,400 pounds for the Stinger. The Stinger was also more heavily armed, carrying two 20mm cannons along with four 7.62mm miniguns.

The miniguns were used against personnel from about thirty-five hundred feet, duplicating the attack pattern of the AC-47. But the Shadow also moved up to seventy-eight hundred feet to attack vehicles with its 20mm cannons.

Fortunately, the introduction of the Shadow and Stinger did not stop work on improvements to the AC-130.

In the winter of 1969–70, a new version of the AC-130 gunship arrived. It was called Surprise Package. The surprise was the addition of a 40mm Bofors gun—originally a Navy antiaircraft weapon—capable of firing up to 120 rounds a minute. By this time, much of the Air Force's attention was focused on stopping truck traffic from North Vietnam into the south through Laos. With its heavier guns, the new gunship was a much more capable truck killer than the earlier planes with their smaller-caliber guns. During the winter of its arrival, the new plane was credited with knocking out 822 trucks, or 7.5 trucks per sortie.

To make the guns even more deadly, the 40mm shells were made with misch-metal liners. The liners work something like the flint in a cigarette lighter, causing sparks. If a truck was not destroyed by the shell, the sparks caused a fire that completed the job.

When the new shells arrived late in 1970, however, the results were disappointing. Terry hurried to the scene and flew several missions to show the crews how to use the new shell effectively. During November, gunship crews attacked 202 trucks but destroyed or damaged only 37 of them. In the first three weeks of December, Terry and his team attacked 532 trucks and destroyed or damaged 361 of them.

The gunship equipped with the 40mm gun was a major development, but the real surprise package arrived in February of 1971. It was the AC-130E. The program was given the code name Pave Aegis, and the plane was called Spectre—the same designation used by today's gunships.

One of the two 40mm guns was replaced with a 105mm howitzer. A proficient crew can pump out eight rounds a minute, until fatigue takes over. A steady three-rounds-a-minute firing rate can be sustained until the plane runs out of shells. Armament then consisted of one 105mm howitzer, one 40mm gun, and two 20mm guns. The plane also had a more advanced fire-control system, a digital computer, and more fuel capacity.

The shells for the new 105mm gun were thirty-one inches long and weighed forty-two pounds apiece. Most important, they were packed with 5.6 pounds of high explosive, compared with only slightly more than half a pound in a 40mm shell. One disadvantage was that the casing of each shell had to be crimped by hand. Otherwise, when the shell was loaded into the gun, which was pointing down toward the ground rather than up in the air like a normal artillery piece, the projectile slipped loose and fell out of the barrel. It took fifteen man hours to crimp a hundred shells, and that was a nuisance, but the effort was a small price to pay for the added firepower of the new gun.

At first, infantrymen and even forward air controllers did not understand the new firepower they had at their command. On several occasions, Spectre crews were put in a holding pattern while jet fighter-bombers were brought in. But the attitude of troops on the ground quickly changed. Once they saw what the big cannon could do, whenever they heard a gunship approaching, they demanded: "Do you have the Big Gun?"

One ground commander was heard to radio: "Okay, all you other guys move off. Big Bertha is here!"

During the enemy's Easter offensive in the spring of 1972, only a single AC-130 had been fitted with the big new gun, but it quickly earned a reputation as a deadly tank killer. It was also incredibly accurate. In one test, half the rounds fired from a ten-thousand-foot altitude landed within twenty-five feet of the target.

During a fierce battle at An Loc in the spring of 1972, Spectre crews were given hand-drawn maps of the town. Troops on the ground then gave them instructions like this: "Go north along Main Street for three blocks, turn east, and hit the second house from the corner."

In that same battle, one ground commander adjusted the fire of the Spectre in twenty-five-meter increments, putting the bullets right where he needed them.

By the time the new gunship with its "Big Bertha" arrived in Southeast Asia, the United States involvement in the war was winding down, and the Air Force was focusing more on the future than on developing new weapons to fight in Vietnam. It was at that time that a momentous decision for the future of special operations was made: the Air Force chose to include the gunship in its post-war arsenal.

While the air commandos were among the first to fight in Vietnam and remained there until the end, they also wrote a long and important chapter in the history of Air Force special operations in a largely secret war over the mountains in Laos.

Colonel Philip G. Cochran, right, and his brother, Cpl. Joseph L. Cochran, who served under him as a member of the 1st Air Commando Group.

Wingate conducts briefing at Lalaghat, India, before attempt to deposit his commandos behind enemy lines. Cochran stands to his rear.

A DC-3 snatches a cable suspended between two posts to take a glider in tow.

P-51 Mustangs of the 1st Air Commando Group over Burma.

1st Air Commando L-5 undergoing repair of battle damage incurred during combat with Japanese forces in Burma.

Soldiers try to coax a balky mule aboard a DC-3 in preparation for a flight behind Japanese lines in Burma.

Air and ground crew members pose beside a YR-4, the first helicopter to be used in combat, in Burma in 1944.

A YR-4 hovers over a B-25 that had crash-landed in India during the Burma Operation.

A Carpetbagger B-24 drops canisters of supplies to resistance forces during a rare daytime operation.

An agent, known as a "Joe," prepares to drop through the Joe hole from a Carpetbagger B-24 somewhere over occupied France.

The Air Resupply and Communications Service, a Korean War–era operation based on the model of the World War II Carpetbaggers, used the SU-16 for flights into hostile territory including, on several occasions, the rescue of crashed U-2 spy plane pilots.

The 581st ARC Wing used the H-19 special operations helicopter for daring missions far behind North Korean and Chinese lines during the Korean War.

An A-1E Sandy prepares for takeoff from Nakom Phanom, an airfield in northern Thailand, near the Laotian border, used extensively by air commandos during the war in Southeast Asia.

An A-1E on a combat mission during the Vietnam War.

In a steep dive, an A-1H releases its bombs on a target in Southeast Asia. Various models of the A-1, originally a Navy plane, were one of the air commandos' favorites.

Brigadier General Henry "Heinie" Aderholt is shown in the cockpit of an AT-28 during one of his tours of duty as an air commando in Thailand. (Courtesy Henry Aderholt)

An H-53 of the type used in the Son Tay raid in 1970 takes on fuel from a C-130 tanker in Southeast Asia.

Despite intensive air attacks, the truck traffic from North Vietnam through Laos into South Vietnam by 1973 had intensified.

Major Bernard F. Fisher and Maj. Dafford W. Myers have good reason to smile after Fisher landed his A-1E and rescued Myers, who had crashed during the deadly battle for the Special Forces outpost in the A Shau Valley in March 1966.

Nimrod veterans of the Vietnam War pose in front of an A-26 at Hurlburt Field, Florida, during their 1994 reunion. The A-26 Invader was used by special forces for three decades, from World War II through the war in Southeast Asia. (Photo by author)

Wreckage of a C-130 at Desert One, destroyed in an accident during the attempt to rescue hostages from Teheran in 1980, symbolized the decline of Air Force special operations in the years immediately after the Vietnam War.

Members of an Air Force special tactics unit fast-rope from a Pave Low helicopter during exercises at Hurlburt Field. (Photo by Rose Reynolds)

Members of the 1723d Combat Control Squadron jump, with their rubber boat, from a Pave Low into the ocean during training exercises. (Photo by TSgt. Lee Schading)

A C-130 of the 16th Special Operations Squadron and a Pave Low helicopter of the 20th Special Operations Squadron fly in formation over Hurlburt Field.

Navy Lt. Devon Jones, pilot of an F-14 that had been shot down, dashes toward the rescue helicopter, passing Sgt. Ben Pennington, a pararescueman who had left the helicopter to assist him. (Photo by MSgt. Timothy Hadrych)

The crew of *Moccasin 05* pose in front of their Pave Low helicopter after their daring rescue deep inside Iraq. From left: TSgt. Jim Peterson, Sgt. Graig Dock, MSgt. Tim Hadrych, Capt. Tom Trask, Maj. Mike Homan, and TSgt. Greg VanHyning.

Four Air Force Pave Low helicopters used their advanced navigation systems to guide eight Army Apache helicopters, like the one shown here armed with Hellfire missiles, for a strike against two Iraqi radar sites to begin the Desert Storm attack on Iraq.

Three Air Force heroes of a fierce shoot-out in downtown Mogadishu during U.S. operations there in 1993 were honored in ceremonies in the nation's capital. From left to right, they are SSgt. Jeffrey Bray, MSgt. Scott Fales, and TSgt. Timothy Wilkinson. Bray and Fales were awarded the Silver Star and Wilkinson the Air Force Cross.

PART 5
Through the Looking Glass

CHAPTER 17
The Secret War

The war over the mountains in Laos was an almost perfect mirror image of the war being waged in Vietnam.

By geography and climate, Laos could have been created as a stage set for a war of fog and shadows, of secrecy and deception. Like a child's image of "the other side of the world," Laos really did look different, like a Chinese watercolor, in muted shades of gray and faded pastels.

Strange pinnacles of rock known as karst soared thousands of feet from valleys of jungle and tiny farms and fields of purple opium poppies. Fog often filled the valleys and drifted past the rocky cliffs. Caves dotted the karst—some big enough to hide large artillery weapons or enough fuel and supplies for an army.

For the air commando crews, finding their way through clouds that were often filled with rocks was always dangerous and sometimes fatal.

In the center of the country, near the border with North Vietnam, is a large relatively flat area covered with what look like large jars left by some ancient people. It is known by its name in French, the Plaine des Jarres—the "Plain of Jars." The American pilots called it the PDJ, for the French initials.

The contrast with the war in Vietnam, especially after 1965, when Americanization began in earnest, was startling.

In Vietnam, the war was public, vividly portrayed on nightly television. The other war was a carefully guarded secret. Even when the broad outlines of what was going on became public, details remained classified. Even today, many documents about that other war are still considered secret.

In Vietnam, the United States military took over the biggest burden of fighting the war. In Laos, most of the fighting—and dying—was done by a group of mountain people known as the Hmong. They even provided much of their own air support, flying mission after mission until they died.

In Laos, the American involvement was masterminded by the civilian ambassador in Vientiane, the capital, and carried on by a strange collection of CIA agents and military men masquerading as soldiers of fortune. For a long time, they succeeded in resisting efforts of the conventional war generals to take over the war, as they had done in Vietnam.

In another important respect, this war on the other side of the looking glass was different. In Vietnam, the South Vietnamese and their United States ally held the big, valuable targets—the cities and the big military bases—while the enemy flowed through the villages and hamlets, able to pick the time and place for combat. In Laos, the situation was the opposite. The Hmong held the mountaintops, while the North Vietnamese and their Pathet Lao allies were tied to the cities, vulnerable supply depots, and roads, where they were subject to attack.

Most pertinent, for this narrative, is that the war, especially in Laos, was very much an air commandos' war, a continuation of the role played by the Farmgate crews in the early days in Vietnam. The commandos flew ancient propeller-driven planes or modified trainers, and they trained the indigenous people to fly and fight the war themselves rather than taking over and fighting it for them. They adopted exotic names for themselves: Butterflies and Ravens were forward air controllers; Nimrods flew the A-26s; Bigmouths broadcast propaganda from the air; and Litterbugs dropped leaflets.

If Laos had been somewhere other than right in the middle of Indochina, it is doubtful that the United States would have become as involved as it did with the native people, helping them to fight off the neighboring North Vietnamese. But Laos, in addition to being one of the Indochinese "dominoes" waiting to fall to international Communism, was, because of its location, also crucial to the situation in Vietnam. For the North Vietnamese, Laos provided a critical link—the Ho Chi Minh Trail—by which troops and supplies moved from the north into South Vietnam. For the United States, Laos provided sites for radar and communications installations guiding bombers against targets in North Vietnam and bases close to the North Vietnamese border for rescue helicopters to go in after downed aircrews.

Quite apart from its strategic importance, many of the air commandos and the CIA officers, with whom they worked closely, thought their work in Laos was important because they had become great admirers of the Hmong and their fierce determination to protect themselves and their way of life from the North Vietnamese.

Ironically, even some of the Americans who worked in Laos with the Hmong didn't really know them very well, despite the fact that they flew with them every day, participated in their ceremonies, and advised them on military strategy. American documents from that period consistently refer to the Hmong as the Meo—a name derived from a term of derision given to the Hmong generations ago, when the people lived in China before moving south into Laos to escape persecution.

There is no doubt of the Americans' admiration for these allies. It was an admiration that did not extend to the lowlanders, the Laotians. The Americans found most of them reluctant warriors, often more interested in coups and countercoups or smuggling heroin than in fighting the North Vietnamese.

Thus, while the formal American presence could be observed in the capital of Vientiane, the military focal point of the United States activity in Laos was in a compound in the hills to the north known as Long Chieng. It was also known as Lima Site 30 and 20 Alternate. The Americans commonly referred to it simply as Alternate. Although the American press, which was barred from visiting Long Chieng, came to refer to it as the "CIA's secret headquarters," Long Chieng was more of a military outpost and staging area. The CIA had its truly secret administrative base back in northern Thailand.

The central figure at Long Chieng was a charismatic Hmong leader named Vang Pao. Although he did not have a high-school education, Vang Pao had a natural flare for guerrilla warfare that impressed the French, with whom he fought against the Vietminh. In 1952, when he was eighteen, the French sent him to a military academy in Vientiane. He emerged as a second lieutenant in time to help lead a rescue force of Hmong resistance fighters on a forced march through the jungles when a large French garrison was trapped at Dien Bien Phu in 1954. But they arrived on the scene the day the French surrendered and turned to retrace their steps into Laos.

Vang Pao preferred to lead by example.

One American pilot watched in amusement as an American Army captain tried to explain to Vang Pao how to use firing tables and other by-the-book methods for firing artillery. Vang Pao looked down and saw an enemy truck approaching. He snipped off a blade of grass and used it to check the distance. He stuck a finger in the air to check the wind. He ordered the gun moved slightly and then gave the order to shoot. A moment later, the truck exploded.

When the bullets were flying, Vang Pao often stood exposed as though he were impervious to enemy fire. He wasn't. On one occasion, he turned just as a bullet tore into his body, inflicting a serious injury. If he had not moved, the bullet would have struck him in the chest and probably killed him.

Although only thirty years old in 1964, he was a kind of father figure to his people.

Major Michael E. Cavanaugh, who flew as a forward air controller in Laos in the late 1960s, recalls the way Vang Pao dealt with his people:

"He was such a people person. People would come in every night and tell General Vang Pao their problems. They were screened before they got in there. . . . He had a little box and he would open up the box and he would take out some kip [the Laotian currency], and he would peel off some big red ones. He would give them the money. . . .

"He was also very strong. We had a forward air controller, one of the Lao backseaters, and he gave wrong information. Gee, talk about feeling bad, one of the Ravens [American pilots flying as forward air controllers] dropped bombs right on top of the friendlies based on what the guy in the backseat told him. General Vang Pao believed the Raven, and of course the guy was scared to death. He said, 'The Raven is lying!' General Vang Pao said, 'Ravens don't lie.' He took him out and shot him. That's it. That was wartime. You goof up, you die. He was upset with him, so he took him out and shot him."

Heinie Aderholt tells a similar story:

"General Vang Pao, he found a traitor? He'd have him tied up out there, and he'd go out every morning and cut off an inch of his hide until he died. He did that so people would know that's what would happen if you were a traitor."

As early as 1960, the CIA arranged for very limited air support for Vang Pao. But he clearly perceived that the key to success in his war with the North Vietnamese and their Pathet Lao allies was what he called, simply, "air"—especially his own planes and pilots, ready to support his forces on the ground whenever they got in trouble.

The answer was Project Water Pump. As it seemed to do routinely when something secret and unusual needed doing, the Air Force called on Aderholt. He set up Project Water Pump at a royal Thai air base at Udorn in March of 1964.

"It was the start," says Aderholt, "of a whole Air Force department that did all kinds of crazy things."

Providing air power for Vang Pao was not the number-one priority when Water Pump was set up. Instead, the original motive was to make it easier to rescue American pilots shot down over the Ho Chi Minh Trail. Because American military people were not supposed to be operating in Laos, the United States arranged for civilian helicopter crews hired by Air America—the CIA front—to fly the rescue missions. But the helicopter pilots were understandably reluctant to go without fighter escort into areas where an airplane had already been shot down.

Thus, the original goal of Water Pump was to teach Thai and Laotian pilots to fly the AT-28 converted trainer—the same plane used by the American Farmgate pilots in Vietnam—and to train them in tactics for suppressing enemy gunfire during a helicopter rescue operation. The Laotians could openly take part in rescue missions. The Thais, as foreigners, temporarily gave up their royal Thai commissions and flew on a kind of pay-per-mission basis.

Vang Pao prevailed on his American friends to include some of his men in the training program, not so they could participate in rescue missions but so they could return and provide air support for his guerrilla forces. But it took a frustratingly long time—three years—before the Hmong volunteers were trained and ready to go into combat.

A major problem was that no one was quite sure how to go about making pilots out of men from the mountains of central Laos. They didn't speak English. Most of them had never driven a car. They were so small that the Americans had to wire chunks of two-by-four to the rudder pedals so the Hmong could reach them. When they reported to the flight line, the would-be pilots brought their helmets, parachutes—and pillows to raise them up enough to see out of the cockpit.

Despite these handicaps, most of them turned out to be superb pilots. On the day the first class graduated, Aderholt arranged a show for Vang Pao, the United States ambassador, and other dignitaries. The pilots roared down the runway in their AT-28s, tucked up their wheels, did a barrel roll, zoomed up, and did another roll before leveling off and returning to land in front of their audience. To be on the safe side, Aderholt had hidden an instructor pilot in the backseat of each of the planes. But the Hmong pilots carried off their flashy show without any need for assistance.

When they returned to their homeland, they called themselves Chaophakaow!, which translates as "Lord White Buddha." It was at the same time a radio call sign and a prayer.

In the cockpit as on the ground, the Hmong proved to be fierce and dedicated warriors. They were also daring, seemingly fearless pilots.

Clyde Howard, who was a young sergeant and one of a small group of enlisted combat controllers, recalls the kind of rough-and-ready combat missions flown by the Hmong.

"Some of them had many, many missions. They flew like cowboys. They'd still have their gear up ten feet from the runway. At the last second, they'd drop their gear. I was hollering at them: 'Check gear down!' They'd do it on purpose just to get me excited. They'd laugh about it. They'd fly all day long—ten missions a day."

One pilot stands out in the memories of Americans involved in that secret war. He was a schoolteacher named Ly Leu who was one of the first to volunteer for pilot training. He would fly from dawn until dusk. When he returned from a mission, he would jump from the plane and help load bombs, in a hurry to get back in the air. Some evenings, when he landed after his last mission, he was so exhausted he had to be helped from the cockpit.

Although he was only a captain, Ly Leu actually served as a general, commanding Vang Pao's small air force. The Americans were fascinated by him. In his off-duty hours, he would play the guitar and entertain them with dirty songs. When he stopped overnight in various cities, he had a wife waiting in each place.

Unlike the Americans, who put in a tour of duty broken by recreational trips to Hawaii, Bangkok, Tokyo, Hong Kong, Kuala Lumpur, or Australia and then went home, the Hmong pilots flew without a break—usually until they died.

They were so aggressive that it scared the Americans just to watch them. One American forward air controller described how they would swoop in at twenty feet off the ground. He said Ly Leu's idea of strafing was to stick a .50-caliber gun in the enemy's ear and pull the trigger. Ly Leu dubbed one of the Americans "the astronaut" because he refused to fly as low as the Hmong did.

Ly Leu was rated by his admirers as the best pilot in Laos, regardless of nationality. He flew as though he were indestructible, but he knew he wasn't. He worried about being hit and trapped in a burning plane. The AT-28s flown by the Hmong at that time did not have ejection seats. In late 1968, he was hit and managed to roll over and drop out of the cockpit just before the plane exploded. He was back in the air the next day with a new plane. But his days were numbered.

Ly Leu was shot down attacking a North Vietnamese bunker while Vang Pao, who was his father-in-law, was controlling the attack by radio from a nearby hill. Cavanaugh vividly recalls the shoot-down and the funeral that followed:

"It was straight north of Long Chieng, south of Muong Soui. . . . There was a pocket of NVA in that area, and we had them. We had them by the short hair. And Ly Leu was on his tenth combat mission of the day. It was nothing for him to fly thirty-minute missions. He would land at Muong Soui, put the bombs on the airplane, and go fly. The target was three miles away. He would drop his bombs, go back and land, and do it again."

On what became his final flight, Ly Leu was targeted by a 12.7mm antiaircraft gun. He always flew low, and, this day, he was right down on the treetops. As he pulled away from the target, struggling for altitude, the enemy gunner followed him up.

"He was pulling off from south to north, and he was real slow, and that gunner was on him. Just rode him to death," Cavanaugh says.

With Ly Leu was a student pilot, being checked out in the plane on a combat mission—what Cavanaugh describes as "one hell of a checkout."

Both Ly Leu and the student pilot were killed, and Cavanaugh and the other Americans went to the Buddhist-style funeral. They saw the two caskets there, surrounded with pictures of the two dead men, family streamers, and flowers.

Following the example of the Hmong, the Americans crawled up to the caskets on their knees, carrying sticks of incense, which they placed in a vase, and then said a prayer.

General Vang Pao, who was devastated by the loss of Ly Leu, was deeply impressed by the way the Americans participated in what, for them, was an unfamiliar and alien ceremony.

Water Pump quickly grew to include more than seventy planes.

In addition to training Lao, Hmong, and Thai pilots, the air commandos also became involved directly in the war.

Howard recalls how they would move planes, people, fuel, bombs, everything they needed, early in the morning and set up operations for the day like a traveling road show. Their main base for these operations was Nakom Phanom (NKP), a base in Thailand about eight miles south of the Mekong River, which forms the border between Laos and Thailand.

"We'd move forward early in the morning. I'd fly in a helicopter and scope out a stretch of road that was suitable for forward operations—fifty or sixty miles inside Laos, near the North Vietnamese border. Once we selected a section of road that was suitable and in friendly territory, we would land.

"I would take a fuels guy, an aircraft mechanic, a bomb loader, and a munitions person. There would be four or five of us there at the break of dawn.

"We'd check the surface, put up markers, bring in the C-7s or C-123s with bombs and off-load them. Then they would launch the AT-28s out of NKP. They would go hit the targets. The targets might be ten miles from where I'm setting up operations. They would drop their bombs, then come back to me, and I would land them on the road.

"I'd control the aircraft in, get them parked over to the side. The others guys would load bombs on them. We had fifty-five-gallon drums of gas, so we'd pump gas into them.

"They had only five or ten miles to go to deliver another load of bombs. We'd do that all day long. We'd turn them as fast as we could turn them. All day long. It was a constant stream. With four airplanes, you really stay busy."

As the air commandos continued to learn their way around, they played a major role, much of it behind the scenes, not only in the secret war in Laos but also in Thailand and, later, in Cambodia.

CHAPTER 18

Butterflies and Ravens

I n the beginning were the Butterflies.
    Butterflies—small winged creatures flitting through Laos's misty valleys and over the mysteries of the Plaine des Jarres. The name was fitting—but only up to a point.

Butterfly was the name given to members of a small group of Air Force combat controllers assigned in mid-1966 to guide attacks by American bombers in support of Vang Pao and his Hmong forces resisting the North Vietnamese on the ground.

The combat controllers, who have since become a vital and integral part of Air Force special operations, were a special breed of warriors: smart, adaptable, willing and able to go anywhere, do anything. They were trained to jump out of airplanes, fight with the infantry, tend wounds, and operate an airport. Direct descendants of the pathfinders who guided the aerial invasions of World War II, the combat controllers still have the main job of going in with Army Rangers to seize an enemy airfield and then to set up an air-traffic control system under combat conditions.

The air commando combat controllers arrived in Southeast Asia early in 1966 as part of Project Lucky Tiger, whose job was to prepare for the introduction of A-26 attack planes into Thailand. But they found themselves called upon to do a seemingly endless number and variety of jobs that no one else could or would do. Acting as Butterflies was only one of these jobs.

Jim Stanford, who now lives in Gravel Ridge, Arkansas, recalls how he and Charles Jones, now a minister in Navarre, Florida, were assigned in mid-1966 to direct air strikes in various parts of Laos.

At the time, Stanford was a technical sergeant and Jones a master sergeant. But for this assignment, they were "sheep dipped," dressed in civilian clothes and stripped of military identification. At first, they were assigned to Vang Pao's headquarters at Long Chieng, later to an even more remote guerrilla outpost in northern Laos.

Although the secret war in Laos is often referred to as a CIA operation, it was also very much of an air commando operation. The CIA air operation, involving civilian crews flying for Air America and Continental Air, was run by Richard Secord. A West Point graduate and one of the early Farmgate pilots, he was on loan to the CIA. Water Pump, which supplied indigenous aircrews and the Butterflies, was run by air commandos. And in Laos, the secret air war was managed by Project 404/Palace Dog, also manned by air commandos. Operating behind the scenes in Vientiane, Project 404 had air operations centers at five locations in Laos.

When Stanford and Jones were assigned as Butterflies, they pretty much ran their own operation.

"We'd have meetings with General Vang Pao," Stanford explains. "He'd tell us where he needed fire support. Charlie and I would go up to these areas with an interpreter. We'd go to sites, recon the targets, call in the ABCCC [an airborne command and control plane—in that era a C-47]. If they were getting overrun, we would try to get all the fighters we could get.

"We also had a squadron of Thai pilots flying AT-28s from Vientiane every day, morning, and afternoon. We had plenty of targets: truck parks, bridges, supply depots, and hordes of troops. It was a daily operation."

Stanford and Jones were not pilots themselves, so they flew with civilian pilots hired by the CIA, flying as employees of Air America or Continental Air. Normally, they flew in an extremely adaptive plane called the Porter Pilatus—a craft almost as maneuverable as a helicopter, able to get in and out of tiny fields roughly hacked out of the jungle or cut on a mountainside. The Porter was also big enough to carry an interpreter familiar with the situation on the ground.

When they reached an area under attack, Stanford or Jones drew a picture of the area on the plane's side window with an erasable marker. The interpreter then marked the friendly and enemy positions, and the Butterfly used this information to guide the fighter-bombers on their attack.

Since the pilots were civilians, they were not supposed to fire any weapons—not even a marking rocket. This meant the Butterfly had to give the fighter pilots precise directions using landmarks on the ground. In the remote areas of Laos where they were operating, however, there were no referees to enforce rules written by politicians half a world away.

The Porter had a bomb bay designed to drop cargo and food. The Americans scrounged hundred-pound bombs—either high explosive or white phosphorous—and loaded them into the bomb bay to drop if they ran out of fighters to direct against targets on the ground.

"We would also drop hand grenades," Stanford says. "We'd take hand grenades, pull the pins, and stick them in these cardboard tubes. The tubes were lashed to the floor with tie-down rings. When you opened the bomb bay, it would hold these tubes in, but all the hand grenades would fall out of the tubes. When they dropped, the spoons would fly off. These hand grenades would just saturate the area. It was like cluster bombs.

"When you were getting overrun, you would do a lot of things. We would fill a bottle with nails, tape a grenade to it, pull the pin, and drop it. Hopefully, it would go off before it hit the ground."

Sometimes, the Butterflies became personally involved in the ordeal of the troops on the ground.

On one occasion in northern Laos, Stanford and Jones were flying out of an outpost under fierce attack by the North Vietnamese.

"You could see the enemy on the ground—huge, huge numbers, hundreds and hundreds of troops," Stanford recalls. "It was one of the few times we could actually see the buildup. Charlie and I, we would describe the targets to the airplanes while we were still sitting on the ground pumping gas out of a fifty-five-gallon drum into the Porter. We'd get enough gas in to get airborne, put the first wave of fighters in, and then we'd flame out, have to land and pump more gas into the airplane and get back airborne. We never had enough time to get enough gas to stay on target the whole time. We'd land on this little dirt strip while it was under attack, pump gas with a hand pump, and take off again."

In this case, the defenders had a wealth of air support. Because of bad weather over North Vietnam, planes scheduled for attacks there were diverted to Laos.

"The ABCCC was diverting all the fighters from North Vietnam," Stanford says. "We had wave after wave: F-4s, A-4s, F-105s, AT-28s. They were coming off the carriers and out of South Vietnam and Thailand. There were flights of four, one after the other, all day. There were tankers out there waiting for them."

Stanford, who also served in South Vietnam and Thailand, found his work as a Butterfly rewarding, despite the dangers.

"It was really a good operation," he says. "It was different from South Vietnam, completely. South Vietnam was too big and political. Laos was not as much political; it was more military. At least at my level, you didn't see the politics as much."

It was Air Force politics, however, that brought an end to the Butterfly operation, although Stanford didn't hear what had happened until years later.

The abrupt change came as the result of a meeting late in 1966 between Aderholt, who was in charge of the Butterflies as part of his Water Pump program of training Thai, Lao, and Hmong pilots, and General Momyer, commander of the Seventh Air Force. It is not a meeting Aderholt is likely to forget:

"He and I had not gotten along well, but I had lunch with him and mentioned the Butterflies. He asked about the FACs [forward air controllers] in Laos and where they came from. I said, 'The people FAC-ing airplanes in Laos are enlisted.' He went about six feet up and hit the ceiling. He said, 'What do you mean? Who is flying the airplane?' I said, 'Air America pilots.' He said, 'That will cease!'"

Although several of the combat controllers had received a special secret training course in the techniques of forward air control and had been doing a good job for several months, Momyer reasoned that only a jet pilot could be trusted to direct an attack by a jet aircraft on a ground target.

The abrupt end to the Butterfly operation did not, however, end the need for effective ways to guide fast-moving fighter-bombers to their targets in Laos. Several expedients filled part of the gap, but they were not a full solution.

Working with the CIA, Vang Pao set up a number of small teams of observers to report on enemy movements. This operation came under Secord, who was running the CIA's air operation in Laos.

By late 1967, there were some eighty teams reporting on enemy supply depots and movements of men and equipment.

Another highly effective technique, introduced later, was the use of several different types of offset bombing devices provided by the CIA and operated by the Hmong.

Clyde Howard was serving in Thailand as a combat controller when the beacons were introduced. He recalls how they were used:

"They gave us about fifty beacons, and we started training our guys. We set up a program of positioning beacons permanently in fixed positions in Laos. We were concerned with the PDJ [Plaine des Jarres], and we only needed about five locations.

"We'd charge the batteries at Udorn and shuttle them up. It was a logistical nightmare, but we made it happen. Guys on the ground did not talk to the airplane. They just kept the beacon on the air. We had all the F-111s. They would take off from Takhli. Everyone going to the war zone would check in with us. If we had any targets, we would divert them to our targets. Eighty percent of the time we had targets."

The F-111s had a sophisticated electronic system that permitted the pilot to punch into his computer the distance and direction to the target from the beacon. Then he flipped an offset switch and aimed at the beacon. The system automatically dropped the bombs on the target. If the pilot forgot to flip the offset switch, the bombs fell on the beacon.

Sometimes Howard or other combat controllers would fly in an airborne control plane to guide the bombers. Other times, they would operate from the ground.

"We'd sit on the mountains under the clouds," Howard recalls. "You could see the troops scuttling across the valley because, with the weather, they knew the airplanes couldn't get them. But with this system, they didn't even hear them. The planes were up at fifteen to twenty thousand feet. All of a sudden, the bombs would fall through the clouds, and the world would come to an end. The enemy called it Silent Death."

Once they got the wrinkles out, the system proved extremely accurate. One night, Howard was flying in a C-130 serving as the airborne control plane when he received a report that Long Chieng was under artillery attack.

"It had to be a 130 mike mike," Howard says, using the phonetic alphabet for *millimeters*. "It was the only thing that would reach that far. One of the [Hmong] forward air guides reported a gun and gave me the coordinates. The next F-111 that came through, I diverted him to that target. When he called bomb release, I told the forward air guide: 'Look toward your target and tell me what you see.' All of a sudden, the bombs blow, and he says, 'You hit the target. You got secondary explosions.' I called Long Chieng and said, 'Are you still taking incoming?' They said, 'No, it just stopped.'"

Each of the F-111s carried twenty-four five-hundred-pound bombs. Normally, they would drop twelve on the first pass and the remainder on the next pass, crisscrossing the target from two directions.

The offset bombing system was later used in the high-flying B-52s but could not be used with fighter-bombers except for the F-111 because the others did not have the required sophisticated electronics. On some missions, however, A-7 fighters flew alongside and just behind the F-111s and dropped their bombs as soon as the pilot saw the bombs emerge from the F-111.

Despite the success of this system, an effective air campaign to support the Hmong guerrilla fighters still required skilled forward air controllers. Early in 1967, Aderholt was back in Florida, assigned to train jet pilots for the air controller job—and back at war with the conventional Air Force.

The basic plane for the forward-air-control job was a single-engine, high-winged plane not dramatically different from the little planes used in Burma more than twenty years before. It was the Cessna O-1 Bird Dog, a plane that had first entered service as an Army observation plane in 1950.

"The Air Force immediately started sending me jet fighter pilots to train as FACs, and they immediately started ground-looping those O-1s," Aderholt recalls. "Every time they ground-looped, I got a message: I was going to get fired.

"We didn't know what to do to stop ground-looping those O-1s. So we got this great acrobatic pilot. He was the best. Were going to get him to train these thirty or forty jet pilots to fly the O-1s. He came in, and he had a football. He threw the football up, and it came down and rolled over and bounced up under a desk.

"He said, 'I just demonstrated to you the landing of an O-1. Nobody knows where that mother is going to bounce when you make a bad landing. If you think you're going to stop ground-looping these things, you'd better stop flying them.'"

At the time, the Tactical Air Command was commanded by a general who had come from the Strategic Air Command. He treated an O-1 damaged in a ground loop just as seriously as he would have treated a B-52 that hit a mountain. At best, somebody got grounded.

"They got hard-nosed about it," Aderholt recalls. "They'd take these pilots, and they'd ground them. Take a hot jet pilot, bring him down here. He washes out a plane that costs fifteen to twenty thousand dollars then, maybe a couple of thousand to repair it. They wash out a guy that cost a million dollars to train. So I said, 'They can't do that to my boys. I can't live with this.'"

Aderholt called an Army general at Fort Rucker, where the Army also flew O-1s, and got him to send down ten planes that had been wrecked.

"We got these spare parts and stored them. And every time one of those O-1s ground-looped, we'd run another one in. So we were cheating."

Aderholt almost got caught when a team from the TAC inspector general's office showed up to count his airplanes. He turned out two planes short. Aderholt asked the inspector to double-check his count in the morning. By the time morning arrived, there were two extra planes on the field. The inspector general threw up his hands and went home.

Many of the pilots who survived Aderholt's FAC school soon found themselves involved in the strange secret war on the other side of the mountain. Theoretically, volunteers for service in Laos were chosen from among pilots who had put in six months as forward air controllers in Vietnam, although that rule was often ignored.

Like the Butterflies before them, the pilots went through the sheep-dip process, shedding their commissions, their formal connection with the United States Air Force, and their uniforms. In the case of the Butterflies, the sheep-dip process was fairly casual because it was no problem to lose a few enlisted men in the paperwork. But the commissioned pilots went through a much more rigorous process that not only severed their connections with the American military but made them feel like some sort of secret agents.

Normally, they flew to Bangkok, up to one of the royal Thai bases used by the Americans and then across the border into Laos. There, they simply slipped into the system without going through Lao customs or immigration checks, without even carrying passports.

They called themselves Ravens. Their Hmong counterparts, trained in Water Pump, chose an even more colorful name, Nokateng—Swooping Bird.

The number of Ravens built up gradually until eventually a total of 191 served as forward air controllers in Laos in the late 1960s and early 1970s.

Of that number, thirty-one died in action—a measure both of the danger of their job and their dedication to getting it done.

Colonel Robert L. F. Tyrrell, who served for a number of years as the air attaché at the embassy in Vientiane, told what he thought about the Ravens:

"You know the biggest problem we had with the Ravens, and God, I used to talk to them quite frequently about not going out there and killing themselves. Because it was my opinion that we could do an effective job without going too gung ho. We had one fellow that had three children, I think it was, that just pressed so hard, and he was right down there where they just knocked him out of the air—where he shouldn't have been—and could've been doing the same thing from a little more altitude. They had a tendency to do that; they were just so motivated to do a good job that they just overextended themselves.

"That was a great bunch. There were a few oddballs along the line, but, for the most part, I really took my hat off to those boys. They did a fantastic job. Because, Jesus, they were out there flying over the ground fire all the time, every day. They realized that it wasn't their war; they were exposing themselves, and they were getting killed, and still they would do this. They just did an outstanding job."

Major Mike Cavanaugh, who flew as a Raven in 1969, was asked if there were rules of engagement governing the operations of the Ravens.

"Absolutely not," he said. "They had the rules, and we had our war. They didn't know, nobody had the guts to go up there and find out exactly what we were up to, what we were doing, and we did the best we could with what we had."

The early Ravens flew the little O-1s that had given Aderholt so much trouble. Later, a number of them checked out in the AT-28, and often they would alternate, flying part of the day in an O-1, the rest of the day in an AT-28.

Whichever plane they flew, they took a Hmong along in the rear seat to help spot targets and communicate with troops on the ground. Several of the Ravens had such a reputation for aggressive flying that the Hmong were reluctant to fly with them. When one Raven in particular approached the building where the backseaters waited for assignment, they would actually hide while he overturned the furniture looking for them.

As they gained experience, the Ravens themselves became expert at spotting signs of the enemy's presence. One Raven liked to take off at first light on a kind of dawn patrol. He would look for the smoke from cook fires that might mark a troop bivouac. Trails where the early morning dew had been brushed off the grass were another sign of human presence. When he returned for breakfast, he had his own list of potentially lucrative targets for the day.

"Once you get a forward air controller's eyes, you begin to be able to see things. . . ." Cavanaugh says. "You can smell where supplies are. One time, I saw bushes which came to a ninety-degree angle. The clever devil that I am, I know that bushes don't grow in ninety-degree angles. That's all I had to go on; I hit it with a set of fighters. I uncovered pallet after pallet of 122mm rockets. They were headed south. They were just stored there, and this was just north of the Plaine des Jarres. I will never forget that, and I learned always to follow my hunch. My hunches were good hunches. I hit that one little area, and we had secondary explosions for two solid days. It was cooking off all during the night, and, the next day, it was still cooking off. All of the rockets were cooking off one at a time and shooting all over the place. It was a very rewarding sight, to be able to catch something like that."

Another time, Capt. Karl L. Polifka zeroed in on what looked like a little lump in the ground out in the middle of the Plaine des Jarres. Intelligence reports indicated it was the entrance to a cave where the enemy had stored five hundred barrels of fuel. Polifka marked the cave entrance and called in a fighter to put a guided bomb into the cave. The intelligence report was right: the bomb set off an explosion that created a fireball a thousand feet in diameter, so hot it drew a rain cloud to the scene.

The job of the Ravens, literally, was to look for trouble. And they often found it, not only in the form of enemy troops and supplies but in the form of barrages of bullets—fired by everything from rifles to high-powered antiaircraft weapons.

Jerome "Jerry" Klingaman, who served with Project 404/Palace Dog, providing target information for the Ravens, tells of his relationship with the Ravens:

"I had problems sending Ravens out to do things I wouldn't do myself," he says. "It helped settle my mind and it kept me aware of what was going on by flying missions with them. I flew with them in the backseat."

Klingaman particularly recalls one Raven, John Mansur, with whom he lived in an old farmhouse. During his tour in Laos, Mansur flew a number of very difficult missions, earning the Silver Star three times.

"On one mission, John was shot right through the helmet. He was up on the PDJ FAC-ing some A-1Es when he was shot through the helmet and blinded. The bullet went in one side of his visor and out the other, right in front of his eyes.

"The A-1Es saw what had happened and started giving him instructions: 'Right wing up. Level. Okay.' That sort of thing. The A-1Es flew him off the PDJ, got him away from the guns, and put him in orbit out there. Anyway, his eyes cleared up, and he was able to make a landing."

Gunners on the ground were not the only worry for the Ravens. They also lived in fear of the jet fighter-bombers diving from twelve thousand feet and streaking through their air space at four or five hundred miles an hour.

Once, when a jet purposely came so close that it forced him down into the weeds, Polifka fired a hundred rounds of .50-caliber bullets across his nose and warned that, the next time, he would shoot him down.

"You know, that sounds stupid now, but I would have had no compunction about shooting one of those guys down if I could have hit him," Polifka said later.

Midair near-collisions occurred several times a week. Most worrisome to the Ravens were the F-105 fighter-bombers. Once committed to a bombing attack, the plane went where it was aimed. If anything got in the way of that "lead sled," as the Ravens called F-105s, that was too bad.

"Once he is coming at you, you can't get out of the way in an

O-1, and he can't turn," Polifka explains. "It would just scare the living hell out of you."

With all the danger from enemy gunners and "friendly" jets, the Ravens were caught short on occasion when they got in trouble because of something as mundane as bad weather.

Cavanaugh used to warn other pilots to make sure they always had enough gas to get to one of the big airfields in Thailand. But he broke his own rule once in the summer of 1969 and almost paid with his life and that of his backseater, a Hmong called Moonface.

He kept calling in fighters on a lucrative target down below until he had only enough gas to get home to Long Chieng. But as he approached the base, he was confronted by a solid wall of clouds, rising to forty thousand feet, boiling with rain and lightning. He thought about landing and spending the night on the Plaine des Jarres but feared he would be captured.

Another pilot suggested landing at Muong Soui, on the edge of the storm north of Long Chieng. The only problem was that the North Vietnamese were in the process of overrunning the field.

Cavanaugh radioed for backup from Dale Brink, a friend who used the call sign Zorro 50. Brink and Rich Rose showed up in their A-1Es and strafed the enemy positions at Muong Soui as Cavanaugh came in for a landing. He describes what happened next:

"I got down, and they [the enemy] were firing right at the airplane. Some of them were on the south side of the runway—it was an east-west runway—and some of them were on the north side of the runway, but they were so close to the runway they couldn't get a good enough angle to shoot me. . . ."

Cavanaugh found an old gas pump the Americans had used when they were flying out of Muong Soui. But the nearby gas barrels were empty. He and Moonface ran two thousand feet down the runway to a bunker where they knew gasoline had been stored. Wrenching open the door of the bunker, Cavanaugh found the most precious barrels of fuel he had ever seen. But the gas pump and the plane were at the other end of the runway.

"Moonface and I took a barrel of gas, and we rolled it uphill two thousand feet at a great rate of speed. It's amazing when you are scared to death how much strength you get," Cavanaugh says.

It was now dark and raining. The enemy soldiers were firing mortar shells at them but kept missing. Dripping with perspiration and rainwater, the two men righted the barrel beside the gas pump and then discovered they had no wrench with which to open the barrel. Desperate, Cavanaugh finally broke the wooden handles off his revolver and used the metal butt to pry open the barrel. Cavanaugh's account continues:

"Moonface was standing around saying, 'No, no, we die. No, no, no, we die.'

"I said, 'No, we are not going to die. We are going to make it.'

"In fact, he was so sure—I am sure he had been told and had seen enough death that he knew that upon death your bowels release, and it's an automatic flush-out when a person dies. So he went ahead and flushed out ahead of time, and he was carrying a load around in his britches. . . . He smelled great, but I couldn't have done it without him."

Cavanaugh set Moonface to pumping while he climbed up on the plane to insert the nozzle into the gas tank. Bullets were going just over his head.

They could fill the tank on only one side because the other had been riddled with bullets. By the time they had enough gas, the wing was drooping noticeably.

When Cavanaugh got into the cockpit, the battery had been hit, and none of his electrical equipment seemed to be working. He reached for the starter switch and thought, Nothing is going to happen. But as soon as he touched the switch, the engine started right up. He aimed at a point at the end of the runway where he had seen a bomb flash a moment before and gunned the engine into the darkness and rain. When it felt as though he had flying speed, he eased the plane off the ground and headed north toward Luang Prabang.

Cavanaugh and Moonface landed there by the headlights of a Jeep. Cavanaugh brought the plane to a stop and sat there shaking.

As the secret war in Laos went on, it gradually underwent a

transformation. Vang Pao's troops, so skilled as guerrillas staging hit-and-run raids on a road-bound enemy, were gradually sucked into battles to take and hold territory or to defend isolated outposts that were of considerable value to the Americans but of little value to the Hmong themselves.

The history of the war in Laos is filled with accounts of fierce, bloody battles for radar installations, known as Lima sites, or little communities of fleeting strategic value. Out in the open, fighting for fixed positions, the Hmong suffered losses their small population could not long sustain.

As early as 1966, in the days of the Butterflies, Lima sites were seen as lucrative targets by the North Vietnamese.

In mid-February 1966, enemy forces overran Lima Site 36, which commanded a major north-south roadway north of the Plaine des Jarres. The site also served as a supply point for the guerrillas. But more important to the Americans, it was a staging site for helicopters standing by to rescue crew members shot down in North Vietnam or northern Laos.

Three months after it was overrun by the enemy, Vang Pao's guerrillas retook the site, and it resumed its role as a helicopter base.

Early on the morning of 6 January 1967, an estimated six to eight hundred enemy troops attacked the site from three sides, cutting off all escape routes for the Hmong defenders and the two American advisers at the site. In the first assault, one of the Americans was killed. The other American, armed with a shotgun and barricaded in the radio shack, called for air support. But the weather was ideal—for the attackers: a two-hundred-foot ceiling with dense clouds shrouded the peaks surrounding the site.

Despite the weather, the pilot of one F-105 jet worked his way under the clouds and buzzed the enemy. But he was forced to fly so low that he couldn't drop any bombs. His presence, however, forced the enemy troops to keep their heads down until two propeller-driven A-1Es, with the call sign of Firefly, arrived. While one orbited above the clouds, the other descended and began firing on the enemy troops with rockets and his 20mm cannon.

At this point, Charlie Jones—Butterfly 44—arrived on the

scene and began directing attacks by other aircraft. As darkness came, Jones estimated that the site could be held if the enemy did not attack during the night and if the weather cleared on the following day.

The night was quiet, and the weather the next morning was better. Vang Pao, who had arrived in the midst of the battle, guessed that the enemy troops had been led into the area by guides and that they would try to find their way out again by the same route. The Hmong general was right: Jones, flying over the likely evacuation routes, spotted a large group of soldiers, carrying at least a hundred dead or wounded, in a nearby canyon.

A flight of Fireflies moved in. Captain John Roberts, the flight leader, later reported:

"We arrived on the scene—the weather was pretty good—talked to the local FAC, Butterfly 44, and he marked an area, a kind of box canyon a little bit less than a kilometer from the actual compound of Lima 36. . . . We really raked this area over. . . .It was a heavily wooded area, but we left it completely blazing and really weren't sure whether we'd done much or not. But later on that afternoon, I spoke to one of our sources here, and he said that he got a report back that it had been quite a lucrative strike."

With heavy air support, Vang Pao's forces were able to hold the site. Their losses were 8 killed, plus 24 wounded—in addition to the one American killed. The enemy losses were estimated at 250 killed. The battle was a "victory" of sorts for the Hmong and their American allies, but there was a growing realization that there would be more occasions in the future where Vang Pao's guerrillas would find themselves defending fixed positions in bloody battles. After the battle for Lima Site 36, the air attaché in Vientiane gave this sober appraisal of the future prospects:

". . . We feel that the enemy will continue to pressure Site 36, but as long as we can count on prompt and sustained close air support, when needed, we can hang on to it or at least be able to conduct an orderly withdrawal. . . ."

In the case of another nearby Lima site, it proved impossible to hold the fort or even to conduct an orderly withdrawal.

For the Americans, the loss of Lima Site 85 on 11 March 1968 was a terrible blow. Although kept secret for many years, the fall of this little mountaintop position in northeastern Laos was one of the most crucial and devastating defeats of the entire war in Southeast Asia for the United States.

Lima Site 85 was located on a fifty-five-hundred-foot ridge known as Phou Pha Thi, about 30 miles from the border with North Vietnam and only about 150 miles west of Hanoi. Partway up the mountain was a short airstrip. At the top was a TACAN (tactical air navigation) station and a radio beacon. It was much like the other Lima sites. But then, early in 1967, it took on a new role and became much more important than the other sites. Prefabricated buildings and tons of electronic equipment were plunked down on the top of the mountain by helicopter.

It was manned on a rotating basis by fifteen Air Force technicians, "sheep dipped" to appear to be civilians. Their job was to operate Commando Club, a system that promised a dramatic improvement in the accuracy of fighter-bomber attacks against North Vietnam. The system was based on the Strategic Air Command's Combat Skyspot radar bomb-scoring system. But, instead of calculating where simulated bombs had fallen, it was used in this case to guide where real bombs would fall.

Although the North Vietnamese probably didn't know just what all the activity at Phou Pha Thi was all about, they saw enough to decide it was worth knocking out the site. Secord, whose job with the CIA was to defend the site, was alarmed to see aerial photos of a new road snaking through the jungle toward Lima 85. He called for air strikes to stop the road dead. He got enough to annoy the road builders, but not enough to stop them.

If an attack came, Secord knew, the defenders—a mixed force of about four hundred Hmong and Thai soldiers—couldn't hold the site. His hope was that air power could hold off the attackers long enough to permit an evacuation of the Americans and many of the Thais while the Hmong melted into the jungles to reform elsewhere. He also planned on the destruction of the radar-bombing equipment, codes, and encryption systems.

The North Vietnamese assault on the site began in a bizarre way in mid-January 1968 when two 1930s-era Soviet-built biplanes made a bombing attack on the new installation atop the mountain. It looked like something out of a World War I movie. The planes were so slow that a helicopter was able to pull alongside one of them while a crewman shot the plane down with an M16 rifle. The other was hit by ground fire and crashed in the jungle.

When the attack by North Vietnamese infantry came in mid-March, it was much more sophisticated than the assault by the two old biplanes. Heavy artillery and mortars hammered the mountain, smashing defenses and destroying electronic equipment. The Skyspot system, which could have directed precise attacks against the enemy, went off the air. As expected, soldiers fought their way through defenses on the steep sides of the mountain. But enemy commandos also managed a feat that was not only unexpected but considered impossible. They scaled a sheer cliff more than a thousand feet high and suddenly appeared among the defenders atop the mountain.

Secord's pleas for air support finally penetrated the higher reaches of the Seventh Air Force in Saigon. On the second morning of the battle, the air was filled with planes, which turned the area surrounding the site into hell on earth for the attackers. The Americans listened to intercepted radio messages from the terror-stricken North Vietnamese. One battalion-level officer radioed: "My men are gone. I'm the only one left. Can anybody hear me? Can I come home?"

An air commando in a propeller-driven AT-28 finally swooped down on the mountaintop installation and destroyed it with his bombs. But the North Vietnamese had already acquired a gold mine of secret technology and top-secret code systems.

Of the sixteen Americans at the site, only six survived, and five of them were wounded. Many of the Thai and Hmong defenders were evacuated by helicopter, and the remainder of the Hmong showed up a few days later at Lima Site 36.

In 1994, an American team located the man who, as a lieutenant, had led the North Vietnamese commandos. He was flown to the top of Phou Pha Thi in a helicopter and pointed out where he and his men had tried to bury three of the dead Americans by covering them with sandbags. Other bodies had been blown apart when the site was bombed to destroy the electronic equipment. No remnants of the dead Americans were found, so they remain listed as missing in action.

The loss of Site 85 came in the aftermath of the enemy's Tet offensive and the assault on Khe Sanh in South Vietnam. Although the destruction of the site—which had controlled a quarter of the bombing missions against North Vietnam—was kept secret from the public, it must have weighed heavily on the minds of officials in Washington. A few days after the fall of Site 85, President Lyndon Johnson called a halt to bombing of the north, and, on 31 March, he announced that he would neither seek nor accept his party's nomination to run for reelection.

Despite the battering they had taken from the air assault, the North Vietnamese regrouped and moved south once more toward Lima Site 36. The battle there was different from the previous battles for this strategic site. The defenders finally received as many as three hundred tactical air strikes a day, with the Ravens guiding saturation bombing attacks whenever the North Vietnamese massed their forces. Companies and even entire battalions simply disappeared as the battle extended into 1969.

At one point, there were only three Ravens available. They flew as many as half a dozen sorties a day, often guiding attacks on enemy soldiers who had given away their own positions by firing into the air. Karl Polifka described the situation:

"They had been taught they could shoot down F-4s with AK-47s [assault rifles], which you can, but you don't start blazing away when they are twelve thousand feet in the air. There are many occasions—we would fly along, you know, at twenty-five hundred feet, three thousand feet, and you were just going somewhere, and you would look down, and here a ridge line would light up. They wouldn't really be shooting at you; they would be shooting at a bunch of F-4s flying somewhere. You had no idea these guys were there; you just proceeded to beat the shit out of them.

"I have no idea how many I killed that way. The CIA said, and they later confirmed, that there were three battalions that disappeared, just disappeared. We know of one case where there were three survivors of a five-hundred-man battalion that straggled into a regimental command post. They were all that was left. We were giving them a very bad time."

Polifka was later told by CIA sources that fifteen hundred North Vietnamese had died as the result of the work of an average of five Ravens during the nine months he was there in 1969.

The concentration of air attacks crippled the North Vietnamese forces so badly that Vang Pao and his guerrillas were able, in 1969, to take control of the entire Plaine des Jarres, which had been under enemy control for years.

For Vang Pao, this was a proud achievement. Although the Hmong were mountain people who didn't choose to live in the Plaine des Jarres in peacetime, control of this central piece of geography took on a kind of symbolic importance well beyond its practical value to the Hmong.

But it was a costly victory. Hardly a building remained standing on the whole plain. And, by taking over this large area, the Hmong completed the transition from guerrillas to defenders of fixed positions. When the Americans left Southeast Asia, the Hmong, drastically reduced in numbers, became refugees, their way of life in the misty mountains of Laos a fading memory.

As one Raven bitterly observed:

". . . The whole damn country is a wasteland, and half the people are killed. They probably have got more maimed and crippled people than they have had in their entire history. So what do you gain; what has he gained?"

The air commandos' support for Vang Pao and his Hmong had, for the Americans, the advantage of drawing North Vietnamese troops into Laos and away from what was seen as the main theater of the war in Vietnam. But the commandos were also involved at the same time in another major effort to disrupt enemy plans by stopping the flow of men and materials down the Ho Chi Minh Trail from North Vietnam through the eastern portion of Laos and into South Vietnam.

CHAPTER 19

The Third War

In between the big public war in South Vietnam and the secret war over the mountains in Laos, the United States and the North Vietnamese fought another long, bloody war along the eastern edge of Laos where it bordered Vietnam. This war, too, was largely secret, with heavy air commando involvement.

The focus of this war was the Ho Chi Minh Trail, the main route for men and supplies headed from North Vietnam toward the battle zones in the south. Although perhaps originally the word *trail* was appropriate, the route soon had more in common with the New Jersey Turnpike than some primitive pathway through the jungle. Between 1966 and the end of 1971, the route grew from 820 miles of existing roads, most dating back to French colonial days, to a complex network totaling 2,710 miles.

The war for control of this vital supply line was a constantly escalating battle. Each improvement in the tactics or equipment on one side quickly brought a compensating adjustment on the other.

At first, supplies were wheeled south on heavily burdened bicycles. The bikes were soon replaced or supplemented by trucks. The standard vehicle was a six-wheel Russian-built ZIL 157 truck, capable of carrying five tons at up to forty miles an hour over

Laotian roads. The driver could even vary his tire inflation while moving to adjust for the condition of the roads.

At first, the trucks moved by day. When that became too dangerous, they traveled at night, with the lights on. When that, too, became dangerous, they drove without lights. Elaborate bamboo trellises were constructed to camouflage truck parks.

In the early years of the war, the United States jet fighter-bombers tried to stop the traffic. But, at the speeds at which they flew, it was hard for them to find trucks moving beneath the jungle canopy. And if they bombed bridges or caused landslides to close the roads, the damage was often repaired before they had returned home.

Early in 1966, as described in Chapter Sixteen, AC-47 gunships moved in. They proved effective truck killers. But they also proved terribly vulnerable. When four planes and their crews were lost in a short period, they were withdrawn, and the Air Force reached down deep in its arsenal for the venerable B-26 bomber that had seen service in World War II and Korea and with the air commandos' Farmgate and Mill Pond operations in the earliest days of the war in Southeast Asia.

But the eight planes that arrived at Nakom Phanom in the spring of 1966 were not the battered old war birds that had been pulled out of service two years before when they began shedding wings. Beginning in 1963, a firm known as On Mark, in Van Nuys, California, had thoroughly overhauled and modernized forty of the planes at a cost of $325,000 apiece. Not only were the wings completely rebuilt, but many other modifications made the plane faster, gave it the ability to carry 60 percent more armament, and increased the altitude at which it could fly. Although it still had some deficiencies, crew members loved the reworked plane. Major Frank Gorski, who had flown in Vietnam as one of the Farmgate pilots, called it "the Cadillac of airplanes—it had everything."

The Douglas Invader had started out as an A-26 in World War II. Then it became the B-26. Upon arrival in Thailand, it became the A-26K. The fiction was that it was an attack plane, there to defend Thailand, rather than a bomber, there to drop bombs on

North Vietnamese targets in Laos. To carry on the fiction, the American insignia on the planes was painted over, and when they did something particularly notable, the public announcement said it had happened in North Vietnam and left out their base and unit identification.

The crews adopted the word *Nimrod* as their call sign, and that soon became the generic term for the crews, the planes, and the entire operation. Unlike most call signs, this one was an almost perfect match for the A-26 missions. In chapter ten of Genesis, the Bible refers to Nimrod, son of Cush, as "a mighty hunter before the Lord." The job of the Air Force Nimrods was precisely that: to hunt trucks and, when they found them, to kill them.

The Nimrods became active on 11 June 1966 as Detachment 1 of the 603d Air Commando Squadron, part of the 606th Air Commando Wing, already operating out of Nakom Phanom with AT-28s, C-123 transports, and U-10 utility planes.

They arrived during the rainy season, which lasts from April into October and makes the roads so muddy that truck traffic is almost impossible. Their first missions were thus orientation and training flights. But they soon learned how dangerous their job could be. On 28 June, the first Nimrod plane was shot down, with the loss of three lives.

Lieutenant Gene Albee was flying as navigator with Gorski (call sign Oilcan Harry) in a two-plane formation with another A-26 that day and saw what happened. The Nimrod crews quickly learned that, as Albee said, "if you made the mistake of taking that black airplane out in the daylight, you got what you deserved."

They were out in broad daylight on this early orientation mission about ten miles from the North Vietnamese border, checking out the Ban Leboy Ford, a shallow place where the trucks drove through the water across a river. It was a natural choke point, where trucks might be lined up waiting to cross the stream. It was also a natural spot for a flak trap.

In the other plane were Capt. C. G. Dudley, the pilot, 1st Lt. A. F. Cavelli, his navigator, and Lt. Tom Wolfe, who was showing them the area. Wolfe pointed out a typical antiaircraft gun emplacement of a type the North Vietnamese had copied from the

Russians. It was in the form of a circle, with the fire-control setup in the center and the guns located in pits around it.

"We were in the lead, but Chuck [Dudley] said he wanted to look at something on the ground," Albee recalls. "We pulled off to the side. We're pulling up, and he rolls in on the guns.

"I heard over the radio, 'I'm hit!' We rolled up back over the top, and he's in flames. We were supposed to follow him in on the guns, but we pulled off immediately. No sense going in, two people doing that."

Albee never did see the guns that got Dudley's plane. He figured that the North Vietnamese had set up a decoy gun position, with logs instead of guns, and hidden the real guns back in the tree line.

"He was really low, down in the trees, when he took this hit," Albee says. "I saw it just before it hit the ground. It was on fire before it hit. And then it was rolling wing over wing and disappeared in smoke and flames. I thought maybe they hosed one of his engines and it caught on fire. That airplane is full of gas, and that aviation gas burns a lot hotter than jet fuel does."

Albee and Gorski called for rescue helicopters and circled the area for about half an hour.

"We finally said, 'Oh, hell, there's no use risking anybody else's life.' So we sent the rescue ships back."

The Nimrods were qualified as forward air controllers, which meant they could identify and attack their own targets. After a while, they knew the area in which they were flying so well that they felt reasonably comfortable operating at night in areas where steep mounds of karst jutted up far above their altitude.

They still worried, however, about the performance of their plane at high altitudes. The plane could struggle up to sixteen thousand feet with a full load of bombs. But if one engine went out, it could only maintain about eighty-five hundred feet. In northern Laos, there were areas where, at that altitude, the pilot would find himself surrounded by much higher peaks of karst. One pilot went over his charts carefully and found only two routes home if he lost an engine in that northern area. And both of those routes would involve weaving through the mountains on instruments.

In addition to bombs and ammunition for the eight .50-caliber guns mounted in the nose, they also carried their own flares so they could illuminate suspected targets. Later, however, the standard practice was to drop a flare—known as a brick—that did not ignite until it hit the ground. There, it looked like a streetlight shining in the jungle and could be used as reference for a bombing or strafing attack.

Although the A-26s were sent to Thailand on temporary duty, they remained there for more than three years, until late 1969. In the early period, the Nimrods normally flew alone. But they soon adopted the practice of flying in two-plane flights—either two A-26s or an A-26 and an AT-28, in a kind of hunter-killer team.

One tactic used was to fly one plane low over the ground, trolling for antiaircraft fire, while the other circled overhead, ready to swoop in if the first plane attracted any ground fire.

Some crews also liked to confuse the enemy by tuning their engines out of synchronization. Albee explains:

"One of the things we did was we'd try and lure activity. We'd go out and fly low—fifty feet sometimes, sometimes between the trees, depending on who was driving. Then we'd go up to a higher altitude and put the props out of synch so they couldn't tell where we were.

"We'd bring the power way back and loiter, just see if anything happens. Often enough it did. It was a pretty good tactic. They couldn't tell where the airplane was. You could hear the airplane, but you'd hear a *rroww, rroww, rroww.* It could be anywhere. Lots of times, they'd start shooting at where they thought the noise was, and in all probability it would be the wrong place."

Using flares to try to expose the enemy or trying to fool him into exposing himself by firing his guns left a lot to be desired for the mighty hunters. What they needed was some way to see in the dark so they could spot the trucks and hit them before they had a chance to hide.

The infantry in Vietnam was using a device called the starlight scope, which intensified whatever faint light happened to be available, such as that from the stars, to pierce the darkness. Aderholt, who was by that time back in Thailand running the interdiction operation out of Nakom Phanom, knew that if he asked for starlight scopes through the normal bureaucracy, he wouldn't get them. Instead, he called his friend Secord and borrowed several from the CIA's stocks.

Major Tom Wickstrom made some practice runs with the scope and found that, as promised, it helped the Nimrods see in the dark. But the bulky, twenty-five-pound scope was an awkward device to hold and keep pointed in the right direction while sitting in the narrow cockpit of an A-26. The solution was to mount a scope in the waist of the plane and aim it down through the open bomb bay. Clyde Howard, a jack-of-all-trades combat controller, was one of those assigned to fly with the Nimrods and operate the scope. He vividly recalls what it was like:

"There was a pilot and navigator up front. I'd fly in the cargo compartment with the bomb bay doors open. I'd watch the road through the starlight scope. If I saw a target, I'd tell them to drop a flare. They'd drop a flare so they could see the target, and then they'd swing around and come in toward it."

Of all the jobs Howard had, operating the scope for the Nimrods was one of the scariest. The scope not only magnified the faint ambient light, but it seemed to turn antiaircraft fire into great balls of fire, headed right toward him. When the plane went into the attack mode, the pilot and navigator were busy and not talking. Alone back in the waist, all Howard knew was that the plane was in a steep dive toward the dark Laotian jungle. Perhaps something had happened to the pilot and navigator. Maybe he was the only one left alive and there was nobody to pull the plane out of its dive. Every time, it was a terrifying few moments before he felt the comforting tug of gravity as the pilot pulled back on the wheel.

As the Invaders, with their newfound ability to see in the dark, racked up a growing toll of damaged and destroyed trucks, the enemy responded with more and more antiaircraft guns. By 1967, it was estimated, there were as many as ten thousand guns along the trail, ranging from .50-caliber to 57mm. Fortunately for the aircrews, many of the gunners were not very good. But enough of them were sufficiently skilled to make life very dangerous for the A-26 crews.

On 22 February 1967, a two-plane flight found a large convoy and set fire to a number of trucks before coming under heavy fire from several guns. One of the planes dove on the guns and fired a long burst of .50-caliber machine-gun fire. But the gunner on the ground was the better shot. Several of his .50-caliber rounds smashed into the plane's starboard engine and set the plane on fire.

The two planes turned toward Nakom Phanom. The damaged plane, piloted by Capt. James McCluskey, with Lt. Mike Scruggs as navigator, made it back across the Mekong River into Thailand. Only a few miles from Nakom Phanom, McCluskey and Scruggs were preparing for a crash landing when the pilot of the other plane, Dwight S. Campell, pulled up alongside. He saw the whole wing on fire and shouted: "Get out! Get out!"

Scruggs jumped first, but his harness caught on the canopy. McCluskey gave him a hard shove and followed him out. Moments later, the plane exploded.

Aderholt, who was at the air base, saw the explosion light up the sky.

McCluskey and Scruggs were both injured but survived. The explosion of their plane, however, engulfed the other A-26. Campell and his navigator, Robert L. Scholl, were killed. It was the only time that two A-26s were destroyed on the same day.

Although the Nimrod crews were authorized to act as their own forward air controllers, they also often had help from Ravens, airborne control planes, and teams on the ground. On occasion, the A-26s acted as escorts for helicopters inserting Army Special Forces road-watch teams near the enemy supply route. These highly secret operations had several code names. Project Shining Brass began in 1965. It was changed to Prairie Fire in 1968 and, finally, to Phu Dung, in 1971. Whatever intelligence they gathered came to the Nimrods indirectly. Often, however, they worked directly with Hmong forward air control teams operated by the CIA in Laos.

"We had some very good results with these people because they were sitting right on the side of the hill," Gorski recalls. "They knew where this stuff was parked and hidden and everything else."

One of the ground teams gave Gorski precise directions for dropping his bombs and then said: "Okay, you go home now, and they'll shoot at you. They'll shoot at you with 37mm."

Gorski asked how he knew the enemy had a 37mm gun.

"He said, 'Well, I sold a gun crew some bananas this evening.' Apparently, the guy was on his way to work, and he sold the bananas to the gun crew, and he was up there talking to me. They're really a strange group, but very effective, very effective."

In their three and a half years operating out of Thailand, the A-26s were responsible for the destruction of hundreds of trucks.

Just how effective they were is uncertain. Certainly, the North Vietnamese were able to move enough men and munitions south to stage the Tet offensive of 1968 and cause heavy casualties to the United States and South Vietnamese for many years.

Albee, who was flying out of Nakom Phanom during 1966, in the early part of the Nimrod deployment, has his own view:

"We liked to think we were real effective. I think we had the effect of deterring a lot of traffic more than we did destroying traffic. I remember seeing movement on the ground, trucks in twos and threes and fours, maybe. But I don't recall seeing any long lines of trucks out there. You read stuff, even back then, about a lot of activity, a lot of trucks destroyed, a lot of damage inflicted on the enemy.

"I think it was a lot of bullshit, myself. There's no way to tell. You could go blow a hole in the road and come back two hours later, and they're running trucks over the road. They had ten thousand people out there with shovels. They had a hell of a lot of trucks. In the thick of the battle, you have a feeling of wanting to have accomplished something. It was a very boring job most of the time. A nasty, boring job. Sometimes, you'd find something to shoot at, and sometimes you wouldn't."

Tim Black, who flew as a pilot there in 1969, toward the end of the Nimrod deployment, says: "The A-26 had the most truck kills of any airplane in Southeast Asia. That is a remarkable statistic when you think of all the planes flying, day and night. We only flew at night. We only had fifteen airplanes—one squadron—flying only at night."

But the toll on the planes and their crews was heavy. Of the thirty planes assigned to Nakom Phanom during that period, twelve, or 40 percent, were lost to enemy action or accidents.

The A-26s stayed longer and did far more work along the Ho Chi Minh Trail than was originally intended. When they were sent to Thailand in mid-1966, they were intended as a stopgap measure until the AC-130 and AC-119 gunships arrived. But it was not until October 1968 that the first AC-130s became operational in Thailand, and a year later that the AC-119s arrived.

At first, the Nimrod pilots were skeptical about the newcomers, but they soon came to appreciate the firepower of the gunships. Tom Wickstrom recalls being ordered to move off to be replaced by an AC-130 during an early test in the fall of 1967. Wickstrom had been trying unsuccessfully to knock out four trucks. Within a few minutes, the gunship not only hit the four trucks Wickstrom had been after but also had four more trucks burning.

With their sophisticated electronic equipment, the gunship crews were able to pick out trucks moving through the darkness, even under the jungle canopy. One device picked up the electrical signal given off by the spark plugs of gasoline-powered engines. If the drivers pulled off the road and stopped, another device detected the heat of the engine even after it had been turned off. The same device pinpointed diesel-powered trucks even though, without spark plugs, they did not give off the telltale electrical signal.

During the trials in 1967, the AC-130s were credited with hitting almost five times as many trucks on each sortie as the A-26s. But in those days, the Pentagon wanted a measure of cost effectiveness for almost everything. In this case, the sharp-pencil experts calculated that the cost per truck destroyed was about the same for the two types of planes—about $5,100 for the gunship and $5,900 for the A-26—considering that the $350,000 Invader carried a crew of two or three, while the gunship cost many millions of dollars and carried a crew of fourteen.

With the initial trials ended, the first AC-130A Spectre gunship began operations out of the Thai air base at Ubon on 27 February 1968 and quickly began showing impressive results. On its third sortie, it destroyed nine trucks and two storage areas. During the year, it destroyed a total of 228 trucks and damaged another 133. Air Force leaders began to believe they at last had a way to stop traffic on the infiltration route into South Vietnam.

In early 1969, with only four planes available, the new gunships were soon accounting for as much as 40 percent of all the trucks destroyed. On one night, a single AC-130 managed to find twenty-five trucks—and destroy all of them.

With the demonstrated ability of the gunships to find and destroy trucks, more planes, and improved models, were moved in during each winter dry season for a series of interdiction campaigns code-named Commando Hunt. In 1969, the gunship force was augmented by the AC-119K Stinger.

In January 1971, a single Spectre destroyed fifty-eight trucks and damaged seven more on a single mission. By March, the Spectres were averaging thirteen destroyed trucks per sortie.

While the gunships had an impressive ability to find trucks by themselves, the interdiction effort was also bolstered by an increasingly sophisticated system of sensors that detected movement and thus told the aircrews where to look for targets. The system was known as Igloo White. It was also known as the McNamara Barrier, for then–Defense Secretary Robert S. McNamara.

While many of the air commandos took a dim view of this complex and expensive system, it was gradually improved to the point where it was making a useful contribution to the interdiction effort.

The success reported by the gunship crews raised a serious question: with all those trucks destroyed, how did the enemy keep fighting? The mystery was highlighted by a message from Air Force officers in the Pentagon early in 1971:

"AC-130 BDA [bomb damage assessment] is the hottest thing in the theater this moment. Seventh Air Force is really concerned about the validity of BDA reported by the AC-130 gunships in their truck killing operation. They stated all aircraft BDA for this hunting season indicated over twenty thousand trucks destroyed or damaged to date, and if intelligence figures are correct, North Vietnam should be out of rolling stock. The trucks continue to roll however."

Perhaps the planes were hitting the trucks but not destroying them. A truckload of rice, for example, might absorb a direct hit by a 40mm gun and still keep rolling. The rules were changed to tighten the conditions under which a truck could be claimed as destroyed.

But the answer may have been that the North Vietnamese were simply replacing trucks faster than they could be destroyed. In each of the first four months of 1971, an estimated eight thousand trucks were spotted from the air, and intelligence reports indicated that North Vietnam was receiving about four hundred new trucks a month from the Soviet Union and other allies.

As the battle along the trail grew in intensity, the North Vietnamese dramatically increased the amount of antiaircraft artillery deployed. In November of 1968, only about two hundred antiaircraft guns were believed to be in Laos. By May 1970, the number had multiplied by 400 percent. Most numerous were the 37mm guns, capable of reaching about 8,500 feet. But there were also bigger 57mm, 85mm, and 100mm guns that could reach as high as 27,500 feet.

To protect the planes and crews, more armor was added to the gunships. And crew members—known as scanners—hung out the rear cargo doors of the planes and looked for tracers headed their way. It was an uncomfortable job, hanging out there battered by the slipstream. The scanners were plagued by colds, ear and throat infections, and sore backs. And it was nerve-racking to see artillery shells headed in your direction.

The scanners quickly learned to tell one kind of fire from another. Rifles and small machine guns made little flashes of light. The 37mm shells looked like orangeish red golf balls. The bigger 57mm shells looked like big white balls, arcing upward. The scanners were always on the alert for surface-to-air missiles (SAMs), which were common around Hanoi, but seldom saw them near the trail.

When a scanner spotted rounds headed his direction, he warned the pilot to swerve. There was usually about three or four seconds available for the warning and the evasive maneuver.

Tactics were also developed to deal with SAMs if they were deployed along the Laotian border. Instrument operators on the plane watched for indications of a SAM launch. They then watched the missile until impact was imminent. At the last moment, the pilot would dive, a maneuver that eluded the missile but put the plane in greater danger from antiaircraft guns.

On 29 March 1972, the SAM threat became a reality when an AC-130 was hit by an SA-2 missile and shot down.

A short time later, on 5 May, five SA-7 Strela missiles were fired at a Spectre flying near An Loc in South Vietnam. Although hit, the plane was able to reach Tan Son Nuht Air Base. The Strela was a frightening new threat—a small heat-seeking missile fired by a soldier on the ground from his shoulder.

The gunship had clearly earned a permanent place in the air commando inventory. But it was also clear that this weapon could be used safely only under certain conditions and with great care.

For many of the gunship crews, the name of the game became truck killing—to the neglect of soldiers in trouble on the ground. There was some justification for this attitude. The enemy would often stage little diversions—a mortar round or two into an outpost—to divert gunships away from the truck route. But some of the veteran air commandos, who knew what it was like to be on the ground facing the enemy, were irritated when they thought the gunship crews were deliberately ignoring soldiers who were really in trouble. This became an increasing problem as the United States withdrawal neared its end—and there were few, if any, Americans among the troops on the ground.

Clyde Howard, the combat controller who had served in Thailand earlier, returned in 1972. He found morale terrible.

Members of the combat control teams (CCT), who had trained some 350 natives of the area as forward air guides, flew with the AC-119 crews to evaluate their students. The crews were rewarded with medals for killing trucks but not for helping out troops on the ground. Howard is still angry about what he observed:

"If this ground controller we had trained, if he requested support because he had troops in contact—they could be shooting at him, it didn't matter. Most of the time, the gunship guys would say, 'Oh, he's bullshitting us. He's not in a jam. He's just calling to waste bullets.' They would tell him, 'Sorry, we have a higher priority target' or 'We're low on fuel.' They'd make up things. They'd say they were low on fuel when they'd just taken off. They'd go look for trucks and tanks. Meanwhile, our troop we had trained, he's back there getting his ass shot off.

"We'd write their ass up. And the general, I forget his name, he used to smoke 'em. After that, they would just tremble at the knees when they saw a combat controller was flying with them.

"I've been on the ground with the same results. They'd say they were low on fuel—had to RTB [return to base]. I'd listen. I'd take notes. When I got back to Udorn, I'd find out what time he took off and what time he landed. It would go straight to Seven/Thirteen Air Force headquarters. It would say, this is what was reported. I was standing on the goddamn ground next to him. Impossible. After that, they were gun-shy. They didn't know where we were. I nailed a couple of them. They didn't like CCT."

By this time, the American involvement in the war was dwindling away. No one wanted to take a chance on getting shot. And no one wanted to take a chance on ending up a prisoner of the North Vietnamese.

There were already too many American airmen in the Hanoi Hilton, the nickname for the main prison in Hanoi, and too many missing—and probably dead—in the jungles of Laos. Many of the air commandos had lost close friends, and they remained willing to take almost any risk to free Americans from captivity. This urge to free the American prisoners was the motive behind one of the most dramatic special operations of the war.

PART 6
Son Tay and the Mayaguez

CHAPTER 20
Destination: Hanoi

In the summer of 1970, United States intelligence picked up alarming reports of increasingly harsh conditions in the prison camps where more than 470 American prisoners of war were held by North Vietnam. The prisoners, most of them aircrew members, suffered from near-starvation diets, long periods of isolation, and, often, outright torture.

The news was particularly bothersome to Air Force officers who had seen far too many of their friends take off from bases in Thailand and disappear into what they referred to as the Hanoi Hilton. By that time, however, Hanoi Hilton was a misnomer. Many of the prisoners were not held in a central compound where they could provide support for one another and where there was some hope they might be treated humanely, as provided for by international law. Instead, many of them were scattered in small compounds in Hanoi and the surrounding area, where their hope for decent treatment rested on the whim of each prison commander and even of individual guards.

It was at this dark period in the prisoner-of-war situation that analysts at Fort Belvoir, Virginia, working on a secret project that involved studying these outlying prisons, came up with a bold proposal. While it would almost certainly be impossible to rescue Americans from the central compound in Hanoi, it might very well be possible to stage a raid that would pluck a significant number of prisoners from one of the outlying compounds.

They passed their suggestion along to the Pentagon and pinpointed a potential target for such a raid. It was the prisoner compound at the Son Tay Citadel, twenty-three miles northwest of Hanoi. Intelligence information confirmed that fifty-five Americans had been moved into the prison in the spring and summer of 1968.

General LeRoy J. Manor, commander of the special operations force at Eglin Air Force Base, Florida, was called to Washington on 8 August 1970 and ordered to plan for a rescue operation and begin putting a team together to do the job.

Manor assembled a remarkably lean and fast-moving crew. Manor, a one-star, was the highest ranking officer involved. His deputy for air operations was a lieutenant colonel, Ben Kraljev. His deputy commanding the Special Forces soldiers who would carry out the rescue was Lt. Col. Arthur D. "Bull" Simons, a soldier with long experience running special operations in Laos and other parts of Southeast Asia.

The rescue they planned was a classic special operation that could have come right out of the history of the Air Commandos and Carpetbaggers of World War II or the ARCS of the 1950s. The Air Force would deliver a fighting force of about fifty soldiers to Son Tay, stand by while the prison guards were gunned down and the prisoners freed and assembled, and then pick up the rescuers and the rescued and carry them all safely back to a base in northern Thailand.

Simons went to the home of the Army Special Forces at Fort Bragg, North Carolina, and asked for volunteers. The men weren't told where they were going or what they were going to do. All they were told was that the mission would be dangerous. Five hundred volunteers stepped forward. Of those, 120 were selected and moved to Duke Field, also known as auxiliary field No. 3, at Eglin Air Force Base. Training began on 1 September, using a mock-up of the Son Tay compound that was dismantled each time a Soviet spy satellite passed overhead.

For the soldiers, the operation was almost routine, in the sense that it called upon skills in which they had long been trained: landing from a helicopter, entering and searching buildings, and suppressing any resistance. For them, preparation for the raid was mostly a matter of repeating every action over and over until it became automatic. And, of course, it involved practicing what to do if anything went wrong until that, too, was automatic.

For the Air Force crews, planning for the Son Tay raid was anything but routine. And, of course, the whole thing would have to be abandoned if the Air Force could not get the soldiers there and bring them and the prisoners back out again.

The requirement that this be a round-trip affair meant the use of helicopters. The Green Berets could not be parachuted onto the compound because they and the prisoners would then be stranded there. And there was no place near Son Tay to land fixed-wing aircraft.

For the core of the operation, Manor settled on a force of six helicopters. That would be enough to carry the raiding force and twice as many prisoners as they hoped to liberate. At every point, he strove to have twice as many aircraft as he thought he needed.

The planners were faced by a daunting dilemma. If the raiding force landed outside the walls of the compound, it was possible that the North Vietnamese might kill some of the prisoners before the raiders blasted their way into the prison. One of the planners, a Navy SEAL who was not going along on the operation, came up with a proposal: crash-land one of the helicopters right in the compound and then leave it there.

His suggestion was adopted, but that added a further complication. The big HH-53 helicopters used for rescue missions—the Super Jolly Green Giants—would be ideal for the mission. But a smaller craft was needed for the crucial crash landing. The decision was made to use an older model HH-3, a machine notoriously slow and underpowered.

All the helicopters were capable of being refueled in the air. This meant the operation could be staged from a base in northern Thailand without the complication of a refueling stop in Laos before hopping across the North Vietnamese border for the run to the target.

With refueling, the helicopters could reach the target and get back again. But could they find the compound? Probably not, since they did not carry navigators and had only rudimentary navigation equipment.

Manor added two MC-130 Combat Talons to his planning to act as pathfinders for the helicopters and for a flight of A-1E Sandys that would come along to suppress enemy antiaircraft fire. The four-engine, propeller-driven Combat Talons were specially equipped for delivering agents behind enemy lines. It was the same type of plane that had carried out the daring leaflet-dropping missions over North Vietnam.

The MC-130s normally carried two navigators, but a third was added for this mission. Still, finding the way, even with a little bit of moonlight, was going to be very, very difficult. There were no lights of cities or highways to use as checkpoints, and the planes were not yet equipped with the kind of inertial navigation system that simplifies the task of those who navigate today's Combat Talons. Night-vision goggles, which make life much easier for today's air commandos, had not yet been developed. The navigators did have a forward-looking infrared system, or FLIR, and that proved invaluable in helping them to find their way.

Getting close to the target was one thing. Picking the prisoner-of-war compound out of the darkness was a more difficult task, compounded by the fact that flood waters from the monsoon rains were capable of changing the contours of the landscape in a matter of hours. The navigators worried, for example, that they might find that the river they relied on to mark one edge of the prison compound had changed overnight into a formless lake.

When they flew practice missions in Florida, the crews found that their dim instrument lights reflected on the canopies of their cockpits and made it almost impossible to see outside. In desperation, they even had the copilot stick his head out a cockpit window to try to see where they were going. It didn't work. With all that wind in his face, it was almost impossible to see anything, and the man with his head out the window couldn't make himself understood through the intercom over the sound of the wind.

They became resigned to doing the best they could without being able to see very well.

Flying the helicopters in formation with the MC-130s posed its own special problems. The pilots of the pathfinder planes were relatively comfortable flying through the darkness with their terrain-following radar, or TFR. The TFR sends a radar beam out in front of the plane to reflect off any obstacles in its path. The pilot then either adds power to climb over the obstacle or flies around it. But the helicopters—even the more powerful HH-53s—could not climb nearly as rapidly as the four-engine pathfinders. This meant the MC-130 pilots had to plan for a very gentle climb over every hill en route.

The most serious problem was posed by the underpowered HH-3. Many pilots would say it is simply impossible to fly the HH-3 in formation with an MC-130. They would be very close to right. But the MC-130 pilots found that, if they flew with their flaps extended about 70 percent at about 107 knots—right on the edge of a stall—the helicopter could keep up. They also found that, flying tucked up behind the bigger plane, the helicopter was, in effect, sucked along by the draft of the MC-130, much as a bicyclist can reach high speeds by pedaling close behind a speeding truck.

When the planning and training were finished, the raiding force itself consisted of two MC-130 Combat Talon pathfinders, five HH-53 helicopters, one HH-3 helicopter, and five Sandy escort fighter-bombers. Each plane had a call sign using the word for a kind of fruit. The pathfinders were Cherry 1 and Cherry 2; the HH-3 helicopter was Banana 1; the HH-53s were Apple 1 through 5; the tankers were Lime 1 and 2; and the A-1E Sandys were Peach 1 through 5. If the North Vietnamese had been listening in, they would have thought they were being attacked by a fruit salad.

It was not until just before the takeoff that the soldiers who were going to carry out the raid were told where they were going. Many of them had not guessed and were astonished to learn that they were heading for the outskirts of Hanoi.

But many of the aircrew members, who had to plan where they

were going and how they were going to get there, were let in on the secret while they were training in Florida. One of the questions that frequently popped up was: Are there really American prisoners in that camp?

An officer from the Defense Intelligence Agency, who said he had access to human intelligence, was sure that the camp was occupied by American prisoners. Although admitting that his information might be as much as a month old, he insisted it was still reliable. But a reservist trained as a photo interpreter, using recent aerial photos, kept pointing to signs that led him to believe the prisoners had been moved: none of the recent pictures showed Caucasians in the prison yard during the times when they would be expected to be outside; weeds and grass were growing on paths that would have been trampled clean if a number of prisoners were being held there.

One of the MC-130 pilots was Ron Jones, then a captain. He recalls wondering whether or not prisoners were present.

"This young captain told us at least a month before the mission went down that he didn't think there were any prisoners there. He said he believed they'd been moved. The decision was still made to go. In my heart of hearts, I believe that the higher-ups knew there were probably not any prisoners there, but they were going to do the mission anyway, for a number of reasons."

Among those aware of the controversy, the dispute over whether or not there were prisoners present at the compound did not seem to make them reluctant to participate. They had trained hard and were ready to go.

Manor and Simons conducted periodic briefings for the brass in Washington. They met with the Joint Chiefs of Staff on 8 September; with Defense Secretary Melvin R. Laird on 24 September; with Henry Kissinger and Brig. Gen. Al Haig at the White House on 9 October. They said they would be ready to go on 21 October.

Kissinger asked Manor how soon he needed a decision.

"Tomorrow night," Manor replied.

Kissinger told him Nixon wouldn't be available to make a decision that quickly. Manor also got the impression another reason for the delay was that a raid at that moment might disrupt negotiations with the North Vietnamese that could lead to release of prisoners.

Manor had picked two "windows" for the operation: 21–25 October and 21–25 November. That would give him a quarter moon thirty-five degrees above the horizon and, if the long-range forecasts were accurate, acceptable weather.

The delay at the White House pushed the date for the operation into November. Manor and Simons were authorized to continue training and to brief a few high-ranking officers who would have to know about the operation.

President Nixon finally took up the matter in early November.

His consideration of whether or not to authorize the raid came nearly two years before the Watergate break-in that eventually drove him from the White House. But already, in 1970, Nixon's Vietnam War policy was under serious attack. The incursion into Cambodia on 30 April not only set off large antiwar demonstrations but also caused serious opposition on Capitol Hill, where, in midyear, the Senate repealed the Tonkin Gulf Resolution that had authorized President Johnson to escalate United States involvement in the war. The decision to authorize a risky mission that could either be a dramatic morale booster or a devastating disaster was a tough call.

"I have often wondered how he would have gone to the American people if we had lost that entire force," Manor says. "If we had been compromised, we could have lost the entire force. It would have been a tough job for him to go to the American people and say he had approved this."

On the afternoon of 18 November, Nixon gave the go-ahead for the operation.

Manor had already assembled his force in Thailand. The final plan called for the soldiers to fly from Takhli to Udorn, in northern Thailand, and board the helicopters there. The next time they would set foot on land, it would be at Son Tay.

It was a lean, compact raiding force. There would be no intermediate stops, no prepositioning of fuel or supplies, no delays en route. They would fly to Son Tay, refueling in the air, assault the

POW compound, spend about half an hour on the ground, and fly directly back out again.

Supporting the raiding force was a substantially larger military operation. In all, the rescue effort involved 116 aircraft taking off from seven airfields and three aircraft carriers. Planes assigned to gather intelligence and assist in communications came from as far away as Okinawa.

Manor believed strongly in using deception to protect his small raiding force. Even though United States policy prohibited bombing attacks on most of North Vietnam, Manor arranged for the Navy to launch a huge mock raid to fool the North Vietnamese into believing that bombing of the Haiphong-Hanoi area was suddenly being resumed in a big way—and thus direct the attention of the defenders to the east, rather than to the west, where the raiding force would enter North Vietnam.

Early in the planning for the raid, Manor received a letter from Adm. Thomas H. Moorer, the chairman of the Joint Chiefs of Staff, ordering everyone in the military to give Manor whatever he asked for, no questions asked. It was the kind of blank check that Cochran and Alison had received from General Arnold as they prepared for their Burma operation a quarter of a century earlier.

Manor was also given the authority to make his own decisions without referring everything back to Washington. As the time for the raid approached, he was faced with a crucial decision. The weather forecasters were anxiously watching the approach of a typhoon that appeared ready to sweep in over the South China Sea, where the carriers operated, and into North Vietnam in the next few days. On his own authority, Manor gave the go-ahead for the raid to be conducted one day early, on 20, rather than 21, November.

Overcoming the natural temptation to climb into a cockpit and lead the raid himself, Manor flew to Da Nang and set up shop atop Monkey Mountain at a major United States communications base. There, he had direct links not only with the raiding force but also with the Navy carriers and the other supporting forces. An open line connected him to Adm. John McCain, the com-

mander in chief, Pacific, in Hawaii—whose son was a prisoner—
and Admiral Moorer in the Pentagon. He was thus in a position
to monitor and, to some extent, control the entire operation and
to make decisions if anything went wrong.

The raiding force took off from Udorn at 10:56 P.M. Three of
the helicopters carried the soldiers. The other three came along
to pick up the rescued prisoners, although one of these was also
designated a gunship to knock out the guard towers.

One of the tickliest parts of the operation came over Laos, before they crossed the border into North Vietnam. The MC-130
pathfinders moved off to the side, and tankers moved in to take
their place. The tankers had only dim lights on their wing tips.
The helicopter pilots first had to find the tankers in the darkness.
Next, they had to nestle into the angle formed by the plane's wing
and its large tail and then lunge forward to insert the drogue pro-
truding from the nose of the helicopter into the funnel-shaped
basket at the end of a hose hanging out from the tanker's wing.

Although aerial refueling is practiced often, it never really becomes routine, especially over the dark mountains of a strange
land, with the dangers of combat in the offing.

The crews of both aircraft worried, understandably, about the
possibility that the helicopter's huge main rotor might strike the
tanker's vertical stabilizer. The tension was most pronounced for
the crews refueling on the right side of the tanker. Since the
drogue protrudes from the right side of the helicopter, refueling
on the right side of the plane forces the pilot to fly about six feet
closer to the tail.

A major concern was refueling the HH-3 helicopter. The chopper was barely able to keep up with the tanker and just didn't have
enough power to overtake the tanker and move into position to
take on fuel. Instead, the tanker pilot had to drop down below
the helicopter so the HH-3 pilot could dive down into position
behind the tanker. Even after weeks of practice, it was still very
much of a white-knuckle feat.

As soon as they had topped off the helicopters' tanks, the
tankers moved off, the pathfinders moved back in, and the raiders
headed east again toward Son Tay.

Manor had planned the entire operation down to the second. Timing was especially crucial on the approach to Son Tay, because there were two radar stations west of the prisoner compound. The raid planners figured they needed at least twelve minutes between any warning and their landing at Son Tay. But the radar stations were far enough west that, if either one had detected the approach of the raiding force, they could have denied the raiders this twelve-minute zone of relative safety.

Intelligence analysts discovered that there was a brief time when both radar stations were looking away from the route of the raiding party. With precise navigation, the two mother-duck pathfinders and their ducklings flew right through the gap and approached Son Tay undetected.

Following the plan, the HH-3 dropped into the compound, hitting the ground so hard that one of the crew members was thrown from the plane. Despite the severe jolt, the crew members and the sixteen Green Berets aboard survived the landing without injury and proceeded with their attack.

One of the HH-53 helicopters—carrying Simons—landed at a compound that had been identified as "the secondary school" but was actually a military installation, about four hundred meters southeast of the prisoner-of-war camp. The soldiers jumped to the ground, and the helicopter lifted off to loiter nearby. The Green Berets immediately became involved in a furious firefight which went on for about four minutes. Then the helicopter pilot returned, picked up the soldiers, and moved them to the POW compound.

Whether the landing at "the secondary school" was a mistake or whether it was done deliberately is still a matter of some controversy. The official version is that it was a mistake, which was almost immediately recognized, and that the raiders began withdrawing after only four minutes on the ground. Another theory, still held by some of those involved in the preparations for the raid, is that there were Chinese soldiers at the other installation and that they were deliberately attacked, in effect sending a message to Beijing: we know you're there and can hurt you if we want to. Manor calls this speculation "fantasy."

Meanwhile, another HH-53 had landed just outside the prisoner compound. The raiders immediately adopted an alternative plan and compensated for the absence of Simons's unit, which had landed at the nearby "school."

The A1-E Sandys that had accompanied the raiding force circled overhead, strafing the approaches to the camp.

Inside what was believed to be the cell block, the Green Berets quickly went from room to room with disappointing results: there wasn't a single prisoner in the compound.

A code word was flashed back to Manor, waiting for news at Monkey Mountain.

"Everything was right on time, all the way through," Manor recalls. "It was working very well until I got the message in my command post that there were no POWs. That was probably the most disappointing message I have ever received. I didn't want to believe it at first. I was hoping it might be garbled, but it wasn't. I gave instructions to extricate the force."

The raiders had achieved complete surprise. But by the time they were ready to board the helicopters and depart, the raid itself and, even more, the Navy's mock assault had stirred the North Vietnamese defenders into furious activity.

Supporting the attacking force were F-4 fighters prepared to fend off any North Vietnamese fighters that might take to the air. Also in the air overhead were F-105 Wild Weasel fighters, whose job it was to provoke the missile crews and then launch their own missiles to home in on the ground-based radar.

Sixteen surface-to-air missiles were launched, and two of the F-105s were hit. Another twenty SAMs were fired at the Navy planes involved in the diversionary raid, but none of them was hit.

Sitting in his helicopter waiting for the withdrawal, Col. Royal A. Brown looked upward.

"They started firing SAMs, and you've never seen as many SAMs as were fired that night," Brown recalled. "I saw two 105s get hit. My job was to see that everybody got out, the rescue forces. I was the last airplane left. I saw the 105s get hit, the first one, like this big ball of fire. I didn't think anybody would get out of that, but he made it back to Udorn.

"The second one got hit. I didn't think anybody would get out of that either, but he kept going. He bailed out over Barrel Roll [an area in northern Laos], and they picked him up.

"It was kind of amazing. We were told that there was a little mountain, not too far from the camp, and if you have to bail out, try to get to this mountain. They thought that would be a fairly safe place, and that was the first place where we started picking up SAM fire that night. Everybody up there has got a gun."

Once the last helicopter lifted off, there was a momentary sense of relief. But the battle was not over.

"Getting out of there was something else," Brown says. "The old saying, remember back in SAC [Strategic Air Command] until the bomb's away, you're working for the government; after the bomb's away, you're working on your own. Getting out of there was difficult. . . . We had a MiG make one pass at us. He fired rockets, but the ground must have broken his lock-on. Just luck it broke. The MiG was coming up real fast. We were trying to find a karst to hide behind when the missile hit a good-sized hill. Blew damn near half the hill up."

Brown's account of the MiG attack is an example of how confusing things can get in the heat of battle. Manor says that, at that point, no MiGs had yet taken to the air. What Brown saw was a United States A-1 firing off a rocket rather than land with the rocket still on its wing.

As Brown later learned, one of the two damaged F-105s managed to make it back to Thailand. The two-man crew of the other plane ejected and parachuted down into northern Laos.

Manor, from his position near Da Nang, took charge of the rescue operation: he ordered the helicopters emerging from the raid to look for the downed airmen as they crossed into Laos. They managed to find the fliers and swooped down for an impromptu rescue of the two men.

When all the aircraft had returned to their bases, the losses were totaled up. The United States had lost one F-105 and the helicopter that was purposely left behind. One of the soldiers had suffered a minor injury.

But the raid had not succeeded in its goal of rescuing prisoners.

On Capitol Hill, Defense Secretary Laird came under scathing questioning by angry senators, incredulous that such a risky operation had been conducted without being sure that there were prisoners there to be rescued. The senators emphasized their anger in a subtle way: they kept Laird in the witness chair hour after hour while they were free to slip out to the rest room as the need arose. Laird wasn't able to offer a very convincing explanation for the apparent intelligence failure. The best excuse he could give was: "We have not been able to develop a camera that sees through the roofs of buildings."

Clearly, there had been doubts about whether the prisoners were still there. Early in the planning, serious consideration was given to having a spy go by the compound to try to determine whether the prison was still in use. But that was ruled out as too dangerous. If the spy had been caught, he might have been forced to send back a false report that would have led the raiders into a trap.

When the American prisoners were released by North Vietnam, Manor met them in the Philippines and learned that the men had been transferred from the Son Tay prison in mid-July, several weeks before he had been given the assignment to try to pull them out.

Was the raid, then, a failure?

Manor doesn't think so.

"A lot of good things did come from it," he says. "The small camps around Hanoi were closed. All the POWs were moved to two big camps . . . old French prisons. There, they were able to live communally. Those who had been held in solitary confinement were released from solitary confinement. When they came out two and a half years later, they were in pretty good shape, much better shape than we expected if we had picked them up."

All the controversy surrounding the failure to find prisoners in the camp tended to obscure the positive features of the raid. As a military operation, both in planning and in execution, the Son Tay raid was almost flawless.

In 1993, Comdr. William McRaven, a Navy SEAL, studied eight

commando-type operations in preparation of a thesis at the Naval
Postgraduate School. They ranged from the German assault on
the Belgian fortress at Eben Emael that opened the blitzkrieg toward the west on 10 May 1940 to the Israeli rescue of passengers
of a hijacked airliner at Mogadishu in 1976. This is McRaven's con-
clusion about the Son Tay raid:

"Disregarding the failure to rescue any POWs, the mission was
almost flawless. Not one soldier or airman was killed or seriously
injured on the raid. This includes the Navy and Air Force airmen
who supported the deception and cover operations. Considering
the difficulty of penetrating a sophisticated air defense system and
then conducting combat operations in unfamiliar surroundings,
the raid on Son Tay should stand as a tribute to the tremendous
preparation and professionalism of the assault force. And, I doubt
any modifications to the plan could have improved the performance of the raiders."

He summed up: "The raid on Son Tay is the best modern day
example of a successful special operation and should be considered 'text book' material for future missions."

Unfortunately, many of the lessons learned and the flying techniques developed in the Son Tay raid were soon forgotten, with
tragic results.

CHAPTER 21

"Utter Chaos" at Tang Island

In the history of American involvement in the long war in Southeast Asia, the incident involving the USS *Mayaguez* is usually accorded a brief passing reference, if that. But in the history of Air Force special operations, the *Mayaguez* affair deserves special attention because of the lessons it holds about how badly wrong things can go if certain basic rules of special operations are forgotten or neglected.

The USS *Mayaguez*, a 10,485-ton American-owned freighter, was sailing through the Gulf of Thailand, far out in international waters about sixty miles off the Cambodian coast, when she was seized by a Cambodian gunboat on 12 May 1975.

For Gerald R. Ford, who had become president nine months before, the seizure was a stinging slap in the face. But two of his key advisers, Secretary of State Henry Kissinger and Defense Secretary James Schlesinger, saw it also as an opportunity to demonstrate that the United States was still a powerful player on the world stage.

The seizure of the ship came at one of the lowest points in American prestige and self-esteem at the end of a seemingly inexorable succession of setbacks.

President Nixon had fled office on 9 August 1974 to avoid trial by the Senate on charges stemming from the Watergate affair.

In Southeast Asia, things had been on a slippery slope for many months. The last American had left Laos on 4 July 1974, allowing the North Vietnamese to take control of the country. Vang Pao and his Hmong people had been disarmed and left at the mercy of their longtime adversaries.

On 16 April 1975, Phnom Penh, the capitol of Cambodia, fell to the Khmer Rouge guerrillas. Americans had fled the city in Operation Eagle Pull.

An even more ignominious and public pullout occurred on 29 April, when the last Americans flew from the roof of the American embassy in Saigon as the North Vietnamese moved in to seal their victory over the south.

For a dinky little nation like Cambodia to seize an American ship on the high seas added an unbearable indignity to this series of setbacks. But, unlike the fall of Phnom Penh and Saigon, it was something the United States, with all its military power, could do something about. At least, that's the way it looked from half a world away in Washington.

Orders went out to the military in the field to take back the seized ship and find and rescue her crew.

At this point, probably few in the American military knew the situation in Cambodia better than the Air Force special operations people. With the fall of Laos, attention had shifted to Cambodia. Heinie Aderholt, who had retired from the Air Force, was recalled to active duty as a general in October 1973 and sent to Thailand to oversee the rebuilding of the Cambodian air force.

"All we were trying to do," he says, "was save Cambodia. We rehabbed all their helicopters. We set all kinds of records for rehabbing. We pulled all the pilots out of the Cambodian air force and retrained them at Water Pump [the unit set up in Thailand years earlier to train Thai, Laotian, and Hmong pilots]. We had guys who had five thousand sorties and didn't know how to work the gunsights. They'd just drop bombs.

"There were some very unusual things we did in that war, and we did them right. But we made them so dogarn classified that we just didn't learn from it."

How many of the Cambodian military who had relied on the United States to help them resist the Khmer Rouge remained alive was in doubt. How many of them still retained any sense of friendship toward the United States, which, they felt, had abandoned them, was also in doubt.

Certainly, the secret bombing and the American incursion into Cambodia in 1970, although their target was North Vietnamese bases in the Cambodian "sanctuary," had also harmed and, presumably, made enemies of many Cambodian peasants.

And then there were the accidents of war that left a residue of bitterness.

Clyde Howard, the combat controller who had operated in Thailand, Laos, and Cambodia, still recalls his dismay when he learned of one such "accident." After the fall of Laos, the offset bombing devices that had been used in Laos were transferred to Cambodia. A number of them were used to direct B-52 attacks. At first, one of the offset devices was set up where it could be easily monitored, at the United States Embassy in Phnom Penh. But the Strategic Air Command was horrified: if a crew forgot to insert the offset into its system, the embassy would be obliterated.

The device was moved to a village in the countryside, and one of the technicians trained by Howard was assigned to monitor it, setting in the coordinates for strikes by the bombers.

"When they found out in Offut Air Force Base [Nebraska, home of the Strategic Air Command] we had a beacon on the embassy, they said, holy. . . . Get that beacon off that embassy! They didn't trust their own crews. They were not required to check in with us, so there was no double check on them," Howard recalls.

"We removed the beacon. Okay, you unprofessional yahoos. We moved it to one of our provincial locations, a village with about three hundred people.

"I came back to the States in June or July 1973. About two weeks after my arrival, I heard a B-52 had wiped out a village in Cambodia. I thought, oh, shit. Come to find out, the aircrew forgot to offset from the beacon. They dropped 108 five-hundred-pounders. They wiped out that little village, with my FAG [forward air guide]."

When the order came from Washington to go after the

Mayaguez, the Air Force special operations teams knew they might encounter a good deal of hostility, not only from the Khmer Rouge but also from other Cambodians who had been armed and trained by the Americans but might now have reason to feel abandoned or wronged by the United States.

Aerial surveillance quickly found the captured ship anchored near tiny Tang Island, thirty-four miles off the Cambodian coast. It was assumed that the gunboat had taken the crew from the freighter to the island and that they were being held there. Since the island was far enough offshore that it could not be readily reinforced from the mainland, it seemed a relatively simple matter to overpower the gunboat crew, free the crewmen from the *Mayaguez,* take back the *Mayaguez,* and demonstrate that some little third-world country couldn't push the United States around and get away with it.

The USS *Coral Sea,* an aircraft carrier, was in the vicinity and was ordered to proceed toward the island. A contingent of Marines was assembled at the royal Thai air base at U Tapao. A combination of special operations and air-sea rescue helicopters arrived and prepared to carry the Marines to the island.

For the helicopter crews, many of whom had been involved in the evacuation of Americans from both Phnom Penh and Saigon, often under hostile fire, in the previous few weeks, the rescue of the crew of the *Mayaguez* seemed almost routine.

But a glance at the map might have raised some concerns. If anything happened to any of the helicopters in the vicinity of Tang Island, the nearest dry land where they could expect a friendly welcome was two hundred miles away, back in Thailand.

The crews were assured that nothing would go wrong. At most, they were told, they could expect to find eleven lightly armed Khmer Rouge soldiers and perhaps a few fishermen on the island.

They did not learn until later that an AC-130 gunship had flown over the island the night before and counted at least fifty campfires.

The helicopters were the best the Air Force had for such an operation. They were either HH-53 Super Jolly Green Giants, of the type used in the Son Tay rescue operation, or a variant of the plane, known as the CH-53. They were large enough to carry a sizable contingent of marines, and they were equipped for aerial refueling so the four-hundred-mile round-trip from U Tapao did not pose a serious obstacle.

The flight to the island was uneventful except when they were fired upon by a ship as they passed overhead. None of the helicopters was hit, but it was not a good omen. As planned, two of the eleven helicopters pulled off and delivered their marines to the deck of a destroyer escort, the USS *Holt*. The Marines later went from the *Holt* to the *Mayaguez*, found the ship unoccupied, and took control.

Meanwhile, the rest of the helicopters proceeded to the island. One contingent of Marines was to land on the east side of the island, where there were some buildings and where the crew members of the American ship probably were being held. The rest of the Marines were to land on the west side of the island to act as a blocking force if the Cambodians tried to escape through the jungle with the captives.

Landing the Marines on the ship was a little tricky. Since the helicopters were so large and the destroyer so small, the helicopters had to hover over the water beside the ship, with one wheel on the deck, while the Marines jumped to the deck.

Gary L. Weikel, then a young lieutenant and now a colonel, was the pilot of Jolly Green 1-1, the lead helicopter, and one of the two landing the Marines on the *Holt*. This is his account of what happened next:

"After all the city evacuations, I felt pretty comfortable that this was really a piece of cake. As it turned out, we were pretty damn wrong on that, because there were about three hundred Khmer Rouge dug in on the island with heavy weaponry. This thing turned to a shit sandwich in a big hurry.

"The first 53s were blown out of the sky with RPGs [rocket-propelled grenades] and recoilless rifles—the first two on the east beach. They were down in the water, on fire, while we were trying to put the Marines on the deck of this little destroyer escort. The CH-53s—Air Force, from the 21st Special Operations Squadron—bore the brunt of that on the east beach. The west beach became the alternative, where the remnants of the force tried to swing around and get in."

But the welcome there was equally ferocious. All the helicopters were badly damaged. One crew tried to water-taxi away from the beach, but their engine quit and they sank offshore.

Only about fifty Marines managed to get ashore on the west beach, and they were in serious trouble.

"Right away, we realized something horrible was going on from listening to the screams on the radio," Weikel says.

By that time, he had unloaded his Marines on the destroyer. But before he could try to help out in the developing battle ashore, he had to find a tanker flying overhead and refuel. Looking down and listening to the radio, Weikel and his crew could tell that the situation had turned to "absolute and utter chaos."

They spotted a CH-53 with its load of Marines still onboard. The plane had been badly shot up and was trying to limp back toward Thailand on one engine. Weikel and another helicopter fell in behind the crippled craft as an escort.

Just as the helicopter passed over the Thai-Cambodian border, the other engine quit, and the pilot autorotated down to a safe landing. While one of the escorts hovered overhead, Weikel and his crew landed to pick up the Marines and the helicopter crew and ferry them back to U Tapao.

Pausing only long enough to refuel, the two escort helicopters loaded on another Marine assault force and headed back toward the west beach of Tang Island.

They successfully landed the Marines on the west beach and then swung around to provide gunfire support for an effort to land another helicopter on the east beach to extract the Marines pinned down there.

The rescue helicopter was badly shot up and limped away from the beach on one engine, fuel pouring out of holes in its tanks.

An HC-130 tanker dove down in front of the helicopter, ready to transfer fuel. But the single functioning engine didn't put out enough power for the craft to stay in position behind the tanker to take on fuel. The tanker pilot pulled back his throttles, trying desperately to fly slow enough so the chopper could plug into the drogue trailing back behind his wing. He slowed so much, in fact, that the big plane stalled out and almost fell into the sea.

The situation seemed hopeless. The helicopter couldn't refuel. It didn't have enough fuel to reach the nearest safe landing place, two hundred miles away in Thailand. Shortly, it would have to land in the sea. Chances of survival from such a landing are not good.

"He was going in the water if we couldn't find a place for him to rest," Weikel says. "In the fog of war, I'm not sure how this happened, but it seems to me we remembered there was a Navy aviation-capable ship heading that way. I asked the HC-130 if, on his weather radar, he saw anything out there that looked like a ship.

"The HC-130 said he saw a single large blob out there. It was either a ship or it was a thunderstorm. It was way out in the Gulf of Siam [Thailand]. We thought, well, if it's a thunderstorm, that's just too bad. If it's a ship, we'll take a chance on it.

"It turned out to be the USS *Coral Sea*. The *Coral Sea* turned into the wind and recovered that bird on a single engine. We landed behind."

Weikel and his crew worked out a last-ditch plan to rescue the Marines and the remnants of the helicopter crews, who had been trapped on the east beach for twelve hours, trading hand grenades with the enemy. The plan reflected the lack of choices available: the helicopter would back in to the beach and stay there until the Marines were aboard, no matter how much damage the enemy inflicted. The chopper had three Gatling guns and a thousand pounds of armor plate, so they had a fair chance of carrying off the rescue attempt.

Even if they couldn't fly, they would water-taxi out away from the island and hope that two small unarmed helicopters from the *Coral Sea* would be able to pick up everyone aboard before the helicopter sank.

As they headed in toward the beach, another helicopter suddenly appeared. It had raced back to U Tapao with a badly wounded Marine and then hurried back to Tang Island—a four-hundred-mile round-trip. The newcomer moved into position near the island to provide fire support for the rescue attempt.

To their surprise, still another Super Jolly Green Giant suddenly appeared on the scene. It was the chopper that had limped out to land on the *Coral Sea*. The ship's crew had managed to get the damaged engine running, patch the holes in the fuel lines, and send the plane back into the battle.

With the other choppers providing support, Weikel used a destroyer that was standing offshore to mask their approach, then did a fast low-level dash toward the beach.

"The survivors popped the red smoke. We saw exactly where to go. We backed in, under some pretty heavy fire," Weikel says. "We set it down in the water with the tail up in the trees. As we were loading, about five Khmer Rouge came out of the bushes and made a hand-grenade rush on us. One grenade rolled under the bird and blew up. It caused some sheet metal damage, rocked us pretty good.

"Our right gunner cut loose with the minigun and killed all five of them. This all happened in about two or three seconds. Just then, when the Marines were still trying to get their wounded up the ramp, a heavy gun opened up to the north of us. The left gunner cut loose. I saw a helmet full of holes roll out on the beach and that gun was silenced.

"We got everybody on and decided to get the hell out of there. We started to slowly lift out of there, and we got heavy cannon fire right under the bird, and there was a lot out in front of us.

"We headed back to the *Coral Sea* because we had a lot of wounded, chest wounds and things like that. Every one of them survived their ordeal."

The rest of the Marines on the west beach were pulled out under darkness that night, with an AC-130 gunship overhead to provide fire support.

After all the agony on the beaches of Tang Island, it was learned that the thirty-nine crew members of the *Mayaguez* were not there after all. They had been taken to the mainland and were soon set afloat in a Thai fishing vessel, to be picked up by an American destroyer.

In Washington, it was announced that one Marine had been killed and that casualties otherwise were light. Defense Secretary Schlesinger declared victory, calling the affair "an eminently successful operation incorporating the judicious and effective use of American force for purposes that were necessary for the well-being of this society." Later, it was acknowledged that fifteen men had been killed and fifty wounded and that three were missing.

By the time they landed on the *Coral Sea,* Weikel and his crew had been up for almost twenty hours and had flown for more than fourteen of those hours. They were ordered not to fly anymore and boarded an HH-53 for the flight back to U Tapao as passengers.

They were happy just to be alive. But, tired as they were, it was hard to rest. The plane was littered with ammunition casings, and it stank of blood and dirt after a day in the jungle. Weikel had time to think.

"The more I thought about it," he says, "the more pissed I got. We had forgotten the lessons of Southeast Asia even though we were still in Southeast Asia. Where the hell was the dedicated helicopter escort we had all through the rescues in Southeast Asia? Example: when the HH-53s did the Son Tay raid, we had A-1 Skyraiders with them. On all our rescues, we had either A-1s or A-7Ds [jet fighter-bombers] dedicated to us for escort.

"Why did we forget that lesson when we were in the very end of the Vietnam War?

"I was also mad because the intel report on the island was so wrong. If we had any doubt as to where the crew of the *Mayaguez* was, we should have sent special operations forces, notably SEALs, in there to do a beach recon, which would have told us, one, they're not on the island, and two, there's a hell of a lot of bad guys on the island.

"They also ignored the AC-130's report. They went down there a night or two before, and they counted fifty campfires on the island. That never registered at all. It was never briefed to us at all."

In the long roller-coaster history of Air Force special operations, with each period of buildup followed by a rapid withering away, the *Mayaguez* incident was a chilling reminder of just how rapidly this delicately honed precision instrument can lose its edge.

PART 7
Hostage Rescue Efforts

CHAPTER 22
Operation Rice Bowl

It was early on the morning of April Fool's Day—1 April 1980—when a small Twin Otter airplane flown by two Central Intelligence Agency pilots landed in the darkness of the Iranian desert more than two hundred miles south of Teheran.

While the pilots settled down to wait, Maj. John T. Carney, Jr., a former Air Force Academy football coach, unloaded a small motorized dirt bike from the cargo compartment of the plane and set off in the darkness to explore the surrounding desert as a potential landing spot for a fleet of transport planes and helicopters preparing to rescue fifty-three Americans who had been held captive in the American embassy in Teheran since the previous 3 November.

Carney was the commander of a small team of Air Force combat controllers who had been working with the Army's Delta Force for some two years, training to combat terrorists or rescue hostages almost anywhere in the world. They were the forerunners of today's special tactics teams. The secret Delta Force—earlier known as Blue Light—was commanded by Col. Charles Beckwith, a legendary Army Special Forces operator. Carney considered himself and his men Beckwith's personal combat controllers.

As he prepared to set out on his scouting expedition, Carney packed onto his bike a small shovel and five small beacons to mark the landing zone. The lights had been specially developed by Carney's team. Normally, a combat control team would set out some twenty lights to mark a landing zone. But Carney's team had found they could get by with only five lights.

Carney adjusted his clumsy night-vision goggles over his eyes and set out to explore the landing zone. Stopping at intervals along the way, he plunged eight-inch lengths of pipe into the sandy desert floor and pulled out plugs of the soil to be analyzed to determine if the area could support C-130 transport planes heavily laden with fuel for the helicopters that would make the actual assault.

He dug shallow holes in the desert and buried four of the beacons in a square about ninety feet on a side. A fifth light, a flashing strobe, was placed about 5,000 feet away to mark the end of the landing zone. The five lights were known as a box-and-one. Only the glass dome of each light protruded above the surface. The lights were designed to be turned on by a signal from the lead aircraft. Even then, they would be invisible to any passerby on the nearby highway, because the lights were both directional and infrared, visible only to someone with special glasses. Those five lights were all the guidance the pilots had. For all they knew, the Grand Canyon could lie just beyond the last light.

"Then I had to survey all this area to make sure there was nothing there, like a rock, that could hit a wing tip and cause us a problem," Carney says. "We knew from overhead photography there didn't appear to be any big obstacles. But you don't need a very big one to cause your undercarriage a problem.

"Once I got my lights set up, I ran all around this area, just kept coming in to make sure there was nothing out there. I ran up and down. It was flat as a pool table. There was a curve in the road, and then it was straight as an arrow, and I used that for reference.

"The only obstacle was a road sign near the curve with an old piece of tin hanging from it. It spooked the hell out of me. It looked like some Arab standing out there. It kept my attention for a while, but it never moved."

While he was at work, Carney saw several cars go by on the lonely road between Tabas, 58 miles to the east, and Yazd, 135 miles to the northwest. He was so busy he didn't bother to count how many. He just flattened himself in the desert until they had passed.

Before taking off on his perilous mission, Carney was briefed on how he would be extracted if something had gone wrong with the airplane.

"If anything happened, they would come in and drop the Fulton recovery kit and snatch me out by a Combat Talon [MC-130]," Carney says.

The Fulton sky hook is the same system that was to be used years earlier to rescue Allen Pope from an Indonesian jail, as described in Chapter Fourteen.

"General Vaught [Maj. Gen. James Vaught, the commander of the Iran rescue operation] said to me one day: 'John, we're thinking about doing a live Fulton recovery. The crews need some confidence in picking up a live body.' What did I think about that?" Carney recalled.

"I said, 'Shit, it seems to me like practicing for a broken leg. It either picks me up or it doesn't. I don't want to practice it, that's for goddamn sure.' I've seen dummies go up in the air and come right back down again.

"I don't know to this day if I would have gotten in that thing. I'd probably have run my little motorcycle until it ran out of gas."

As it turned out, there was no reason for Carney to be plucked from the desert. When his hour-long survey was done, he rode back to the plane and awakened the pilots, and they flew away.

Carney's one-man survey of the potential landing site confirmed that it could be used as a refueling point for the helicopters that would carry Beckwith's Delta Force into downtown Teheran.

More important, the decision to send Carney into Iran was a crucial factor in moving the rescue operation—under the code name of Operation Rice Bowl—from talk and paperwork to action.

"You need the help of a lot of other agencies, and there wasn't a lot of help being given to General Vaught," Carney says. "Another agency was given the task of getting me in and out of there. That was General Vaught's way of getting everybody serious, getting them involved.

"When the president okayed the reconnaissance mission, then everybody had to get involved. There was no time to sit back and debate it. It was kind of ingenious on General Vaught's part."

Planning for the rescue operation had begun some five months earlier, immediately after the Americans had been taken hostage.

It did not take a military genius to realize that this was very close to a mission impossible. A sizable commando force would have to be inserted right into downtown Teheran, a city where virulently anti-American mobs roamed freely, deep inside Iran. They would have to fight their way into the embassy building where the hostages were being held, and search it carefully to make sure all the hostages were found. And then some way would have to be found to get the rescuers and the rescued safely out of a city and a country that were by now thoroughly aroused.

Lee Hess, then a major on the air staff at the Pentagon and now a retired colonel, recalls searching for the closest friendly air base. They found a field in a remote section of southern Turkey, near the Iran border, that was not being used by the Turks. It would be a perfect staging area for the rescue effort—or at least as close to perfect as was possible in these circumstances. But would the Turks permit the use of their territory for a raid on another Muslim nation? Probably not. Someone suggested that the United States, which routinely conducted military operations from Turkish bases, just go ahead and use the field and not tell the Turks. The State Department, already noticeably cool to any rescue attempt, quickly signaled thumbs down on that idea.

Because of the need for secrecy, the five members of the Joint Chiefs of Staff took a personal hand in planning the operation. To head it, they chose General Vaught, an Army Special Forces veteran. Vaught understandably thought in terms of his own experience and the Army way of doing things.

When the Army moves a force by air, it uses something known by the inelegant designation of FARRP—which stands for "Forward Area Refueling and Rearming Point." Depending on the distance to be covered, the Army might use a series of FARRPs, hopscotching its way toward the objective.

Air Force special operators, on the other hand, tend to think in terms of a single long jump to the objective, refueling in the air, if necessary, rather than stopping at a FARRP.

This was the pattern in Burma; in long behind-the-lines penetrations in Europe during World War II; in ARCS operations during the 1950s; and in the Son Tay raid. Even in the *Mayaguez* operation, Air Force helicopters flew from a base two hundred miles from the scene of the action, although, in that case, they had no choice.

Whether there was a choice in the Iran rescue effort that might have avoided the use of the FARRP technique is still a matter of debate. But, at the time, with an Army general in charge, there seems to have been little thought given to any alternative to the use of the Army's hopscotch method.

As the plan evolved, Beckwith's 138-man Delta Force assembled on the island of Masirah, off the coast of Oman in the Arabian Sea, to be flown to the refueling point, designated as Desert One, in three MC-130 Combat Talon transport planes. Three C-130 transport aircraft, modified to carry internal fuel bladders, were loaded with eighteen thousand gallons of jet fuel, preparing them to serve as filling stations for the helicopters that would carry the soldiers on to Teheran. One of the troop-carrying MC-130s also carried three five-hundred-gallon rubber bladders of fuel as a backup.

Eight RH-53D Sea Stallion helicopters—a Navy version of the basic bird used by the Air Force in the Son Tay and *Mayaguez* operations—were assembled aboard the USS *Nimitz*, which took up position in the Arabian Sea, about fifty nautical miles off the south coast of Iran. Since the planes were a type used in minesweeping, Marine helicopter pilots familiar with minesweeping were chosen for the operation, although one Air Force officer served as a copilot.

The plan called for the helicopters to make three stops. The first would be at Desert One, the site checked out by Carney. There, the helicopters would be refueled, and the soldiers would transfer to the helicopters. They would then fly two hours and ten minutes to a drop-off point. The soldiers would hike five miles to a hiding place in the hills outside Teheran. The helicopters would proceed on to another hiding place of their own. The penetration of Iranian air space, the refueling, the flight to the drop-off point, and the flight to the hiding place would take about eight hours, and it would all have to be done within the hours of darkness. At that time of the year, it would be dark for only a little over nine hours, so timing was critical.

After hiding all day, hoping they and their helicopters would not be detected, the soldiers would be taken on the second night of the operation to the embassy in trucks to conduct their raid. At the proper moment, the helicopters would leave their hiding place and fly to a soccer stadium adjoining the embassy. Once the Delta Force had found and rescued the hostages, they would all climb into the helicopters for the flight to the Manzarïyeh airfield south of Teheran.

Meanwhile, a hundred Army Rangers, flying from Wadi Kena in Egypt, would have taken over the field. Overhead would be gunships to help in securing the airfield and, if needed, to push mobs back away from the embassy during the rescue operation. They would also prevent any Iranian fighters from taking off from another nearby airfield.

As soon as Manzarïyeh was captured, two big C-141 transport planes, one of them equipped as a flying hospital, would land and stand by to carry the Delta Force and the rescued hostages out of Iran.

It was a highly complex operation, involving scores of aircraft operating from widely scattered air bases and an aircraft carrier and requiring precise timing and coordination.

As the complexity grew, so, too, did the number of opportunities for things to go wrong.

Although the raiding force itself was made up of Army soldiers and the helicopters would be flown by Marines, the success of the operation as a whole depended heavily on the skills of the Air Force special operations units involved.

Unfortunately, Air Force special operations had fallen into one of its recurrent periods of neglect following the Vietnam War. The signs of disintegration in capability were already evident at the time of the *Mayaguez* incident five years earlier, and things had gotten progressively worse in the meantime.

For a period of years, special operations had been assigned to the Tactical Air Command, dominated by fighter pilots. They had little interest in, or appreciation of, special operations except as a source of money and promotions. Funds were siphoned off from special operations to pay for new F-15s and F-16s for the fighter pilots. And, with special operations swelling the size of the Tactical Air Command, there were more opportunities for promotions. As the special operators saw it, the promotions all went to the fighter pilots. Carney himself was passed over for promotion twice before his skills were finally recognized and he was advanced to the rank of colonel earlier than normal.

Except for the assignment of Carney and his handful of combat controllers to work with Beckwith and Delta, the Air Force had given little thought to its possible role in efforts to combat terrorism and to rescue hostages.

The attitude of many in the Air Force was summed up at the time by Gen. Larry D. Welch, a fighter pilot who was then vice–chief of staff and later chief of staff: "We can lose any number of terrorist encounters and low-intensity conflicts without endangering the nation one whit. But, fail to deter or lose a conventional or nuclear war. . . ."

As a result, when the hostages were taken by the Iranians, the Air Force had failed to develop a sophisticated helicopter suitable for such a long-range rescue effort. Specialized transport planes and gunships left over from the Vietnam War had been shunted off to the reserves.

Moreover, except for the link between the combat controllers and the Delta Force, little thought had been given to coordinating Army, Navy, Air Force, and Marine units to work together on such an operation, and they had done little training together.

General Vaught thus had to create a rescue force out of bits and pieces of the military. He also had to do his job in the greatest secrecy. Everyone agreed that the rescue effort had to come as a total surprise to the Iranians. The slightest hint of what was up would doom the effort to failure. As a result, Vaught was extremely limited in his ability to reach out to combat veterans who might have helped increase the odds of success.

Hess, who was deeply involved in the planning for the rescue, recalls with some bemusement how he was also helping to develop several other contingency plans headed by generals and admirals who were kept in the dark about the rival plans. In some cases, for example, the different plans called for using the same tankers that were integral to the success of the other plans.

Secrecy also had a strong impact on training for the operation. Key phases of the rescue effort were practiced in the most realistic ways possible, but there never was a full-scale practice session with all the actors on stage at once.

To pull together the Air Force portion of the effort, Vaught chose Col. James H. Kyle, a veteran Combat Talon pilot with a thousand hours' combat flying in his logbook. Shortly before the rescue attempt got underway, Kyle was also named the on-scene commander at Desert One.

As early as mid-December, rehearsals began at a Marine airfield at Twentynine Palms, California. Kyle stood at the side of the blacked-out field as the time came for the arrival of the first C-130. An overcast had blotted out the moon, cutting visibility to zero. It was not until the plane had landed, using infrared landing lights, and moved into position to unload a planeload of Rangers, that Kyle heard its engines and realized the plane had landed undetected by those awaiting its arrival.

The training was as realistic as possible, but it was conducted in separate compartments. Those involved in various parts of the effort spent hours thinking and talking about what might go wrong and how to avoid problems, but they seldom had the chance to sit down with those involved in other phases of the operation to work out the glitches.

While the Delta Force practiced by themselves on a mockup of the embassy, the helicopters and C-130s exercised in the western desert. The AC-130 gunships that would provide overhead support flew off to Guam, thousands of miles from the rest of the task force, to practice low-level gunship operation.

The secrecy was so tight that aircrews involved in a deception operation related to the rescue didn't know that's what they were doing. They also weren't asked for their advice, which might have been helpful.

Ron Jones, the pilot referred to in Chapter Fifteen who flew leaflet-dropping missions over North Vietnam, was operations officer of the Seventh Special Operations Squadron, a Combat Talon unit stationed in Germany. Jones was by then a lieutenant colonel. Early in 1980, the unit was sent on temporary duty to Wadi Kena, an air base in the Egyptian desert, for training. The decision made sense. Because of objections from the citizenry, they were running out of areas in Europe where they could practice one of their most vital skills—low-level flying at night. Egypt offered vast spaces where such flights would disturb no one but an occasional camel herder.

Wadi Kena was also, unknown to Jones and his colleagues, to become a major staging area for Operation Rice Bowl. The flights by the Seventh SOS accustomed people in the area to seeing C-130s lumbering overhead, so that, when the planes involved in the rescue operation arrived, they attracted little attention.

"None of us related what we were doing to what was going on in the States, primarily because we didn't know what was going on in the States," Jones recalls. "We flew against the Egyptians' surface-to-air sites. They had SA-2, SA-3, and SA-6 missiles, plus they had the MiG-21 interceptor.

"The Seventh SOS deployed on an operation to England just about the time the task force was coming into Wadi Kena. I was picked as USAFE [United States Air Force in Europe] liaison officer to the task force. They'd been there a week or more, and I arrived a week or so before the mission.

"I didn't know what was going on. I walked into the big hangar that was their operations center and asked what was going on. I was told, 'We don't have time to tell you. Go around, look over people's shoulders, and figure it out.' I spent most of a morning and afternoon looking over people's shoulders, trying to figure out what was going on.

"There was a very cavalier—and I don't mean to call attention to myself when I say this—but there was one thing that will always stick in my mind was how cavalier the people were in planning this mission with regard to being able to operate out of somebody else's country.

"Four or five days before the mission was to go down, General Gast [Lt. Gen. Philip Gast, an Air Force officer who was deputy commander of the operation] was there in the mission ops [operations] center talking about a phase of the mission and the various operating locations.

"I said, 'Well, General, how do you plan on getting out of here?'

"He looked at me, and he said, 'Well, we're just going to go out and take off with no clearance, and we're just going to fly out of country. What's the problem?'

"I said, 'Well, you've got a big problem, General. One of the things is, you've got an SA-2 battery that sits about two or three miles off the end of this runway that does not require authorization to fire. You go flying airplanes off of here, you're going to end up with some smoking holes in the ground. Did you ever think about coordinating with the Egyptians?'

"He said, 'You've got my attention.'"

At that time, the Egyptians had only recently signed a peace agreement with Israel. The memories of the 1967 war, when much of their air force was destroyed on the ground in a surprise attack, and the violence of the 1973 war were still fresh. Jones vividly recalled one training mission.

"One night, we flew a couple of airplanes against the Aswan High Dam. They had SA-2s, SA-3s, and SA-6s at the dam. They locked on our airplanes with all those systems. [A lock-on by the missile's guidance radar is the last step before firing.] It was the first time some of our crews had ever seen an actual lock-on by any of those systems. We were flying terrain-following at a thousand feet. We dipped down to 250 feet, and they lost us. They couldn't maintain the lock. It scared them to death. They said, 'Don't you ever do that again. You'll always fly at a thousand feet so we can see you.' We flew at a thousand feet from then on."

What was particularly worrisome was that the individual Egyptian antiaircraft sites had authority to fire without checking with any higher headquarters. Egyptian friends told Jones they feared a hostile plane could get through their defenses in the time it took for a SAM battery to get permission to fire. Jones was very busy the next few days:

"I stayed busy for the last four or five days coordinating with the Egyptians, without telling them in so many words what was going on, just telling them there would be a large contingent of airplanes departing at approximately this time, exiting the country at this point, and then they'll be returning at approximately this time. I believe, without that notice, the Egyptians would have fired on them."

The rescue operation, as it began to unfold late on the afternoon of 24 April, was like a carefully choreographed ballet, with every intricate movement beautifully coordinated.

The C-130s slated to serve as filling stations at Desert One—so heavily laden with fuel that they could hardly take off—and the Combat Talons flew from Wadi Kena to Masirah. AC-130 gunships and C-141 transport planes stood by at Wadi Kena to help take over the airfield at Manzariyeh and carry out the evacuation after the rescue effort.

One Combat Talon carrying Beckwith and part of his force, plus Carney and his team, took off first from Masirah at dusk on 24 April, with the rest of the force scheduled to follow about an hour later.

In a completely separate movement, the eight helicopters lifted off from the deck of the *Nimitz* and headed toward the Iranian coast. They were ordered to fly as low as possible, sneaking in under the Iranian radar. The helicopters did not carry navigators, and the pilots depended on being able to see the ground.

As the lead MC-130 approached Desert One, Carney leaned forward between the pilots. It had been twenty-four days since he had buried the beacons in the desert. If, for any reason, the lights failed to function, the rescue effort would be doomed at the start. A member of Carney's team sent the signal to turn the lights on. Suddenly, four lights appeared in a square on the desert floor, with a fifth light blinking to mark the end of the landing zone.

The first plane lined up on the beacons and settled down to a smooth landing on the desert. Carney and his six-man team roared out the rear of the plane on their motorcycles and raced across the road to set up a second box-and-one to delineate a second landing strip on the other side of the roadway. It was their job to line the C-130s up in refueling slots and, when the helicopters arrived, to move them in behind the C-130s.

A team of Rangers followed them out the big cargo door on their motorcycles to set up roadblocks at each end of the area to stop any traffic that happened along. They had no sooner reached their blocking positions than an intercity bus carrying forty-three passengers and a driver showed up. It was quickly decided that the people would be put aboard one of the planes and flown out when the planes left, to be returned after the rescue operation had been completed.

Carney describes how the situation unfolded at Desert One:

"While the bus is getting sorted out, we're establishing the second landing zone, and the 130s are coming in. We were landing the even-numbered ones to the north side and the odd coming in to the right. Then we're waiting for the helicopters to come in so we can marshal them up behind the 130s."

The first helicopter came in more than twenty minutes late. The aircraft crews unreeled hoses attached to fuel bladders in the C-130s and began refueling the helicopters as soon as they arrived.

The helicopters, flying just above the desert floor, had run into a hazy cloud of dust that blinded the pilots. One of the helicopters had a malfunction and was abandoned. Its crew was picked up by another helicopter, and they continued on. Another helicopter turned around and returned to the *Nimitz*. The helicopters straggled in to Desert One far behind schedule, the last arriving eighty-five minutes late. But six of them arrived, and that was the minimum number needed to continue on to Teheran.

The scene was one of barely controlled chaos. The propellers of the C-130s and the rotors of the helicopters continued to spin, churning up dust and making so much noise that communication, even with radio, was difficult. Men moving about the refueling area appeared only as faint shadows.

Carney's account continues:

"In the course of refueling the helicopters, a helacious ball of fire breaks out up where the box lights are, up at the bend in the road. A fuel truck was coming through, was barreling down on the roadblock we had up there. One of Charlie Beckwith's guys told a young Ranger to stop the truck. He did. He unlocked an antitank weapon, fired it, and blew the tank truck up, dead on the approach to the north runway.

"Now, we've got this fireball up there, and everyone is stunned. What has happened? Everybody is thinking, We're getting attacked."

For the pilots arriving on the scene, the truck fire was a shocking surprise. They were wearing night-vision goggles, which intensify even the faintest lights, such as that from the stars. Suddenly, they were blinded by a huge fire on the ground.

"When you look back at that, that was an awesome, awesome task," Carney says. "Those C-130 crew members did an outstanding job. Here they've got to land in the desert with all sorts of sand blowing around. Now you've got a fuel truck on fire.

"Can you imagine flying into that area and seeing that big ball of fire? You know damn well they think that's an aircraft crashed. They come in and land anyway, grease it right in there. We couldn't have one guy turn around and go back on us. That was fuel we needed. I don't think they've ever been paid the credit for what they really did. I was certainly proud of the job they did."

To Carney, the scene looked like something out of the movie *Apocalypse Now*. But he saw six helicopters lined up being refueled—and that was the number needed to continue the mission.

"I remember standing in the middle of the road with Colonel Kyle and Colonel Beckwith. We're kind of congratulating each other," Carney says. "I remember Kyle saying good luck to Charlie. As he heads for the helicopter, we see people coming off the helicopter. I ask what the hell's going on."

One of the six helicopters had a malfunction in its electronics and could not go on. Carney knew that doomed the operation, and he turned his thoughts to the task of getting everyone back out of Desert One.

The first task was to reposition the helicopters so the C-130s could move out of the area and prepare to take off. As the aircraft began to move, the air was filled with blinding dust and sand.

One of the helicopters lifted off the ground, then suddenly lurched forward and clipped the tail of one of the C-130s. The chopper rose up, spun around, and came down hard on the cockpit of the C-130. The two aircraft were engulfed in flames at the point where they came together.

Five members of the C-130 crew were in the cockpit. They all burned to death. Three crew members in the back of the helicopter also died.

But the pilot got out of the helicopter, and some of Beckwith's commandos, in the back of the transport plane, also escaped before the craft was consumed by flames.

As the fire worked its way through the transport, it reached ammunition brought along by the commandos. Shells began cooking off, spraying the entire area with bullets. By some miracle, none of the other fuel-laden planes was hit.

"You're never fortunate if you lose even one person," Carney says. "But I must say we're very fortunate we didn't lose many more in that mess. I have to hand it to those 130 crews. They sat there and waited for us to move them in an orderly fashion and get them out of there. That took a hell of a lot of balls to just sit there and wait for instructions. We had to run over to them and tell them. We gave them the sequence, told them how we were going to get them out of there."

Carney climbed into the last aircraft with Kyle. One of Carney's men made a circuit of the area on his motorcycle to make sure no one was being left behind. While they waited, Carney and Kyle debated whether to try to destroy the helicopters that were being abandoned.

"Kyle's decision, which was a good one, was if we fool around destroying helicopters, we'll get a piece of shrapnel through an engine in the last plane out of Dodge City. We jumped in the airplane and took off," Carney says.

Eight men had been killed and five more injured. Five intact helicopters, as well as the wreckage of the helicopter and the

C-130 that had collided, were left behind in the desert, along with some classified documents that were left in the helos by the Marine aircrews as they scrambled for the exits. The documents were later found and exploited by the Iranians.

The failure of the rescue attempt was a terrible embarrassment for the United States and especially for its military forces. And the failure to extract the hostages contributed to President Carter's loss to Ronald Reagan in the 1980 election.

The postmortems began almost immediately.

At the most simplistic level, Americans asked why, with hundreds of billions a year in taxpayer dollars, the military couldn't pull off the simple little task of rescuing a few hostages held by a ragtag group that described themselves as militant students. The failed rescue attempt was often compared unfavorably with the raid in which Israeli commandos rescued 106 hostages held by terrorists at the Entebbe airfield in Uganda on 3 and 4 July 1976.

What this question failed to recognize was the great complexity and difficulty of the Iranian operation. Carney summed it up this way:

"You're trying to pull off what is probably the most sophisticated damn operation in the annals of military history. People want to compare it with Son Tay or Entebbe. Bullshit. There was no comparison. Entebbe, they're in and out, bingo, bango, they're gone. Son Tay the same thing. This thing, you're talking, over a forty-eight-hour period, an absolutely complex mission."

A six-member commission was named by the Joint Chiefs of Staff to study the rescue attempt. The group was headed by Adm. James L. Holloway III, a former chief of naval operations. It included men with long experience in special operations, including Gen. LeRoy Manor, the commander of the Son Tay raid a decade earlier.

The Holloway Commission unanimously concluded that "the risks were manageable, the overall probability of success good, and the operation feasible."

But it also criticized a number of aspects of the operation and its planning and raised serious questions about other aspects.

While recognizing the need for secrecy, it implied that the

emphasis on secrecy was overdone, resulting in the failure to seek advice (Manor had not been consulted about his Son Tay experience) and a lack of communication among those involved.

It also concluded that there should have been more than the eight helicopters in the original launch from the *Nimitz*—at least ten and perhaps as many as twelve.

The Holloway group also strongly implied that the operation would have had a greater chance of success if Air Force pilots experienced in long-range, low-level flights in the dark had been brought in to fly the helicopters.

At the time, the group found, there were two hundred Air Force pilots available with current or recent experience in long-range flight and aerial refueling. Their Air Force helicopters would not fit in the elevators on a carrier because their rotors could not be folded. So they would have had to learn to fly the Navy's Sea Stallion version of the basic H-53 helicopter. The Holloway Commission found that would have been fairly simple.

Air commandos who have studied the Iranian rescue attempt agree that the decision to give the helicopter job to the Marines was a matter of spreading the work around to avoid interservice jealousy and that the logical choice would have been to put experienced Air Force pilots in the cockpits, even if they had to put them in Navy uniforms, remind them they were on a "ship" and not a "boat," and teach them to say *head* and *ladder* instead of *rest room* and *stairs*.

Manor, who frequently lectures on the Son Tay and Desert One operations in classified briefings for military audiences, is convinced that the helicopters should have flown right along with the C-130s, as they did at Son Tay, or that they should at least have been provided with a C-130 pathfinder to lead them to the refueling spot on time.

"The Marines who flew the helicopters were in a difficult position," he says, "and they did a real good job considering the position they were placed in—following the contour of the terrain. We asked why they were flying that low. They said they had been briefed that radar detection could compromise the mission.

"But the C-130s, on approximately the same route at approximately the same time, were flying at a much higher altitude. Their route took them over the weather phenomenon the helicopters flew into. They did not receive the same warning, that they could be detected by the radar.

"In my estimation, being detected by the radar was not a big problem. So the helicopters could have had it much easier if they had been given the same information as the C-130 pilots and flown at a much higher altitude. It would have been much easier.

"I think if I had been planning it, I would have arranged for the helicopters and the 130s to fly in one formation, which is what we did on the Son Tay operation. The helicopter crews don't carry navigators, and they were on their own. They don't have the sophisticated equipment you find on the Combat Talon. Here, the Combat Talons were flying essentially the same route. And they have a couple of navigators on their crew.

"We asked, why didn't you marry the two together? Well, we were told, the speeds aren't compatible. Well, the speeds were compatible for the Son Tay operation. Here's an example where we don't capitalize on lessons that are learned. It's true a C-130 normally flies faster than an H-53. But the 130 can reduce its speed and make it possible for a 53 to fly with it, and we've done it. We flew formation with the C-130 to Son Tay."

Gary Weikel, the helicopter pilot who had a firsthand experience of the decline of Air Force special operations capability during the *Mayaguez* operation, is one of the most outspoken in his contention that the Iran rescue operation was basically flawed, relying on the Army's hopscotch method rather than a simpler in-and-out operation following Air Force doctrine.

"Why, in 1980," he asks, "did we have that ridiculous Desert One scenario, and why did we not go back to Son Tay? In Son Tay . . . they flew straight into North Vietnam, no landings, no intermediate operations, or anything else, and did the assault on the prison. And then they rolled back and came back on out. It was slick. All you had to have was intelligence on one place. You didn't have to have all these moving parts and all these ground operations. But then, ten years later, we forgot all about that. There were so many moving parts in that thing, so many tactical ground operations. . . . The damn thing almost had to be doomed to failure.

"Why didn't we do it the Son Tay way? Where we use refuelable helicopters, and we fly in there, kick their ass on one location, and come on back out? Instead of doing all these crazy, ponderous operations?"

Weikel's criticism should probably be seen more as a theoretical argument for doing things the Air Force special operations way than as a workable alternative to Operation Rice Bowl. The fact is that the Air Force at that time didn't have the aircraft or an organization that could have moved in on short notice to carry out the hostage-rescue effort. Manor puts the blame largely on the Air Force:

"In the decade of the seventies, we allowed our capability to dissipate. To zero. When this happened in Teheran, we didn't have the capability. We could have taken B-52s and bombed the hell out of Iran, but that wouldn't have solved the problem.

"What we needed was the capability to go in there and do something. The capability didn't exist. The only capability that had been developed and maintained was Delta. It had a tremendous capability, but there wasn't the means to get it where it was needed. The Air Force is largely at fault for not having maintained that capability."

The ignominious failure at Desert One got the attention of top Air Force officers. Within a short time, major efforts were underway to equip the Air Force to go back in again and succeed in the rescue of the hostages.

CHAPTER 23

Back to Teheran

Two months after the disaster at Desert One, the nighttime rest of the residents of Lubbock, Texas, was shattered by the roar of aircraft and the staccato chatter of automatic-weapons fire at Reese Air Force Base, a training base on the edge of the city.

It sounded like war, and alarmed citizens jammed switchboards at the police and sheriff's offices, demanding to know what was going on.

A quickly devised cover story blamed the uproar on an exercise by the Texas National Guard. In reality, it was a full-dress rehearsal for the first stage of an audacious new plan to go back into Iran to rescue the hostages, and Reese Air Force Base was a stand-in for Teheran's Meherabad International Airport.

No sooner had he returned to Washington than General Vaught was ordered to prepare for a second rescue attempt. Richard Secord, one of the original Farmgate pilots and, by then, a general and a top official in the Pentagon, was tabbed as his deputy for air. Since much of the operation would involve aircraft, Secord had a major role to play.

They quickly assembled a huge force: nearly four thousand troops and more than a hundred aircraft. Whereas the original rescue attempt had relied on eight helicopters, Secord rounded up ninety-five helicopters from both the Air Force and the Army.

Under the new plan, two Ranger battalions—more than fourteen hundred men—would be flown in to take over the Meharabad airport. They would be followed quickly by a stream of transport planes carrying additional troops and helicopters. As soon as the planes landed, the helicopters—already fueled and fully armed—would be rolled out and prepared for flight. The goal was to have them airborne, on the way to rescue the hostages, within two minutes.

Overhead there would be AC-130 gunships and Navy F-14 fighter planes to make sure no Iranian fighters interfered with the operation.

No wonder the people of Lubbock thought they were under attack!

Because of uncertainty about where some of the hostages might be kept, there were a dozen contingency plans for finding and moving the hostages to the airfield. Secord later described the operation as "the Carnegie Hall of raids." Unlike the earlier rescue attempt, which relied on stealth and assumed relatively small casualties among the Iranians, Secord foresaw the force blasting its way in and out of Teheran, inflicting heavy casualties as it did so.

Of the ninety-five helicopters conscripted for the operation, the bulk of them came from the Army. They ranged from the new Black Hawk, a powerfully armed troop carrier, to tiny scout helicopters with racks attached on the sides to carry several Delta Force soldiers.

The Air Force contribution to this force was modest in terms of numbers. Because of the neglect it had suffered in recent years, Air Force special operations had few helicopters in its arsenal. But the Air Force had one noteworthy piece of machinery that was just being added to its inventory. It was called Pave Low III. The Air Force uses the term *pave* for a variety of radar systems. Since the aircraft relies heavily on radar for its performance, it was called Pave. *Low* was added on because the plane spends most of its time within a relatively few feet of the ground. And the *III* indicated this was the third attempt to develop such a machine.

The Pave Low was the same basic aircraft as the Super Jolly

Green Giant rescue helicopter used in Vietnam. In fact, the "new" helicopters were the same machines that had flown in Vietnam, but thoroughly rebuilt, with a dazzling array of new technology that made them capable of going places and doing things that no other aircraft, new or old, could do.

In fact, this new machine, which was to become a mainstay of Air Force special operations in coming decades, was not originally designed for use by special operations, and when some of the air commandos saw it, they said they didn't want it.

Thirteen years before, in the spring of 1967, the Air Force began work on what eventually became Pave Low. The effort was spurred by the frustrating failure to rescue many of the airmen shot down over North Vietnam and Laos. The practice then was to send in the rescue helicopters as soon as a pilot went down. But when dark came, they had to return to their bases and wait until first light to resume the rescue attempt. Too often, the downed flier was no longer there in the morning.

The Air Force put the situation in bureaucratic language: "... there was an urgent requirement for an integrated system to enable a rescue vehicle to penetrate hostile territory at low level and perform search and rescue under conditions of total darkness and/or adverse weather in all geographical areas including mountainous terrain."

As the program developed, another requirement was added: "Additionally, the rescue vehicle must have a low-level capability to penetrate hostile territory against radar-directed weapons."

Colonel Frank Pehr, who later joined the program as the chief test pilot, recalls talking to fighter pilots, who were incredulous about requirements for the new helicopter.

"We went to the fighter community, and we said, 'You go in and attack targets, and we'll come rescue you if you get shot down.' And they said to us: 'You think *you* can survive in areas where we are attacking targets? *We* can't survive there.'

"And that's a good point. We are taking an aircraft that has very limited dynamics compared to a fighter, in terms of speed and velocities and maneuverability, and we're supposed to go into this high-threat area where they have been shot down—and survive.

Well, that's a big issue. I'm not claiming we can do that, but that was our charter.

"So we were very concerned about what it would take to survive there, not to attack anything, but just to survive there. What we would like to do is go there and come back without anybody knowing we had been there. This helicopter is not the best vehicle to do that. But a stealth airplane doesn't hover very well, and it is difficult to pick up a survivor. Right there, you have a compromise. You need hover capability to get in there and do the job. How are you going to do it without someone seeing you, knowing you are there, and shooting you down? It's hard."

As the Air Force struggled with the problem, the solutions remained elusive—and the cost kept going up. Two programs were canceled in the face of technical failures and rising costs. Finally, Ronald Terry, by then a colonel, heard of the Pave Low program. Terry and a small team of dedicated engineers and fliers had developed the gunship, from the early AC-47 to the AC-130 Spectre, with its sophisticated electronics and powerful 105mm cannon. Terry was looking for new challenges—and the rescue helicopter was just about the biggest technological challenge the Air Force had to offer.

Terry and his team took over the program and immediately began looking for devices already in service that could be adapted for use in the Pave Low instead of asking industry to invent new systems—"reinvent the wheel," as Terry put it. Even so, adapting existing equipment to the exacting demands of the rescue helicopter posed some very difficult problems.

A key requirement was the ability to fly very low in the dark. This meant some kind of terrain-following radar to look out ahead and warn the pilot before he ran into a mountain or a cliff. Texas Instruments had developed such a system, and it was used in the A-7 fighter-bomber.

But when the A-7 pilots were questioned, they admitted they didn't really trust the system to guide them in the dark, close to the ground. So the system would not only have to be adapted to the very different demands of operating in a helicopter, as opposed to a much faster jet fighter, but it would also have to be made so reliable that aircrews would trust it to do the job.

Texas Instruments officials agreed to try.

Then Pehr drew on his combat experience, flying Jolly Green Giants out of Da Nang, to add a new demand. Instead of the two-hundred-foot clearance the Texas Instruments experts were aiming for, he said he wanted to fly safely at one hundred feet. They told him, no way! They would never trust their radar to fly at one hundred feet.

Terry put the radar in a test helicopter, and Pehr took it out to see how low he could fly. They proved that they could operate safely, in the dark, at one hundred feet.

Special navigation systems were adapted for use in the Pave Low. They were so accurate that it was possible for a pilot to find a downed flier and hover overhead while a cable was lowered to pick him up—all without the pilot ever being able to see the ground.

Subsequent tests went so well that the go-ahead was given to modify eight of the fifty-some HH-53 helicopters in the Air Force inventory into the new Pave Low configuration. To hold down costs, the job was given to the naval air rework facility at Pensacola.

The first production model was rolled out on 13 March 1979—thirteen years after the need for such an aircraft was first officially recognized.

Ironically, by that time serious questions were being raised about whether the Air Force really needed such a super flying machine.

"We had a system that was so good I felt it was too good for the rescue mission and would not last in rescue," Pehr explains. "The rescue mission is a humanitarian and a morale mission. We've done studies, and we've determined that it's cheaper to train new pilots than it is to save pilots. Rescue doesn't get funds for its mission. You have to try to justify it from a morale standpoint or a humanitarian standpoint. But it is not necessarily going to win wars.

"This aircraft was developed to satisfy a combat rescue mission which at that point in time did not exist. But it was so good it had a number of applications that should be exploited. One of those was a tremendous special operations role. It was something they could use. But they didn't seem to be very interested."

That all began to change in a dramatic way immediately after Desert One. At that time, there were the eight Pave Low helicopters that had been modified, plus another one that had also been modified with a little money left over from the work on the original eight. Not all the helicopters were fully fitted out with all their new equipment. The Pave Lows were all based at Kirtland Air Force Base in Albuquerque, New Mexico, along with the first class of experienced pilots learning to fly the new plane.

Abruptly, the unit was ordered to report to Hurlburt Field in Florida, the longtime headquarters for the air commandos, as soon as possible, with helicopters, maintenance people, and the pilots in training. The order came on a Friday. On Sunday, they flew to Hurlburt.

At that time, Hurlburt was a kind of sleepy backwater. The wing commander was a maintenance man without combat experience, and Secord was underwhelmed, to say the least, by the whole operation. Suddenly, things changed. The frantic pace of operations reminded old-timers of the days in the early 1960s when Jungle Jim was gearing up.

The pilots who had been in training soon found themselves checked out and upgraded to instructors. Pilots found themselves flying lower in the dark than they normally dared fly in the daytime.

This was all part of something with the code name of Honey Badger. Although that was the overall designation for the huge rescue operation then in preparation, the helicopter crews still think of Honey Badger as their own special operation. In fact, they didn't know what all the excitement was about or even who was in charge. This, of course, was all part of the secrecy that surrounded the whole renewed rescue effort.

One of the unusual demands on the Air Force pilots was that they learn to fly their planes in formation. While Army helicopters often fly in large formations, this was not a skill the Air Force felt a need for. The Air Force pilots were happiest when they were as far as possible from any other object, especially another flying object with big rotors twirling around.

The pilots were told they not only had to fly formation, but they had to do it at night. To make it a little easier at night, they were issued the first generation of night-vision goggles, known by the initials *NVG*. They were big cumbersome contraptions, weighing seven or eight pounds, and designed for a tank driver, not an aircraft pilot.

John F. "Jack" Kelly vividly recalls one of the first times he used the night-vision goggles. When he arrived at Hurlburt, he was a second lieutenant, but he also wore command pilot wings. He had been an Army warrant officer, with many hours of flight time, and had recently switched over to the Air Force and been commissioned. Flying formation was, for him, nothing new. But doing it at night was still a challenge.

"We were in formation," he says, "heading southeast down over the panhandle of Florida and then across the Gulf of Mexico to Tampa. I was copilot to a fairly high-time instructor pilot. We were number-two aircraft in a formation of seven or eight helicopters.

"It was just sunset when we left. The sun went down, and we started flying across the gulf. As it transitioned from sunset to dusk to night—I think I had one previous mission using NVG—I told the instructor I would put on the NVG and pilot the aircraft.

"I turned my head from the aircraft I was following, and, of course, with the NVG, I couldn't see anything in the cockpit. When I turned back to look outside, all that was out there was lights. That's all you could see with the NVG. They were poor quality in those days.

"I picked up these lights and started flying on them. I see the formation's turning to the right. I'm starting to descend and turning to the right, trying to pick out the lead aircraft. The guys behind me are doing the same thing, following me around. Finally, I asked my flight engineer, 'What's my altitude?' He said, 'About a hundred feet.'

"At that time, I realized I was flying formation off a shrimp boat. I had the whole rest of the formation behind me trying to join up on the shrimp boat. By that time, the lead aircraft was about five miles down the road. Those are the kinds of things we learned, experimenting with NVGs."

The intensive Honey Badger training continued through the fall until, with the election of Ronald Reagan as president and the likelihood of the release of the hostages (they were actually released moments after he was sworn in), preparations for the rescue effort were called off.

Miraculously, the crews survived their demanding training and dramatically realistic practice sessions without the loss of a single aircraft or crew member. Ironically, on their return to their base after a final rehearsal, one plane became unbalanced because of a faulty fuel-transfer system, went into an uncontrollable spiral, and crashed.

While the Honey Badger training was in progress, the Air Force set in motion another even more audacious plan for a possible rescue of the hostages.

Instead of a massive operation involving thousands of troops and scores of airplanes, this plan called for a single C-130 to land in the soccer stadium adjoining the United States Embassy in Teheran to deliver a rescue force and then fly away with the hostages and the rescuers—a total of more than a hundred people.

As anyone familiar with airplanes would quickly realize, landing a four-engine transport plane in a soccer stadium—which is about the same size as an American football stadium—and then taking off again fully loaded is contrary to the laws of physics.

Ron Terry, who had done the impossible with the gunships and again with the Pave Low helicopter, was called in to do the impossible again.

The project was given the code name of Credible Sport.

Lockheed Aircraft, which manufactures the C-130, put its most experienced people on the job, working around the clock, seven days a week, to modify several planes at its plant in Marietta, Georgia. The flaps on the wings were taken apart and reworked so the plane could make its final approach into the stadium at eighty knots, rather than its normal landing speed of more than one hundred knots. A special refueling rig was attached to the top of the plane.

Colonel Ron Jones, who was still with the 7th Special Operations Squadron in Europe, was the leader of one of three crews brought in from Europe, Hurlburt, and the Far East to train to fly the specially equipped plane.

"It was truly an amazing thing to see," he says.

The plane was fitted out with eight motors from a rocket system, known as ASROC, used by the Navy to fire torpedoes at distant targets. They provided eighty thousand pounds of decelerating force to stop the plane. To cushion the landing, the plane was also fitted with eight Shrike rocket motors, which were fired straight down just before the plane touched the ground.

For takeoff, rocket motors provided 180,000 pounds of thrust for the first four seconds and 20,000 pounds of thrust for another twenty seconds.

In a test in October 1980, the plane set a record for short-takeoff-and-landing aircraft. Within ten feet of the point where the brake was released, the nosewheel was six feet off the ground. The entire plane was airborne within 150 feet, and, by the time it had gone the length of a soccer field, it was 30 feet in the air and flying at 115 knots. A small rocket motor in the tail pushed the tail up to help the pilot level off from the steep climb out of the stadium.

The plan was for the plane to dive in steeply, clearing the stadium wall by eight feet, land, taxi to the other end of the stadium, turn around, and prepare for takeoff. With the power of its rocket motors, there was no reason to worry which way the wind was blowing.

Jones asked what would happen if the nose gear had been damaged on landing.

"The engineer says, 'Don't worry. When you hit that switch, it doesn't make any difference. You're going out of there.' You just pointed it wherever you wanted to go and hit the button. Once you cooked those things off, you were going where you pointed."

Inside, the plane was braced with a massive steel box frame to absorb the violence of the landing and takeoff. Special aluminum seats were designed so the hostages could be strapped in quickly, braced for the takeoff.

The first prototype was completed and ready for testing in six weeks, and the test program was wrapped up in another three weeks.

A final full-scale test of the system ended with a disappointing accident. The test plane had taken off from one of the auxiliary fields at Eglin Air Force Base, gone through its paces, and returned for a landing. The flight engineer, sitting between the pilots, had the job of firing the rocket motors to stop the plane after it had landed. Unaccountably, he pushed the button while the plane was still about fifteen feet in the air. It stopped right where it was and smacked down onto the runway, breaking off a wing. Fortunately, a fire engine was standing almost at the scene of the accident. The aircraft crew escaped without serious injury, and the plane was spared further damage from fire.

Thought of using the Credible Sport system in an actual rescue was dropped at about the same time those involved in Honey Badger stopped their preparations.

Further tests on the plane were conducted in the following months, but it was never used in an actual operation. This was in contrast to the Pave Low helicopter system. By the time the Honey Badger exercises were completed, the Air Force had this new weapon in its arsenal along with crews highly trained to get the most out of the new machine. It was the beginning of yet another period of renewal and the beginning of the modern era in Air Force special operations.

Chapter 24
Not Quite Ready

When the United States decided to invade the tiny Caribbean island of Grenada in October 1983, the first thing that was needed was a "pair of eyes" on the ground to check out the condition of the Point Salines airfield.

Was the airfield, which was under construction, suitable for landing large troop-carrying aircraft?

Was the field defended? If so, how many guns did the defenders have and where were they located?

The obvious choice to provide that "pair of eyes" was John Carney, the same combat controller who had scoped out the desert landing area for the hostage rescue effort three years earlier.

To Carney, this sounded like a piece of cake. No landing in the desert in the dark; no scooting around on a motorcycle; no worry about getting back out again.

The United States was still at peace with Grenada, even though the prime minister had been killed in a leftist coup and there were grave concerns for the safety of a group of American medical students studying on the island.

As he pictured it, Carney would take a tourist flight to the island, slip into penny loafers and a pineapple shirt, perhaps sip a piña colada, and casually take a look at the airport. A brief telephone conversation would suffice to pass on his assessment. Then he would catch the next flight home.

Somehow, what should have been a simple one-man reconnaissance foray turned into a big and, eventually, disastrous military operation—one that failed in the end to get any close-up look at the situation at the airport.

Carney was ordered to report aboard a Navy vessel and then proceed with a group of SEALs in a small boat to the island, where they would creep ashore to report on whether planes could land at the airport or whether troops would have to be parachuted in.

He and a couple of other combat controllers flew to a nearby island, took a taxi to the dock, and boarded a Navy vessel, which then took up station off the Grenada coast. Even this looked to Carney like a two-man job, but that was not the way events unfolded.

To help the combat controllers get ashore, the Navy sent two planeloads of SEALs from SEAL Team Six. The special antiterrorist unit was created after the failed hostage rescue effort had drawn attention to the possibility that, with international terrorism on the increase, rescue operations might be required in unpredictable parts of the world on short notice.

The SEALs had expected to parachute into calm seas in the daytime, climb into boats that had been dropped with them, and join up with Carney on the ship. The air drop was delayed, and the weather report was wrong: the SEALs were dropped at night into wind-whipped waves topped by whitecaps. Four of the SEALs disappeared into the dark waters and were never found.

"I've jumped in the water at night, probably over a hundred times," Carney says. "It's probably one of the most difficult tasks I've ever done. First of all, you have the difficulty of finding the boat that dropped in with you. If the sea state's high enough, you can't see a guy swimming four yards from you.

"Then, it's pitch black. You get to the boat, and it's not easy to navigate out there, to know where you're going. The recovery of the people is the most difficult. They don't jump in a neat little package. They get dispersed a hundred yards apart, probably.

"It was pathetic. They're firing weapons. I did see one pin flare.

We're trying to pick these people up. The current's washing some of them away. It was pathetic, absolutely pathetic. It takes a herculean effort to stay afloat out there. I was absolutely shocked when I saw this thing coming down."

Carney and the surviving SEALs made two unsuccessful attempts to reach the island. Even though he never made it ashore, he was able to see enough through binoculars to tell that at least a small airport-seizure team of Army Rangers would have to parachute in to try to clear the runways and provide enough protection for subsequent planes to land. He even heard broadcasts over the island radio station urging people to hurry to the airport to repel the invaders.

By this time, five MC-130 Combat Talons carrying the Rangers were already airborne. Lieutenant Colonel James L. "Jim" Hobson, Jr., commander of the 8th Special Operations Squadron, was at the controls of one of the Talons. He was supposed to be the third plane in line, coming in to land thirty minutes after the first two planes had dropped the initial runway-seizure team.

"We were told the cloud cover would be five thousand feet broken, with five miles visibility," Hobson recalls. "We were holding about seventy-five miles west of the island, stacked a thousand feet apart. There was lightning, all kinds of shit. We were using night-vision goggles to maintain separation from each other. Every time there was a bolt of lightning, you couldn't see shit for five minutes."

While the big four-engine planes circled, praying there would be no midair collision, they received word that all the Rangers would be parachuted. The troops in the back of Hobson's plane had expected to step out of the plane onto the runway, so they were not wearing their parachutes. Hurriedly, they donned their jump gear and prepared for the jump.

As the first Combat Talon approached the airfield, its inertial navigation system malfunctioned. The aircrews had been warned, "Whatever you do, don't drop the Rangers in the water." Without his navigation system working, the pilot of the lead plane decided to pull off. Hobson received radioed orders to fly to the island as quickly as possible and drop his Rangers.

In the hurried preparations for the invasion of the island, the Air Force crews and the Army commanders received separate, and quite different, intelligence briefings. The soldiers were told to expect significant resistance. The aircrews were told there were only two 23mm guns on the island, and neither was at the airport. It sounded almost like a routine training drop.

Because of the briefing they had received, the Rangers said they wanted to jump from five hundred feet altitude. That would give them only about ten seconds of "hang time" between the moment their chutes opened and the time they hit the ground.

"About a mile off the end of the runway, a searchlight came on and shined on the airplane," Hobson says. "I'll never forget this: the copilot looked at me and he said, 'This ain't going to be a surprise!' Right over the end of the runway, we called, 'Green light' [indicating the troops should begin jumping]."

The loadmaster, watching out the cargo door, said, "They're firing rockets at us!" Every time he keyed his mike, the other members of the crew could hear the weapons firing over the intercom. Actually, what looked like rockets to the excited loadmaster were 23mm tracer shells—a familiar sight to an earlier generation of air commandos, flying over the Ho Chi Minh Trail.

Even in the brief time the Rangers were suspended in their chutes, they could hear bullets whizzing through the risers that connected them to the canopies overhead. Remarkably, none of them was hit.

As soon as the last chutist cleared the door, Hobson broke right and dove toward the water. The guns turned to zero in on the plane, following him down the runway, inflicting several hits.

"I radioed back and said, 'Hey, you better get a gunship in here. There's a lot of resistance down there.' It doesn't make sense to lose an airplane with all those guys in the back as long as you can get a gunship in here," Hobson says.

Under the rules of engagement, the Americans were not supposed to fire unless they had been fired upon first.

"But once they unloaded on me and the guy behind me, it was open warfare," Hobson says. "The gunship came in and took care of it."

For the crew of the AC-130 Spectre gunship, it wasn't quite that simple. As engineer aboard the plane, CMSgt. Mike Hozenbackez was sitting between and just behind the pilots, looking out the windscreen as they approached the airfield about dawn. During the night, the defenders on the ground had heard the plane but could not pinpoint it with their searchlights. As soon as daylight broke, they could see where to shoot.

"We were told there was only one triple-A site," Hozenbackez says. "When we got there, we counted six. The tracers were coming past the windscreen. We wondered why we didn't get hit. I could see the triple A coming up on both sides of the windscreen. It was 23mm, orange and red tracers, coming up at us. When you see it come past the windscreen, you know it's close, but we didn't get hit."

The job of the gunship crew was to suppress all the antiaircraft fire so the Rangers could get in safely. The last gun refused to be silenced. The gunship poured both 20mm and 40mm shells in his direction, but he kept shooting right back.

"We kept raining down on him, and he kept raining back up at us. I wondered, Are we going to shut this guy down or not?" Hozenbackez says.

The crew saw another AC-130 gunship orbiting nearby and called for help. But the other crew said they didn't want to get in the same orbit with another gunship.

"When we all landed at Barbados, those other guys came over," Hozenbackez says. "We said, 'How come you guys didn't come give us a hand?' One of them said, 'Man, you should have seen that from where we were. Fire was going down, fire was coming up. Like two guys dueling it out.'"

As soon as all the guns appeared to have been put out of business, the Combat Talons began landing. But some of the enemy gunners were just playing possum. With the big transport planes on the ground and vulnerable, they opened up again.

"One of the Talons got pinned on the runway, and a 14mm started firing at him, shooting across the runway," Hozenbackez says. "We told him to take off. We marked along the runway as he took off. We gave him an armed escort right down the runway."

After the Rangers landed, the gunships continued to provide fire support for them.

One group of Rangers radioed that they were pinned down, hiding under a cement truck, taking fire from a group of Cubans barricaded in a nearby house. They asked for help.

The gunship crew fired at the house with their 105mm cannon, but the shells burst as soon as they hit the house rather than penetrating. They then set the shells on delay so they penetrated the house and went off in the basement. That quickly ended the threat to the Rangers.

At another point, the gunship crew knew they were taking fire, but they couldn't see where it was coming from. Finally, the right scanner spotted the gun. The pilot called him to the cockpit to point it out. Where he pointed was a house, and the pilot was reluctant to fire.

"Then the guy made one mistake," Hozenbackez says. "He fired while we were looking at him. We rolled in there and took that out. We Winchestered [fired off] all our bullets."

By the time the crew landed in Barbados to pick up another load of bullets, they had been in the air for thirty-one hours.

While Hozenbackez and his crew members were clearing out opposition at Salines, other gunships were busy protecting a small group of SEALs who had been delivered by helicopter to the governor's mansion on a hill overlooking the capital city of Saint George's. Their job was to escort the governor-general, Sir Paul Scoon, and his family and aides to an airfield in the city below. But they found themselves cut off and outgunned by Grenadan forces who circled the mansion with armored personnel carriers.

The gunships fired within a few feet of the SEALs guarding the perimeter of the compound, knocking out the personnel carriers with pinpoint fire and repelling at least one determined infantry charge against the defenders.

For the air commandos and for the military's special operations community generally, Grenada was a test under fire of the lessons learned since Desert One three years before. Many of the forces performed as expected. The Air Force gunships probably saved the day at both Salines and the governor-general's mansion. Hobson won the Air Force's Mackay Trophy for the most meritorious flight of 1983.

But it was also clear that there were many lessons yet to be learned. The nation's special operations forces were, to put it charitably, not quite ready.

Intelligence information was incomplete and contradictory, if not totally lacking, as demonstrated by the conflicting information about the defenses at Salines provided to the Rangers and the Air Force crews.

Communications among Army, Air Force, Navy, and Marine units were sometimes impossible. Even members of the same services had difficulty talking to one another.

In Washington, the invasion was declared a victory. In a sense, it was. On very short notice, the military had gathered a formidable force to descend on Grenada. Within days, the defenses had been neutralized and the endangered medical students had been removed to safety.

But many of those who took part in the operation were deeply disturbed.

Shortly after the operation, John Carney, then a lieutenant colonel, retired from the Air Force.

"I was disturbed just how it got so screwed up and messed up," Carney says. "I just didn't like identifying with it. Here we've got all this money put into this, and things are starting to come along, and we pull off what was really stupid. It was just dumb. It was insidious. It just bothered me. I never could live with it. I said, 'Let's get the hell out of the community.'"

To those involved and to key members of Congress, the Grenada operation demonstrated just how far the military's special operations community had to go, both in terms of their capabilities and especially in terms of being able to work effectively together.

For the air commandos, this meant the rest of the decade of the 1980s would be a difficult, contentious, and eventually rewarding experience.

Within sixty days of Carney's retirement, a general with whom he had worked closely in the past had talked him into coming back on active duty. In the next few years, the small cadre of combat controllers Carney had at the time of the Iranian hostage rescue attempt was expanded into three special tactics squadrons based in the United States, Germany, Great Britain, and Japan. In the process, one of the most serious deficiencies of the special tactics teams was corrected.

The combat controllers thought of their basic job as going in with the Rangers on an airfield-seizure operation, making sure that the runways and taxiways were clear, controlling the flow of aircraft bringing in additional troops, and marshaling the planes on the ground. All this would be done in the dark and possibly under fire.

But what about those who were injured or wounded in the original drop or subsequent firefights?

Even before Grenada, Carney had been mulling that question in his mind.

"It was apparent to me we didn't have a dedicated rescue force," he says. "We, the controllers, didn't have the capability to be fixing broken legs on the runway. That's not our job. We had to clear the runway and get this airflow going in there."

The Air Force Rescue Service had trained a number of men to give medical treatment to an Air Force crewman shot down behind enemy lines, help him aboard a rescue helicopter, and stabilize him on the flight back to a friendly base. But, as part of one of the military's frequent reorganizations, plans to purchase newer helicopters to carry the rescue forces were canceled in favor of buying more fighter aircraft. The Air Force ended up with eighty-six pararescuemen—known as PJs—with only antiquated helicopters to take them to the war.

Carney blended them with his combat controllers into the new special tactics teams and then trained them all to do one another's jobs—as well as to help out other units in the field.

"Some of the senior NCOs and I realized we had to be trained to fill in wherever we had to," Carney says. "You can't be a burden to these guys you're going in with. Charlie Beckwith always told us, 'We're not going to drag your knuckles through the streets.'

What he meant was, you'd better be able to help if we ever need it. I started sending the guys to some of these esoteric weapons schools, field trade–type schools."

They learned to swim like a SEAL, jump like a paratrooper, fight like a Ranger. Plus, they were good communicators and aircraft controllers.

"The whole idea was that we would never be a burden to any force that was sent anywhere in the world to do a job," Carney says.

"A classic example: We were on an exercise. They had a Brit who was the commander. It was an airfield seizure out West. They were clearing buildings. He ran out of people to clear buildings. He walked up to one of the special tactics guys, and he said, 'Mate, I want you to take your men over there and clear that building.' My guy says, 'We're not Army. We're Air Force people. We know how to do that, but that's not our job.' But this young guy, he takes his guys, and they go clear the building."

While Carney was busy building the special tactics teams into a highly trained combat controller–rescue force, the whole Air Force special operations capability seemed to some of those involved in danger of disappearing.

In the mid-1980s, the chief of staff of the Army and the chief of staff of the Air Force agreed to transfer the Air Force's helicopters to the Army. If that happened, how long would it be before the Army also took over the tankers needed to refuel the helicopters, the Combat Talons needed to carry the Army Rangers, the gunships needed to provide firepower—in effect, all of Air Force special operations?

At the time, Gary Weikel had recently been assigned to the air staff at the Pentagon after flying the Pave Low. He decided to do something to prevent what seemed to him a disastrous abandonment of special operations by the Air Force brass. He thus inserted himself at the center of a battle that could have been just as dangerous to his career as his role, as a young helicopter pilot, in the *Mayaguez* affair had been to his life.

"The Air Force generals don't like helicopters in general because the Air Force fighter-pilot leadership believes the service's destiny lies in higher, faster, and further, not the dirty ground wars in Southeast Asia and the stuff that special operations gets involved in," Weikel says.

"They view that whole Vietnam era as a tremendous delay in the destiny of the Air Force. They did not like to have to buy all those goddamn helicopters and those AC-130 gunships, and AC-47s and AC-119s and A-1 Skyraiders that were piston engined. In their view, that delayed introduction of newer generations of fighters, diverted their resources. They don't like to even think about wars like that, and they do not like special operations. To a certain extent, they think it was the special operations community that got us embroiled in Southeast Asia in the first place."

Weikel "went over the hill" and asked a friend in the office of the secretary of defense for advice. The friend gave him the name of a staffer on Capitol Hill who had been an Army Special Forces trooper and who might be able to do something to block the plans of the Army and Air Force chiefs. But he warned Weikel, "You'd be taking your career in your hands to do something like that. If the Air Force found out about you doing this outside their direction, you'd be toast."

Weikel decided to do it anyway. He and the staffer hit it off. Together, they worked to draft legislation that would protect Air Force special operations. Meanwhile, civilian officials in the Pentagon also set up roadblocks to the plans of the top generals in the Air Force and Army.

Their resistance was well timed. Key members of Congress were deeply disturbed by what they had heard in classified briefings about the Grenada operation and were searching for ways to strengthen the nation's ability to deal with hostage taking, hijacking, and other small-scale emergencies in various parts of the world.

The result was legislation creating the United States Special Operations Command, a separate military organization, combining Army, Air Force, and Navy commando forces, with its own budget and headed by a four-star officer. It began operations in April 1987. Air Force special operations was upgraded, becoming the Twenty-third Air Force—but it still reported to the Military Airlift Command as well as to the new joint command. It was not until 1990 that the separate Air Force Special Operations Command was created.

The setup was not exactly what Weikel and his co-conspirators had envisioned, but it was much better, in their view, than the disastrous direction in which things had been headed.

With the reorganization came money for a new Combat Talon transport plane and a new gunship. Of special interest to Weikel, it also authorized the conversion of all the Air Force's HH-53 helicopters to the Pave Low configuration.

As the legislation was moving toward final approval, Weikel, somehow having survived his part in the insurrection, was assigned to command the 20th Special Operations Squadron at Hurlburt, getting the Pave Low force up to speed for the next call to action, wherever that might be. And Hobson was being groomed to become commander of Air Force Special Operations, the first true air commando to hold that post.

CHAPTER 25

Panama—Getting It Together

When Major Clay McCutchan set off for Panama on 17 December 1989, it was his fortieth birthday and he had the bittersweet feelings of anyone passing life's halfway milestone. But he was happy nevertheless, looking forward to a welcome break from the cool winter weather in his home in Florida's northwest panhandle. What he didn't realize was that, before the week was over, his country would be at war, a war from which he would emerge court-martialed and disgraced—or a hero.

McCutchan is the pilot of an AC-130 gunship in the Air Force reserves. A bachelor, he had volunteered at the last moment for a training assignment in Panama, relieving the crew of one of the active-duty gunships assigned there over the holidays.

Although there had been rumblings of trouble between the United States and Manuel Noriega, the Panamanian strongman, war was far from McCutchan's thoughts as he approached Howard Air Force Base, the big United States base in the Canal Zone. He considered himself a very ordinary pilot and reasoned that a more skilled flier would have been sent in his place if war were imminent. He looked forward to a pleasant couple of weeks of nighttime training flights, with swimming and tennis filling his days.

What he did not know was that a highly successful full-scale re-hearsal for the invasion of Panama—secretly developed under the code name of Blue Spoon—had been held at Hurlburt Field, a few miles from his home, only a couple of days earlier—on 14 to 16 December. And then President Bush had given his approval for the operation, to be known publicly as Just Cause.

As soon as he arrived at Howard, McCutchan noted the steady stream of aircraft descending on the airfield and sensed that something was up. In recent days, a Marine had been killed and a Navy lieutenant and his wife had been held and mistreated by Noriega's men.

On Monday, McCutchan and his crew were let in on the secret plans for the invasion. Seven AC-130s from the active-duty Air Force would fly in from Hurlburt to knock out key defensive po-sitions. But at the moment, the two reserve planes were the only AC-130s in Panama. If the conflict occurred ahead of schedule, the reserve crews would lead the way. That night, they flew over the Commendancia, the nerve center of any opposition to the American operation, and photographed it in case they were called on to attack.

When they returned to Howard about midnight, two active-duty gunships had arrived from the States. Five more were sched-uled to arrive shortly. The invasion was scheduled for the night of 19–20 December—Tuesday night into Wednesday morning.

Although McCutchan later referred to Operation Just Cause as the "all-time great gunship war, a gunship war from beginning to end," it was really a broader affair, drawing on the full range of Air Force special operations: Combat Talons dropped Rangers to capture airfields; an Air Force special tactics team accompanied Navy SEALs in the attack on another airfield; Pave Low and Pave Hawk helicopters backed up the forces on the ground; nine spe-cial operations tankers circled endlessly, keeping other planes in the air.

The task of the special operations forces was to spearhead an invasion whose goal was to oust Noriega from his position, return him to the United States for trial on drug charges, and install a new government.

The operation would be the first large-scale test of how well the Air Force had learned the lessons of Desert One and Grenada.

Unlike Grenada, where the entire operation had been carried out on the spur of the moment, planning for the Blue Spoon invasion had been lengthy, and there had been time for intense training and elaborate rehearsals. On training assignments in the Canal Zone, aircrews had had the opportunity to fly over, drive by, and walk around their targets, studying them at their leisure.

Active-duty gunship crews had, for months, practiced firing at mock-ups of the targets, such as the Commendancia, that they would hit in the opening moments of the invasion, although the crews considered them routine training exercises and doubted they would ever be called on actually to attack those targets.

With the arrival of the active-duty gunships, the two reserve crews were shifted into a backup position. McCutchan's assignment was to stand by to protect Howard if it came under attack. One of the fears of those planning the operation was that a mortar attack, if not a full-scale assault, on Howard could shut down the base or so disrupt operations that aircraft involved in the invasion would not have a safe place to land.

Sitting in his plane, strapped in and ready to go on a moment's notice, McCutchan's big worry was not the Panamanians but all the American aircraft milling about in the dark. Howard was completely blacked out, and so were the planes. Crew members relied on their night-vision goggles to help avoid running into one another. It was the first time anyone had ever conducted a major military operation in total blackout conditions. McCutchan was especially sensitive to the possibility of a taxiing accident. Several months before, he had run over a fire extinguisher and had been demoted from aircraft commander to copilot. Only after a hurried check ride had he been reinstated as an aircraft commander in time for the Panama assignment.

Surprisingly, Howard did not come under the kind of attack that had been feared. McCutchan and his crew were ordered into the air to respond to calls for help from troops on the ground. As they took off, they could see tracer bullets from machine guns fired by the Panamanian defense force arcing clear across the city.

"There was a terrific firefight at a police station just north of Howard," McCutchan says. "We could see the enemy and the Marines, but we couldn't join in the fight because we couldn't establish radio contact. The frequencies weren't correct."

In an attempt to make up for the lack of communication during the operation in Grenada, the military had burdened the aircrews with more radios and separate frequencies than they knew what to do with. One pilot described the documentation for the multitude of radio frequencies as looking like "the Bronx phone book." In the AC-130s, with their large crews, three men shared the task of monitoring the radios. In the helicopters, with their smaller crews, the copilot became totally occupied with trying to maintain communications, leaving all the flying to the pilot.

For most of the night, McCutchan's crew flew in circles and waited for assignments while watching tensely for the sight of other planes in the dark—especially other gunships shooting down. Flying at forty-five hundred feet, they were the lowest gunship.

"This meant everything above us was shooting down, and everything below us was shooting up," McCutchan says.

They finally received an assignment to aid a group of civilians pinned down by a sniper. They quickly silenced the sniper with four rounds from their most accurate gun, the 40mm weapon.

"The whole night was very frustrating," McCutchan says. "We didn't really get to shoot that much. We only put four rounds down."

Finally, when he had only about an hour's worth of gas left, McCutchan was directed to the Fort Amador causeway. Looking down, the crew could see a big firefight in progress. They could even tell the good guys from the bad guys. But they couldn't establish radio communications to get permission to fire in support of the Americans.

"It was just so frustrating I couldn't believe it," McCutchan says.

To compound the situation, the crew of McCutchan's plane suddenly became aware there was another gunship above them, shooting down through their orbit. They got out of there in a hurry.

As they turned away, they saw several armored cars. This time, they established radio contact and were given permission—in fact they were ordered—to fire on the armored cars. McCutchan gripped the trigger, eager to shoot.

"That's when my sensor operator and fire-control officer saw about thirty or forty people show up around these armored cars," McCutchan says.

Looking through their infrared and television sensors, the experts on McCutchan's crew became convinced the men they saw around the armored cars were friendly troops. But the orders from the ground were explicit: "They're enemy, and you're cleared to kill 'em."

The crew decided to use their 20mm guns on the troops and hit the armored cars with their 40mm. But the fire-control officer continued to insist he was seeing friendly troops.

"I'm leaning forward, and I wanted to get the job done, and I wanted to shoot so bad I could taste it," McCutchan says.

"The FAC is shouting at us to shoot. We go back to the command post and they're telling us: 'You are ordered to shoot. Confirmed enemy.'

"I would have shot. But based on what my fire-control officer was telling me, I had to trust him. And I did. So I didn't shoot. I was convinced I was going to get court-martialed because we disobeyed a direct order to fire."

The plane had been in the air for five and a half hours. McCutchan figured it was time to get on the ground before someone made a serious mistake. As he parked the plane, he looked out and saw his squadron commander waiting on the apron.

"He said, 'Why didn't you shoot?' We said, 'We thought they were friendlies, we weren't sure.' He said, 'Well, you're either in a lot of trouble or you're a hero.'

The exhausted crew members tumbled into bed. Sometime after noon the next day, the squadron commander awakened them. "You guys are heroes," he said. "They were friendlies."

Army Green Berets had stopped and captured the personnel carriers, and it was American troops gathering around the vehicles that the sensor operators in the gunship saw.

Members of the crew all received medals. McCutchan and

three other officers were awarded the Distinguished Flying Cross—for having the guts not to shoot.

How difficult it is to tell friend from foe, even with the sophisticated equipment carried by the AC-130 gunships, was demonstrated in another incident that same night.

One of the active-duty gunships backing up troops at the Commendancia was told of the approach of an enemy armored personnel carrier in the dark. The crew of the gunship spotted the vehicle with both television and infrared sensors and fired.

Several days later, the commander of the gunship unit visited the Commendancia to examine the damage done by his men. An infantry officer mentioned damage to one of his vehicles.

It was an American personnel carrier that had been hit by the gunship. There were no deaths, but there were several injuries from this "friendly fire" incident.

General George A. Gray III, who was then a colonel commanding the 1st Special Operations Wing, says American troops and vehicles were supposed to be marked with special "gun tape" visible to the gunship crews. But in this case, trying to penetrate the smoke of the battle down below, the crew was switching back and forth between their television and infrared sensors. The special marking tape can be seen on the TV screen but not on the IR display.

Gray later looked at the recorded images of what the crew members were seeing. "Whenever I see the trigger getting ready to be pulled, there's no gun tape," he says.

The incident was not discovered until several days after it occurred and was not made public until six months later. When the official records of the incident were requested under the Freedom of Information Act, the Air Force replied that all the records, except for a small collection of newspaper clippings, had been destroyed.

One other incident that night spoiled an almost perfect record for the gunships as they rode shotgun for the troops down below. In several cases, Panamanian troops surrendered, even though they outnumbered the Americans, when they were told a gunship was overhead.

One of the gunships was assigned to circle overhead as Navy

SEALs attacked the Paitilla airfield to prevent Noriega from escaping in a jet parked there. Two special tactics combat controllers went with the SEALs, landing at the foot of the Paitilla runway in rubber boats. The Air Force men stayed with the command unit while one of the SEAL platoons advanced up the field toward the hangar where the jet was kept.

Suddenly, the SEALs came under murderous fire from a small group of Panamanians hiding in the darkened hangar. Four SEALs fell mortally wounded, and nine others were injured.

The special tactics controllers called for help from the gunship but could not make contact. They could hear the Spectre continuing to circle frustratingly overhead during the brief firefight. Whether the gunship could have helped in any event is doubtful. By the time the gunship could have fired, the SEAL platoons had already been badly mauled. And, by that time, the SEALs were so close to the hangar that the gunship could not have fired without risking hitting them as well as the Panamanians.

Looking back on the incident later, Gary Weikel, commander of the 20th Special Operations Squadron, a Pave Low helicopter unit from Hurlburt, was frustrated that he had not been able to have one of his Pave Lows accompany the SEALs on their mission.

With their ability to see in the dark, the crew of a Pave Low would have been a perfect escort for the SEALs, peering ahead and telling them exactly what kind of resistance they could expect to encounter as they approached the hangar. And if they saw trouble ahead, they could have provided a withering curtain of support with their guns.

But Weikel was short of helicopters to carry out all the assignments his unit had that night. He blames the shortage on interservice rivalry.

Months before the actual invasion, Weikel foresaw that his unit might be called upon to go into action in Panama. He put special emphasis on training down there.

"I wanted to lull them into complacency," he says. "It was like a page out of the Egyptian attack on Israel in the 1973 war. The Egyptians, for interminable days and weeks, practiced Suez Canal crossing exercises, bridging exercises. The Israelis got desensitized to it and didn't pay any attention to it. And one day, they came. That's kind of what I was doing, grabbing a little bit of the element of surprise to ourselves, to have this aircraft appear in some numbers down there, particularly since it's such a unique airplane, with the blisters and the bubbles and the guns all over."

While stepping up training in the Canal Zone, Weikel tried to find out what kind of military operation was planned.

"For six months, I had been trying to query the system to find out what other special operations forces were down there so I could provide support to them," Weikel says. "I was rebuffed at every turn. I was told I was going to take only five Pave Lows down there, even though I had twelve available at Hurlburt that were ready to go.

"I was given a lot of cockamamy excuses. It turned out, if we had known SEAL Team Four was going to be down there, I could have brought down a couple more Pave Lows to provide support for them. When they got in trouble, they could have had immediate fire support and extraction capability. As it turned out, I broke one of the five Pave Lows loose and sent him over with an Air Force MH-60 Pave Hawk to support the SEALs, to reinforce Team Four, and to evacuate the casualties and the wounded.

"I detailed a Pave Low to provide almost full-time fire support, sniper suppression, all during the next few days. Every time the Pave Low would go away, the SEALs would catch fire. Every time the Pave Low would come back, all the firing would stop."

One of the four SEALs who lost their lives at Paitilla might have survived if he had been evacuated and received prompt medical attention. But the "golden hour" in which his life might have been saved was lost because there was no helicopter immediately available to evacuate him.

Weikel credits the Army helicopters with doing an extremely good job during Operation Just Cause. But he adds:

"I was very unhappy we didn't have more Pave Lows down there. We could have covered all these other special operations units involved. Army aviation has been jealous of the Air Force helicopter community. There has been very bad blood between them over the years. After 1984 [when the plan to transfer the

Air Force special operations helicopters to the Army was blocked], they were pissed that the Air Force had gotten all these superb helicopters and had gotten all this attention. And they didn't want any more Air Force helicopters invited to the war than what we had."

Weikel's five Pave Low helicopters flew nonstop from Hurlburt to Panama, a grueling fourteen-hour ordeal with aerial refuelings along the way. The Pave Low, unlike a fixed-wing airplane, has no automatic pilot. That means hands-on flying every moment the craft is in the air. The crews had earned a long rest when they landed at Howard.

But Weikel, remembering his fourteen-hour combat day during the *Mayaguez* incident, had insisted on training extra crews. Counting crew members assigned to squadron headquarters, he actually had enough men to provide two-plus crews for each plane. Almost as soon as they arrived at Howard, the Pave Lows were ready to go into action. And the squadron was able to keep its planes in the air around the clock, unlike Army units, which had to ground their helicopters while the crews rested.

Although the Pave Lows had special targets to hit when the operation began, they were put on standby at Howard because the shooting started earlier than expected. In the next few days, the unit flew more than three hundred combat sorties, crisscrossing over the fighting down below.

Weikel was disturbed by the lack of fixed-wing escorts for the troop-carrying helicopters and Combat Talons—another lesson from the war in Southeast Asia that had been forgotten.

After dawn on the first day of the operation, the Pave Lows were assigned to move a unit of soldiers across the city.

"The sun is up now, and we were concerned," Weikel says. "Here we are in the daytime with absolutely no fighter escort, with an elite Army force onboard. Here we are flying across skirmish lines in the daytime. We had forgotten all our lessons from Southeast Asia. We forgot about the tactical side of the house. Where was the escort? When the MC-130s went in to do those drops, they were unescorted. Why? Would we ever have done an unescorted mission into Khe Sanh [site of a bitter battle in 1968]? No way! Those missions into Laos and North Vietnam with helicopters? No way!"

The helicopter crews also had the same kind of difficulty with communications experienced by those flying the gunships.

"Communications were completely screwed up," Weikel says. "The problem was that, even though we had excellent radios and communications gear, we had so many people talking on the radios, lots of people just routinely asking situation reports from their forces, that they were stepping on each other and not enabling key communications to pass through.

"Another problem was that, sometimes in the excitement of battle, guys forgot some portion of their call sign. For example, there was a call went out that *Five-one*'s hit and going down. Trouble is, there's an *Alpha* through *Zulu Five-one* out there. Everyone who has a *Five-one* out there is going to come up on the net at the same time. When they're all doing that, you can't use that radio to find out what happened to the *Five-one* that's in trouble.

"The lesson from Desert One was that there wasn't enough communication. Now they've got too much talking. The dedicated special operations community was always trained that you only communicate by exception. If you're out there and everything is going according to plan, you aren't going to say anything. The only time you're going to come up on the radios is when something is not going according to plan or you need something. That did not seem to be adhered to, and that is another legacy of Desert One we inherited in our own force."

For the 1720th and 1724th Special Tactics Teams, their support of the Rangers in simultaneous nighttime jumps to seize two airfields was the first test in combat since the pararescue PJs had been melded in with the combat controllers more than two years before.

Sergeant Gordon W. Tully was with the Rangers in the second plane over the Rio Hato military airfield that night. Each of the two lead planes carried a five-man special tactics team, to provide redundancy. First out was the "bike chaser," whose job it was to follow a small motorcycle, with its own chute, to the ground and then set out to check the condition of the field. Then came the team leader; an air traffic controller; a command and control communicator; and finally a PJ whose job was to place an infrared strobe light at the far end of the runway. Other members of the team set out the same kind of box-and-one, with five infrared lights, that Carney had placed for the Desert One landing.

"As we came inbound, about an hour out, we were notified that yes, the runway was blocked," Tully says. "Ten minutes out, we open the doors, a little earlier than normal. As we ran in towards the airfield, the F-117s [Stealth fighter-bombers in use for the first time] made their strike. They struck the airfield. We had two AC-130 gunships overhead, giving us extremely close air support.

"As I came under the canopy, I saw the runway was blocked. There was no shooting yet. Even though they knew we were coming, we still took them by surprise, due to the tactics we used, running without lights. Fifteen aircraft dropped, one minute in trail.

"The first team dropped three hundred yards right. I dropped right next to the runway. I was derigging my equipment as Chalk Three flew over. [*Chalk* is a term used to distinguish aircraft loads.] There was still no shooting. I was putting on my rucksack when Chalk Four came over. The triple A started hot and heavy."

Before the mission, the crews had been told to expect fire from four antiaircraft guns. After the battle, Tully took pictures of twelve antiaircraft guns, all of which had been firing.

"Chalks Four through Fifteen all were hit by triple A, some of them quite heavily," Tully says. "I remember 130s going over with cones of three or four tracers on them. People were shot inside the aircraft, but not a single 130 went down.

"You could only see the planes when they were right over the airfield. Running in and out, you couldn't see them. As they passed over, the triple A guns would fire. As they passed off into the darkness, the triple A would go up and down the sticks of jumpers. As they reached the ground, they'd use grazing fire across the airfield.

"When they did grazing fire, I would have to get down flat. It is quite intimidating having a machine gun do that. But then the next aircraft would come over, they'd go right back up, and I could jump up and move forward.

"One of my jobs was to assure the approach end of the runway was clear. I had to drag a few friendly casualties off the runway. One guy had a broken hip, probably a jump injury. He was being given buddy care by one of his mates. We grabbed his load-bearing equipment and dragged him off the runway, much to his distress. We did that more than once. We had to get those reinforcements in or people would die."

The PJs, meanwhile, set up aid stations to treat wounded and injured—both Americans and Panamanians. During the airfield operation, they helped 146 wounded or injured soldiers.

Even after the airfield was seized by the Rangers, hostile fire continued. Despite the gunfire, two Combat Talons brought in supplies for the Rangers and then remained on the runway, refueling Army helicopters from their own fuel tanks.

The invasion of Panama came after the creation of the United States Special Operations Command in 1987 by a Congress angered by problems revealed at Grenada. But the air commandos were still in the Twenty-third Air Force—a part of the Military Airlift Command. On 22 May 1990, the unit was transformed into a command of its own—the Air Force Special Operations Command, reporting to the overall United States Special Operations Command.

When the brief, intense operation in Panama was reviewed, it was clear that Air Force special operations had made impressive strides. The Spectre gunships had proved invaluable in supporting troops on the ground. The Pave Lows, flying around the clock, had proved themselves in combat. And the combat controllers and pararescuemen had worked smoothly together in their new special tactics teams.

The operation also emphasized once again the importance of well-trained and well-equipped reserves, quickly available to support the active-duty units. The 711th Special Operations Squadron, the reserve unit of which McCutchan and his crew are members, added to the number of gunships available. The 193rd Special Operations Group of the Pennsylvania Air National

Guard, a unit that specializes in psychological warfare, added a capability that would otherwise have been lacking in the operation.

There were, of course, still problems to be worked out. Communications needed a lot more discipline. Techniques for telling friend from foe to prevent "friendly fire" incidents were still far from perfect, as the incident involving the gunship at the Commendancia and McCutchan's narrow decision not to fire demonstrated. There were still no dedicated fixed-wing fighter escorts for transport planes and helicopters.

Crew fatigue surfaced, as it does in every conflict, as a major problem. McCutchan's crew was finally grounded and forced to rest, and one man—the scanner, whose job it was to lean out into the slipstream to watch for antiaircraft fire and other planes—had to be hospitalized. Only units, such as Weikel's Pave Low squadron, that had trained extra crews were able to keep their planes in the air around the clock.

And, for many air commandos, there was a new worry about their independence now that they were part of the Army-dominated United States Special Operations Command.

A problem that hardly anyone foresaw was about to make its appearance in a new theater of combat in Southwest Asia.

As the buildup that preceded the war with Iraq began, special forces units were among the first to arrive in Saudi Arabia. But Gen. H. Norman Schwarzkopf, the Desert Shield–Desert Storm commander, displayed a good deal of doubt—to many it seemed outright hostility—about the role the special forces would play in the war. For a while, it seemed as though they might throw a war and the air commandos would not be invited.

PART 8
New Challenges

CHAPTER 26
The Gulf War and Beyond

Colonel George Gray, commander of the 1st Special Operations Wing, was gloomy and frustrated as he flew back to his base from a meeting with General Schwarzkopf late in 1990.

Gray and the other special operators reporting to Schwarzkopf had come up with what they thought was a workable, if not elegant, solution to one of the most serious problems facing those planning the imminent air assault on Iraq.

No matter how they looked at the map, there was no way to approach Baghdad without penetrating a ring of radar stations in position to give timely warning of an attack. Eventually, the defenses could be destroyed, but the losses in the first wave of attacking aircraft would be painfully high.

The plan seemed a simple one to the special operators: Pave Low helicopters, skimming over the desert under the cover of darkness, would deposit teams of Green Berets close to two key radar stations commanding the southern approaches to Baghdad. Striking without warning, the Army Special Forces troops would hit both radar sites at the same instant, putting them both off the air moments before the first aircraft roared through the gap.

It was not a routine operation, but it was the kind of thing the Air Force and Army had long trained for. It was precisely the kind of surprise attack behind enemy lines they had prepared, during the long years of the Cold War, to carry out in Europe.

But Schwarzkopf said no, there would not be any cross-border operations by special forces: "There isn't going to be anybody on the ground prior to H-hour!"

Perhaps it was partially the ingrained suspicion of special operators on the part of the traditional Army and Air Force. But there was also reason behind his refusal. By their very nature, small-scale operations behind enemy lines, once they were launched, slipped out from under the control of commanders back in headquarters. And there was always the danger that such a small unit might get into trouble and have to be rescued.

Other possibilities for breaching the radar barrier ran through Gray's mind. Bombers might be used to hit the radar sites. But how could they be sure, flashing by in the darkness at high speed, that the job had been done—and done right? Pave Lows could find the radar sites in the darkness, but their machine guns were designed for defense, not for blowing away an installation as large and complex as a radar site.

Looking out the plane window, Gray noted a line of Army Apaches. The Apaches were heavily armed helicopter gunships, but they didn't have navigation equipment good enough to find a precise target at long range in the dark. The answer to the problem suddenly came into Gray's mind: use Pave Lows as pathfinders to lead the Apaches to the targets, where they would crush the radar sites with missiles and guns and then hover long enough to make sure the installations had been destroyed.

This was an elegant solution. It did not risk a small, elite force on the ground. It promised to open a gap in the radar net moments before the first attackers flashed through. And it held out the hope that aircraft losses in the first strike would be kept to a minimum.

Schwarzkopf liked the plan. He authorized training of the crews. But he told them they could not fire any Hellfire guided missiles for practice. The weapons were expensive, and he would need all he had in the upcoming ground battle to knock out enemy tanks.

Gray told him: "With all due respect, sir, I can't take the mission unless I can rehearse with Hellfires. Most of these kids have never shot a live Hellfire before."

Schwarzkopf agreed: "Okay, you're right. But you call me every time you shoot a Hellfire."

The plan called for a total of twelve aircraft to carry out the attack, with four Pave Lows leading two flights of four Apaches against each target. Although only one pathfinder was needed to find each radar site, an extra Pave Low went along on both flights just to be on the safe side.

They were following the successful model of the Son Tay raid, and not the example of Desert One, where too few helicopters were dispatched.

Major Bob Leonik, who was tabbed to fly one of the Pave Lows, along with Lt. Col. Richard L. Comer, commander of the 20th Special Operations Squadron, was reminded of his high-school days. As a teenager, Leonik was a trumpet virtuoso, so skilled that he had an offer from the Dallas Symphony and had to decide, when he finished high school, whether to go to college or embark immediately on a career as a professional musician. He chose to go to college, but his instincts as a musician stayed with him.

"My father taught me that being able to play a musical instrument is the basis of everything else you do in life," Leonik says. "If you could master a musical instrument, you could apply that to other things in life. That's what the Pave Low was, a musical instrument. I had hoped to go from being a performer to becoming a conductor. Being an aircraft commander was the closest thing to being a conductor, especially when you're working with a Pave Low crew. I saw the same things you see in an orchestra."

Even flying in the desert reminded Leonik of his experience as a musician. In pilot training, the emphasis was on flying in places like Vietnam, with jungles, rivers, and bodies of water to use as landmarks. But here in the hazy, featureless desert, there was little to go by.

"In the desert," Leonik says, "you have to be concerned with subtle changes. It was like reading a piece of music."

For four months, the crews trained for the mission, with special emphasis on what to do if any of a long list of things went wrong. Although they weren't told their actual targets until just before the attack, they had a pretty good idea of the role they would play in starting the war.

Leonik didn't use musical terms in talking to his crew, but that's the way he thought.

"If I used those terms, they would think I was crazy," he says. "I didn't use the word *staccato,* but I defined it. I told them to make their calls 'crisp, clean, clear.'"

There was something very appropriate and traditional about a trumpet player leading the charge. It was reminiscent of the way the bugler signaled the attack by a squadron of horse cavalry.

"We had a graduation exercise, simulating all the distances we were going to fly," Gray says. "We went to a Saudi range and shot off something like four hundred thousand dollars, worth of Hellfires in our graduation exercise."

Gray and several other officers crowded into Schwarzkopf's office. He was on the couch. Gray sat on the floor. The others stood behind him. They explained the plan to Schwarzkopf again.

Schwarzkopf listened quietly and then turned to Gray and demanded: "Can you guarantee me 100 percent?"

"I thought about that a bit. It was obvious I was thinking. He had just put an awful lot of heat on me right there," Gray recalled. After a long pause, Gray replied: "Yes, sir, I will."

"Okay, Colonel, you can start the war," Schwarzkopf replied.

The two sites to be attacked were about eight to ten miles inside Iraq and about fifteen miles apart. Since one was a little further from the border than the other, the six-ship formation led by Leonik and Comer took off about twenty minutes early.

As they headed north, the Apaches tucked in as close behind the Pave Lows as they dared. Flying without lights, the Apache pilots relied on their forward-looking infrared to fly tight formation on the Pave Lows.

For Leonik and his crew, it was just like a training mission. But it was a little chilly. Someone turned on the cabin heat. Suddenly a stray current ran through the electrical system and knocked out the alignment of their inertial navigation system.

"The very thing we were up there to do was just dropped off the line," Leonik says. "So now what do you do? You're sitting there in the middle of a piece, and your bow just broke. Or you just lost a string. Or the middle valve on your trumpet locked up. Is there a way you can get through the piece without a middle valve? That's where all the training paid off."

The crew used their radar to pick out a known landmark up ahead and then updated their navigation system as they passed over it. They were back in business.

For Maj. Ben Pulsifer, flying another Pave Low leading the second flight of Apaches to the other target, everything went smoothly.

"The ride in was uneventful," Pulsifer recalls. "We just headed north toward a point. It just seemed like another practice run. But as we approached the border and the mileage counted down, we sat back as a crew and thought, Wow! We're about to penetrate Iraq and kick off a war involving a million people on both sides! It was quite daunting to do that. It was just overwhelming to start something like that."

As planned, the lead Pave Lows in each flight dropped a bundle of chem lights [small marker lights that use a chemical reaction to cause a greenish yellow glow when activated] at a predetermined point. The Apaches used the lights as a reference point to update their own navigation systems and turn in for the attack.

The Pave Lows swung away and flew back toward the border, still close enough to rescue crew members if any of the Apaches were shot down.

As he pulled away to the west, Pulsifer's tail gunner, who was crouching on the ramp at the rear of the plane, spotted a SAM launch.

Pulsifer broke abruptly toward the SAM. Such a maneuver causes the missile to turn so sharply that it stalls out or loses its lock on the target. The crew members were wearing night-vision goggles, but it was still hard to see, hard even to make out the line between earth and sky in the hazy darkness.

"We punched off our countermeasures," Pulsifer says. "That one, obviously, didn't get us, didn't come near us. The danger we found was that we were flying about eighty feet at the time. It was just pitch-dark. As I made my break and rolled out level, I rolled out about forty feet off the ground. We survived the missiles but almost impacted the ground. There was a good lesson to learn there about making a break."

But there wasn't time for the lesson to sink in.

"As we came back to our holding point, my right scanner suddenly yelled out, 'SAM, four o'clock!' I made a break. He actually saw, from one of the Bedouin camps out there, saw the launch of the missile and saw it coming at the helicopter. We made a break and defeated the missile, this time not more than, oh, two feet above the ground. So we decided to move our orbit point a little bit because we didn't like orbiting there right above the SAM launchers."

From what they could see, the missiles appeared to be SA-7 shoulder-launched missiles.

Orbiting near the border, the Pave Low crews were close enough to see the explosions at the two radar sites, where the Apaches had struck within ten seconds of each other. But they weren't close enough to confirm that the targets had been destroyed. They began to receive messages demanding a report, but they had to wait themselves for a report from the Apaches.

At one point, Colonel Comer, flying in Leonik's plane, came on the air and told everyone to shut up—"We're trying to get something done out here."

Finally, the word came that the targets had been destroyed—so thoroughly that they never came back on the air. The Pave Lows flashed the code word *California,* indicating the gap in the radar barrier had been created.

"About this time, in the FLIR system, we could see some of the low-level aircraft start to streak across the border," Pulsifer recalls. "We saw a couple of the F-15 Strike Eagles, the low-level attack birds. Everybody else was coming in at high level. Our hit was twenty minutes prior to the start of the war. About twenty minutes after our hit, everything started to explode to the north. You could see tracer fire up in the sky. It looked like a wild Fourth of July up there.

"We had gone to an HC-130 to refuel. As we headed north on the track, you could see all the explosions. Our follow-on mission was to go pick up any pilots shot down. The initial run-in was no big deal because we had rehearsed it so much. But as we were getting the gas and watching all the bombs going off and the tracer fire, I began to go: 'Wow, I don't want to go back up there. It looks pretty nasty.' Then I started to get that tightening of the stomach. This would be pretty intensive if we had to go up there.

"Not long after we got our gas, we were looking to the south, back over Saudi. And all of a sudden, all these strobe lights started coming on. As the guys came back across the border, they would come up with their anticollision lights. To me, that was probably one of the most spectacular sights I've ever seen. Just to see the sky fill up with all these airplanes coming back safely. Within twenty minutes of that, we got a call telling us to go ahead and come home. That was just an incredible feeling, that all those guys got in and out, and they weren't going to need us at all."

Although planners of the air assault on Iraq had calculated that they would lose at least thirty-five planes in the initial assault, only one plane was shot down.

But many of the planes coming back were in trouble, either because they had suffered battle damage or, in the great majority of cases, because they were running dangerously low on fuel.

At Al Jouf, the Saudi airfield just south of the border, a special tactics team had set up shop, prepared to conduct a frantic aviation triage operation, sorting out the planes that were about to crash-land, those that were about to flame out for lack of fuel, and those that had just enough fuel to find a tanker or go on to a field farther south.

For members of the special tactics team, it was a postgraduate course in combat control. They had already paid their way by taking over the uncompleted King Fahd airport and turning it into the busiest airfield in history during the buildup for the war. On some days, they handled as many as eighteen hundred aircraft. But nothing in their previous experience matched the urgency of the operations that night at Al Jouf.

Sergeant Tully was in the tower at Al Jouf as the planes came

streaming back from the attack on Baghdad and targets throughout Iraq. Plans called for refueling the planes in the air, but Tully
and the other sergeants had told the brass that wouldn't work—
and they were right.

"I had six battle-damaged aircraft simultaneously and eighteen
emergency-fuel aircraft," Tully recalls. "They can't divert anywhere else. I don't know how many minimal fuels I had."

His most pressing problem was a Navy A-6 bomber that was not
only on fire but was still carrying bombs that the crew couldn't
release. Tully cleared the plane for landing. The crew made it
onto the ground, stopped, jumped out, and left the burning plane
on the runway. Hundreds of planes, many of them low on fuel and
five of them suffering battle damage, were headed toward the
field.

Tully stacked the battle-damaged planes at two thousand feet
apart. He broadcast that he didn't even want to talk to planes with
minimum fuel—only those with battle damage or those about to
flame out for lack of fuel.

One Navy F/A-18 pilot reported he had less than two minutes'
fuel remaining and asked for the best bail-out location. Tully told
him to wait while he brought in a battle-damaged Tornado. The
crew of the British Tornado said they were at twenty-eight thousand feet with neither engine working.

The Tornadoes, flown by British and Saudi crews, had drawn
one of the most dangerous tasks in the entire assault—low-level
attacks on the heavily defended Iraqi airfields.

"The Brit got a restart in one of his engines, so I put the F/A-
18 pilot number one," Tully continues. "Meanwhile, the runway
is still blocked by a burning aircraft with hung ordnance—a cluster bomb. We tried to get the Saudi fire crew to push it off the
runway with their fire truck. They couldn't understand why we
wanted to destroy this aircraft when their job was to save aircraft."

One of the Americans ran out, wrapped a chain around the
burning plane's landing gear, jumped in the fire truck, and
pulled the plane out of the way.

"I had already lined up the F/A-18 pilot," Tully recalls. "I had
him on his approach with the runway still blocked. If he couldn't

land, I was going to sidestep him to the parallel taxiway and start landing planes there, which is not a safe thing to do. He was three miles out when they started to move that aircraft. They got the aircraft off just before I had to sidestep him to the taxiway. And I had my other five battle-damaged aircraft coming in behind him. He landed on the runway and flamed out, ran out of gas. He took it off the end of the runway into the desert. Just to get out of the way.

"The Brit Tornado came in right after him. He turned left at the end of the runway and ran off into the desert."

Four refueling points had been set up at both ends of the runway and taxiway, and there were two fuel trucks. As the fuel-hungry planes came in, a number of them were barely able to taxi off the runway before they ran out of fuel. At one point, six F-16 fighters flamed out while waiting in line on the ground for fuel. Trucks brought fuel to them.

At the fuel stations, the planes kept their engines running, in a process known as hot refueling, so they could move rapidly out of the way and make room for the next plane in line.

"We refueled hundreds of aircraft," Tully says. "We saved a lot of people that night."

Although the Pave Lows were not called upon to conduct combat rescue operations on the night the air war opened, such a call came four days later, on 21 January 1991, when a Navy F-14 was shot down south of Baghdad.

Two Pave Lows and four other rescue helicopters were on alert at the 'Ar'Ar airfield near the Saudi-Iraq border. Captain Thomas J. Trask, his copilot, Maj. Michael Homan, and their crew in *Moccasin 05* had been on alert since noon the day before. They had waited through the night, hoping that, if a plane were shot down, they would be able to make the rescue attempt under the cover of darkness. But it was after dawn when they received word that two Navy planes had gone down during the night. A daylight rescue mission deep into Iraq would be a highly risky venture.

But, with a heavy fog limiting visibility to one hundred feet, the crews of the two Pave Lows decided to use the cover of the fog to make the rescue attempt. Theirs were the only helicopters able to fly in such conditions. They decided to split up. Trask and Homan would try to find the crew of the F-14, believed to be down in the desert some 60 miles northwest of Baghdad, 130 miles into Iraq. The other Pave Low would wait for more information and then go looking for the crew of the other plane. Only later did they learn that only one plane was down.

"We were relieved we had all that cloud cover," Homan says. "We figured the worst part would be going through the defenses right at the border. All the shots we had taken up to that point had been right at the border. You couldn't ask for a better cloaking device than that fog.

"We got up to the border, and that's when the fog just cleared away. You felt like you were standing naked out in the street."

They continued north, at one point skimming past an antiaircraft position so fast the Iraqis did not have time to shoot. But they must have sounded the alarm.

Suddenly, the AWACS plane, which was monitoring the whole area with its powerful radar, broadcast an urgent message: "*Moccasin Zero-five.* Snap one-eight-zero now!" An Iraqi MiG fighter was headed in their direction.

The advice from the AWACS, to turn and flee toward the border, would have been useful if they had been flying a supersonic jet, but they were flying at only 140 knots, and they were already sixty or seventy miles from the border and the sheltering fog. Trask and Homan quickly decided that, if they turned around, they would just be shot down a few miles closer to the border. They continued north and then found a depression in the desert, where they hid as the jet passed by far overhead.

A few minutes later, the AWACS reported more trouble: a "slow-mover"—an Iraqi helicopter—was headed in their direction. Two A-10 fighters were refueling, preparing to escort the Pave Low. Homan radioed for them to hurry up, but he wasn't as worried by the helicopter as he had been by the fighter. The crew rather looked forward to taking on an enemy helicopter with their .50-caliber machine guns. But moments after the radioed request for the A-10s, the enemy helicopter returned to its base—an indication the Iraqis were listening in, monitoring the progress of *Moccasin 05*.

The Iraqis were also, obviously, listening for signals from the downed crewman, later identified as Lt. Devon Jones. But there weren't any signals. Jones was saving his batteries and trying to avoid detection, assuming he would have to wait until after dark for rescue.

Trask and Homan searched as best they could. They checked out a number of discarded fuel tanks. They even found, and stopped to examine, an old Soviet-made ejection seat. Finally, they turned, disappointed, toward 'Ar'Ar for fuel.

As they sat in the hot-refueling pit, they heard a one-sided conversation that sounded as though an A-10 pilot were talking to someone on the ground. As soon as their tanks were topped off, they headed north again, this time toward a spot twenty-five miles farther north than they had gone before. Their route took them skimming a few feet over a busy highway and so close to an enemy airfield that they could see the hangars and the parked planes. Everyone in that part of Iraq must have known they were coming.

Because they were so low, the helicopter pilots couldn't hear the downed pilot, but the A-10 pilots were in contact and knew where he was. Homan asked one of the two A-10 pilots to fly directly over the pilot and then go vertical, marking the spot.

"We were headed right toward him when he popped right straight up," Homan says. "We were about a mile and a half out when we spotted a vehicle. It was traveling real fast out in the desert. This guy was kicking up a pretty good dust cloud."

The truck was probably carrying soldiers with direction-finding equipment, heading right toward the downed pilot. The helicopter crew didn't want to take on the truck themselves because they still weren't quite sure where Jones was. They moved out of the way, and Homan radioed a terse message to the A-10s: "Smoke the truck!"

The planes hit the truck and set it ablaze. Then they told the Pave Low to head directly toward the column of smoke coming from the truck. That's where the downed pilot was. As they approached, taxiing fast, Jones broke from the shallow hole he had dug with his fingernails and ran toward the helicopter. Ben Pennington, a pararescueman, jumped out to aid him, but Jones said later that he never even saw Pennington as he ran for the helicopter.

Sergeant Timothy B. Hadrych, watching from his gunner's position at the left window of the helicopter, saw that the truck was still rolling forward. He decided not to shoot because he was afraid of hitting Jones.

"I was not about to put a lot of bullets out there and shoot the guy we were trying to rescue," he says.

Instead, Hadrych leaned out with a cheap little camera he had brought along and snapped two extraordinary pictures of Jones running toward the helicopter, with Pennington in the foreground.

Jones survived his ordeal with only minor injuries. But he was extremely lucky, not only to avoid capture but to survive the downing of his plane in the first place. The F-14 was hit by a missile that knocked off the tail and sent the craft into a tight, flat spin. The spin was so violent that, when he was rescued, the whites of Jones's eyes were still red from the G forces he had experienced just before his ejection. He and his backseater both managed to eject. The other crewman was captured several hours before Jones was rescued.

The rescue was the first successful pickup of a downed pilot from Iraq. For their exploit, the crew received the Mackay Trophy for the most meritorious Air Force flight of the year. Trask and Homan were awarded the Silver Star, and Hadrych and the other crew members each received the Distinguished Flying Cross.

Despite the initial reluctance at headquarters, the rule against cross-border commando-type raids was gradually eased. Eventually, the air commandos were involved in dozens of such operations, many of them attempts to find and knock out the elusive Iraqi SCUD missiles. For the Air Force special operators, it was a familiar role, reminiscent of operations in Europe and Burma half a century before.

One of the most challenging assignments was to deliver Army Green Berets deep inside Iraq with vehicles and enough supplies to permit them to remain and move about for as long as ten days.

The Army had rigged special all-terrain vehicles for the mission. They weighed ten thousand pounds or more. A Pave Low carrying such a vehicle, a team of Green Berets and their supplies, and a full load of fuel weighed close to fifty thousand pounds. At that weight, the helicopter could fly, but it couldn't hover.

Mike Homan was commander on the first two-aircraft mission carrying the heavy vehicles.

"The technique we came up with was to find a good level area and then start our approach two or three miles back from the point where we intended to land," Homan explains. "We would set up a single-ship approach, just ignore the other aircraft because we couldn't stay in formation at those weights.

"We'd take it down and roll it in to a landing. We'd try to hit about fifteen knots, twenty miles an hour. We'd touch down at that speed and hope we didn't hit a rock, because we couldn't slow it down anymore. You didn't want to hit the brakes, either, because that would put additional stress on your gear."

On the first mission, Homan flew as commander in the second plane. Major Corby Martin led the way, freeing Homan to command the overall operation.

Before takeoff, the crews had been told they would be landing in a large area of flat land. But when they got there, they saw rolling hills stretching out in front of them. The pilots of the two choppers picked out their own landing spots independently. Once committed to a landing, there was no chance for a change of mind because of the heavy weight they were carrying. The weight also meant they couldn't hop over any obstacles that might suddenly loom out of the dark.

"I was on Corby's left rear, about three hundred yards back," Homan says. "Corby spotted a rising sand dune right in front of him, which he didn't see until he got right up on it. The last I saw of Corby's airplane, it was flaring up like this [Homan gestures sharply upward], and there was a big cloud of dust. The last I saw, he was up there, falling. I thought he was a goner.

"I was just a few feet off the ground myself. I actually closed my eyes because I was expecting a fireball. Just an unconscious reaction. Then I opened them right away and thought, Boy, was that stupid!

When Homan opened his eyes, there was no fireball, just a big cloud of dust. In an amazing feat of airmanship, Martin had managed to regain control and land his plane.

"I was glad to see dust over there, but I didn't expect him to be able to fly out," Homan says. "I figured he hit the ground too hard. We hit hard ourselves. The gunner in the back actually got his arm banged up."

The soldiers quickly streamed out of the rear of the helicopters, rolled out their vehicles, and prepared to depart on their mission.

To Homan's surprise, Martin's plane lifted off and headed toward home.

After a week or more, the helicopters flew back in to pick up the Green Berets. By that time, the soldiers had burned off fuel in their vehicles and consumed the rations they had taken with them, making the loads just a little lighter on the takeoff for the flight home.

Although, on most of the missions, the role of the Air Force was to deliver the soldiers behind enemy lines and then pick them up again, on several occasions, Air Force special tactics team members went along on operations to coordinate close air support if the troops came under attack.

Sergeant Steve D. Jones, a special tactics air controller, volunteered to go in with two dozen British commandos to destroy a buried fiber-optic communications cable about thirty-five kilometers from Baghdad. Jones's job was to coordinate air support if it was needed.

Preparations for the mission involved an elaborate escape and evasion plan in case something happened to the helicopters.

"A big part of the planning was the E&E plan," Jones says. "Each man, in addition to team equipment, had a big rucksack full of survival gear, with food and water. There was a big lake nearby. Every man had fins and a mask and a wet suit so we could swim. If we started getting overrun, we could get in this lake and swim across it.

"Our plan was to make it across the lake. Then they had specific areas, designated safe areas, where folks would link up. And we had specified contact times."

The two helicopters carrying the teams took off about 8 P.M. from a base just south of the border and skimmed the surface on the way north. At one point, they passed a few feet above a motorized convoy so quickly the Iraqis below didn't realize what had happened.

After a flight of about two hours, they touched down. The "dig teams" went to work with metal detectors and then pick and shovel to burrow down through the hard desert surface to the cable. They placed two hundred pounds of explosives in the hole—far more than enough to rupture the cable. While the diggers worked, the helicopters stood by a short distance away, their engines running.

After about half an hour on the ground, the skyline over Baghdad lit up with the glow of tracers from the defenders' antiaircraft guns.

"We were just all amazed at that amount of triple A," Jones says. "It was a pretty impressive light show."

Their amazement quickly turned to concern, however, when guns at a nearby town joined in the shooting. The commandos could see the tracers arcing toward them and burning out as the shells fell toward the ground—about where their helicopters waited. As soon as the explosive was buried and the fuse set, they hurried to the helicopters.

Jones was on the rear ramp of one of the choppers when the explosive went off, creating a huge glow in the dark night.

The commandos finished their job and took off about midnight, refueled in the air on the way out, and touched down back in Saudi Arabia two hours later.

The air commandos were beginning to feel pretty good about

their contribution to the war, far out of proportion to their small numbers. But then on 31 January, disaster struck. An AC-130 gunship—call sign *Spirit 03*—was shot down with the loss of its fourteen-man crew. It was the largest single loss of the air war.

The plane, piloted by Maj. Paul J. Weaver, was one of three Spectre gunships involved in repelling a cross-border attack by Iraqi forces against a United States Marine outpost at the border town of Khafji. The other two planes had been above the battle scene for some time, knocking out a number of armored personnel carriers and trying to target several missiles that could be fired against the Marines.

Spirit 03 arrived on the scene at 5:25 A.M. with orders to break off by daylight—about 6 A.M.—to return to base. Commanders didn't want to risk one of the big, relatively slow-moving planes after it had lost the cover of darkness.

A log kept by the crew of another gunship, included in a report on the loss of *Spirit 03*, indicates the crew of the doomed plane flew into an area the other plane had left because of heavy antiaircraft fire. Excerpts from the log tell the story:

". . . passed to *03* we encountered heavy triple A from [deleted] and recommended he not fly further east along the border than that. Fully explained the threats.

"Blacklist [code name for the radar-control plane] offered us seventeen trucks at [deleted]. We refused due to triple A threat we had just left.

"Then they offered FROGS [free rocket over-ground missiles] at [deleted] which we also declined due to same Triple A.

"We left the area RTB [return to base]. We heard *03* accepting tasking to take out FROGS and was heading NE."

The official report of the loss of *Spirit 03* records an increasingly urgent series of messages transmitted to the plane reminding the crew to leave the area by daylight and return to base. The first message was sent at 5:30 A.M., about the time the plane took up its station over the battle scene. Others were recorded at 5:45 and 6:05. At 6:10, the squadron commander told the AWACS plane, "I want *Spirit 03* to RTB now."

At 6:19, the commander of the AWACS unit, call sign Jeremiah, stepped in and told the AWACS crew, call sign PONCA, to order *Spirit 03* to return to base. The following dialogue was recorded:

"PONCA: *Spirit 03*. Jeremiah directs you to refill.

"*03*: Roger, Jeremiah directs us to refill.

"[Voice of copilot. Analysis of database charts . . . suggests that *Spirit 03* continued to engage targets and appeared to be evading/disengaging/reengaging for approximately the next three to five minutes. At about 0623, the following transmissions were recorded:]

"PONCA: *Spirit 03*, confirm you know you are supposed to refill.

"*03*: Roger, roger. [Copilot's voice described by controller as hunky-dory voice or as calm, unconcerned.]

"PONCA: *Spirit 03*, confirm you are in a left-hand turn to the south.

"*03*: Roger, roger. [Same calm voice.]

"[Immediately following this last transmission, a weak and panicked different voice was heard to say, 'Mayday, Mayday.' PONCA transmitted, '*Spirit 03*, radio check' three times with no reply. Over the next two minutes, the data trail of *Spirit 03* faded away. No further radio transmissions or radio beacons from *03* were ever received. Search and rescue efforts were initiated, but neither wreckage nor bodies were ever located or recovered.]"

Months after that report was written and after the fighting was over, the wreckage of *Spirit 03* was found on the ocean bottom off the Kuwaiti coast on 4 March, and remains of the crew members were recovered.

Gray, who was the wing commander, says an examination of the wreckage indicated the plane had been hit by an SA-16 missile. The plane went into a spin so violent that none of the crew members could escape, and the plane hit the water's surface so hard that it exploded into small fragments. The largest piece a diver saw when he examined the scene was only fifteen feet long, and most of the other pieces were much smaller.

This is the way Gray assesses what happened:

"This gunship, *Spirit 03*, was the third gunship that went up. They were basically told, when it becomes six o'clock in the

morning, it's time to disengage. We don't want you up there after the sun comes up.

"He was up there having a wonderful time, shooting the you-
know-what out of the bad guys. He was bingo fuel. He was just
about Winchestered on all of his ammunition. We had been asking specifically, through the AWACS, for him to disengage at 0600.
We had made several phone calls to the tactical air control center. I would call there, say, 'Get your controller to call AWACS. We
want to remind *Spirit 03* we want him off station and heading for
home at 0600.'

"He was on target, had no threats he was able to pick up. He
got the call about 0623 to RTB from the AWACS. They got a roger.
. . . Right after that, they got hit by an SA-16. They were on the
way home."

Gray was asked if his account meant the plane had stayed
twenty-three minutes after it was supposed to have headed home.

"That becomes a judgment call," Gray says. "I'm up there, I'm
doing good work, I'm getting cheered on by the USMC, which
he was. There's nothing threatening me and my airplane. I probably would have stayed there myself."

The plane's flight recorder carried the sound of a muffled
thump and an indication of a fire in an engine while the plane
was at eight to ten thousand feet.

"I can almost guarantee a wing came off," Gray says. "You wrap
up fast when that happens. With any kind of controlled airplane,
you would be able to get most everybody out."

Although the other gunships had reported 23mm antiaircraft
fire severe enough to keep them out of certain areas, Gray says
there was no intelligence indicating the Iraqis had SA-16 missiles
of the type that brought down *Spirit 03* until ten days later, when
an A-10 landed with an unexploded SA-16 warhead in its wing.

"We had no intelligence to indicate those kinds of systems in
the area of operations," Gray says. "None. Zero."

There was, however, plenty of warning that the Iraqis were
equipped with shoulder-fired SA-7 missiles—an estimated one for
each fifty soldiers. Unlike radar-guided missiles, such weapons are
impossible to detect until they have been fired, and they are es-

pecially dangerous during the daylight hours, when the soldiers can see what they are shooting at.

Not all the special operations involved shooting at the enemy. The Combat Talons carried out one of the most basic traditional duties of air commandos, dating back to World War II, by dropping 17 million leaflets over Iraqi defensive positions. The leaflets urged the enemy soldiers to surrender—which thousands of them did—and warned them what would happen if they didn't.

The "what would happen" involved intensive air strikes by fighter-bombers and carpet bombing by B-52s. But the Combat Talons also contributed their share by dropping eleven BLU82 Daisy Cutter bombs. The fifteen-thousand-pound bombs, too big to fit in the belly of a bomber, were carried in the cargo compartment of an MC-130 and then rolled out the big rear door as the plane passed over the target at sixteen to twenty thousand feet, above the range of most enemy antiaircraft weapons.

The big bombs were used not only to crack the morale of the Iraqi forces but also to blast gaps in the formidable minefields along the border. Dropped at night, and often two or three at a time, the bombs made a noise that could be heard for many miles and created a mushroom cloud of dust and debris similar in appearance to that from a nuclear explosion.

One British special forces team located 110 miles from the site of the first Daisy Cutter explosion radioed to its headquarters: "Sir, sir, the blokes! They've just nuked Kuwait."

As the Iraqi forces retreated, four special tactics team members were among the first into Kuwait City. At the international airport, MSgt. Wayne Norrad climbed the stairway in the darkness to the top of the fourteen-story control tower, sweeping the area in front of him with the antenna of his hand-held radio to detect wires attached to possible booby traps.

Equipment in the tower had been wrecked, and there was no electricity. Looking down, Norrad could see the field was littered with unexploded ammunition. The Iraqis had scattered vehicles and large baggage carts to block the runways.

Sergeant Steve Jones and his teammates, along with a group of Marines, set about clearing the runways.

"After we got the big stuff off, we got in line and went down picking up all the little stuff," Jones says. "One of these unexploded cluster-bomb bomblets was lying on the taxiway. A buddy of mine, named Gus, reached down and picked it up and threw it off into the dirt. It didn't explode, but I said, 'Gus, if you ever do that again, make sure I'm not standing next to you.'

"We're trained in demolition. We can blow up unexploded ordnance. Moving it was the trick. We could have jury-rigged a stick and noose, behind some kind of barrier, and moved it. But it took time. We had airplanes coming."

Clearing the runways turned into a three-hour job. Jones then joined Norrad in the tower. While Norrad controlled the incoming planes, Jones supervised the ground crews, parking the planes so they did not block the taxiways.

Even though it was only about 2 P.M., there was so much smoke in the air from burning oil wells that visibility was down to half a mile, and incoming pilots were given the choice of whether they wanted to land or not.

After the fighting was over and most American troops began heading home, some of the air commandos were ordered to stay behind.

"I went over on 20 September, and I was there until April 31 of 1991," said Sergeant Hadrych. "We were there for Desert Shield, Desert Storm, and what we affectionately called Desert Shaft. I think they called it Desert Calm or something. It didn't seem like we were ever, ever going to leave. I had 221 days in-country, straight. I was not happy."

But Hadrych concluded that one mission—the one in which he helped rescue Lieutenant Jones—made it all worthwhile.

Other special operations units set up shop in southern Turkey as part of Operation Provide Comfort—helping to protect Kurds living in northern Iraq from Saddam Hussein's forces. In both 1992 and 1993, Air Force special operations helicopter crews won the Cheney Award for the outstanding military humanitarian aircraft mission of the year. In 1992, two MH-60 helicopters—a smaller aircraft than the Pave Low—flew through heavy enemy fire in a futile effort to rescue a Turkish pilot whose plane had crashed. In the 1993 operation, a Pave Low flew through a blinding storm for six hours to evacuate a critically ill French soldier from a United Nations mission in Iraq.

The operations in Desert Storm and northern Iraq were part of the strange new world created by the end of the Cold War. No longer was the Soviet Union the one big potential enemy to worry about, and no longer could the world be divided easily between the good guys and the bad guys. It was a new world in which special operations forces would be increasingly called upon to undertake urgent missions in unexpected parts of the world.

On 3 October 1993, three members of the 24th Special Tactics Squadron—a combat controller and two pararescuemen—found themselves in such a situation and became embroiled in one of the bloodiest firefights involving American troops since the Vietnam War.

The three were among a group of eleven members of the squadron attached to Joint Task Force Ranger, a two-hundred-man-strong Army unit operating in Mogadishu, Somalia, in support of a United Nations effort to quell the fighting between rival warlords.

Sergeant Jeffrey Bray, the combat controller, was the first into action that afternoon. He accompanied a Ranger unit that fast-roped from a helicopter to the ground in a crowded section of downtown Mogadishu to capture a group of men believed responsible for attacks on United States troops. Despite coming under fire, they quickly rounded up the men and called for a truck to pick them up.

Moments later, an Army Black Hawk helicopter was struck by a rocket-propelled grenade and crashed three hundred yards from Bray's position. Bray and a Ranger platoon moved toward the crash scene under heavy fire, racing against Somali forces heading in the same direction.

When the Black Hawk went down, the two pararescuemen—MSgt. Scott Fales and TSgt. Timothy Wilkinson—were in another Black Hawk circling nearby, members of a fifteen-man search and rescue security team. As their plane hovered above the crash scene, members of the rescue unit fast-roped to the street,

forty feet below. As Fales and Wilkinson, the last two men, prepared to go out the doors, the helicopter was hit by a rocket-
propelled grenade. The pilots held the plane steady while the two
men slid down into the blinding dust cloud kicked up by the rotor blades.

Fales and Wilkinson, with two units of Rangers, fought their way
to the downed helicopter. They found it on its side, the two pilots
dead. Moments later, Fales was shot through the leg. Wilkinson
helped free a trapped crew member, and then he and Fales, despite his own injury, set up an aid station near the tail of the helicopter and began treating the wounded men.

Bray had found a sheltered area nearby to treat the wounded
members of his unit. But he needed help. In response to a radioed
call, Wilkinson sprinted forty-five meters through heavy fire to
Bray's position. Later, he ran back to the helicopter for more supplies and then crossed again to Bray's position.

Bray, meanwhile, directed fire from helicopter gunships circling overhead.

It was seven o'clock the next morning before a rescue force
fought its way to the scene of the fighting to pull the survivors,
the wounded, and the bodies of the dead out to a makeshift aid
station.

For his heroic actions, Wilkinson received the Air Force Cross.
Fales and Bray were awarded the Silver Star. The eight other special tactics team members received the Bronze Star.

The Americans had lost eighteen men killed. Another eighty-
four were injured.

It was a disaster that never should have happened.

The Rangers had been sent into the worst possible situation—
a crowded city in which gunmen mingled with crowds of civilians
in an area bisected by streets and narrow little alleys. They had
neither armored vehicles to protect them from gunmen wielding
automatic rifles and grenade launchers nor an AC-130 gunship
overhead to serve as an escort.

A Spectre gunship, operating above the range of the Somali
weapons, could have provided pinpoint support for the unit. But
the gunships that had been stationed in Somalia earlier had been

sent off to Italy in case they were needed to back up United Nations forces in Bosnia.

In September 1995, a Senate Armed Services Committee report blamed political considerations for the failure to have AC-130 gunships available to back up the Rangers. Senate investigators found that senior officials wanted to hold down the numbers of Americans in Somalia and to avoid the appearance of unnecessary damage to civilians in Mogadishu. General Colin Powell, then chairman of the Joint Chiefs of Staff, was quoted as saying that, when they were used earlier, the gunships "wrecked a few buildings, and it wasn't the greatest imagery on CNN."

The report concluded: "It is difficult to understand the decision to omit the AC-130 gunships from the Joint Task Force Ranger force package. The AC-130s were part of all the force package options and were included in all of the training exercises. This decision is inconsistent with the principle that you fight as you train."

Veteran air commandos, while proud of the heroism of the men involved, were sickened by the failure of leadership that had put them in such an impossible position.

Colonel Gary Weikel expressed what many of his colleagues felt:

"We had a Holloway Commission after Desert One in 1980. But we lost a lot more people in this Mogadishu operation than we ever lost in 1980. Where was there someone in the government looking at what really happened? Nobody ever forced the military to look at what the heck it just did and account for it and try to figure out, is there a better, smarter way to do this to make sure we don't do this dumb-ass stuff again?

"They were just as happy to have this whole thing brushed away, hand out a bunch of medals, try to make everybody feel as good, in damage control, as possible, and then move on. As a professional military guy, I'm unhappy that we didn't address how could we do that differently so the outcome would be different. Let's face it, besides all those kids we got killed and injured, which far and away exceeded Desert One, we failed. And we caused a significant shift in U.S. foreign policy."

As Air Force special operations moves into its second half century, it has probably never been better off physically. While the military has suffered slashed budgets almost across the board, money has continued to flow to the Air Force Special Operations Command, as evidenced by the new buildings under construction at its headquarters at Hurlburt Field.

A new unit—the 6th Special Operations Squadron—has been formed to specialize in helping other nations in their internal defense—a mission very much like that of the old Jungle Jim in the early 1960s. The command also operates an Air Force Special Operations School at Hurlburt, with students drawn not only from the Air Force but from other services, foreign countries, and civilian agencies.

On the runways, the command can boast of a fleet of the most sophisticated aircraft in the world. There is a new gunship with radar-guided weapons that can be aimed and fired independently at two separate targets simultaneously and with electronic equipment so precise that the crew can follow an individual bullet to the ground. The Combat Talon transport plane and the Combat Shadow tanker have navigational equipment that permits them to fly closer to the ground in clouds and darkness than most pilots dare to fly in the daytime.

The Pave Low helicopter and the smaller Pave Hawk are equally advanced technologically.

But problems do lie not too far in the future. The Pave Lows were originally built in the 1960s, and, although drastically modernized, they are nearing the end of their useful life. The special operators would very much like to see them replaced with the V-22 Osprey, a plane whose engines rotate on fixed wings so that it can take off vertically like a helicopter and then speed off like a normal fixed-wing plane. Although debate over funding for the Osprey has focused on its use by the Marines, it is even better suited for special operations, where its speed, coupled with its ability to take off and land vertically, makes it an ideal replacement for the Pave Low.

"The Osprey makes a whole lot of sense," says George Gray, who has been promoted to brigadier general since his duty in Desert

Storm. "In Iraq, it took me two hours to get a Pave Low up to pick up that pilot and two hours back. And we had to run tankers into Iraq. With the Osprey, you could do it all in an hour and a half total, at 250 knots instead of 150 knots. That's a big difference. Special operations has a much greater need for that plane than the Marines."

The plane has, however, been plagued by technical problems of the kind common with a new type of aircraft and opposition even within the Pentagon. Whether it will be available to replace the Pave Low is an open question. Without it, the special operators will have a critical gap in their arsenal.

Another gap is evident on the parking aprons at Hurlburt. There are no fixed-wing escorts to fill the role of the Spads of the Vietnam era or the P-51s of the World War II battles in Burma.

One proposal that has been made is to transfer a squadron or two of A-10 fighter-bombers to special operations.

"The A-10 fits in as an escort. I pushed for that when I was commander of the 1st Special Operations Wing," says Gray. "But I was turned down. There are a lot of A-10 folks excited about the possibility of getting into special operations."

But James Hobson, who led the airdrop in Grenada and, in 1994, became the first career special operator to head the Air Force Special Operations Command, says that's not going to happen.

Hobson, now a major general, says his superiors at the United States Special Operations Command don't want to get in the business of owning any more airplanes.

"We don't need our own," he says. "We need A-10s chopped to us for specific operations. But I don't think the command needs to buy and pay for its own A-10s. We train together all the time. But we don't need to own those guys."

Other officers fear, however, that the A-10s might not be available when they are needed—or that they might not be available at all—if special operations doesn't "own" them. Although the A-10 is powered by jet engines, it is designed to fly low and slow, killing tanks and supporting troops on the ground. It is an ungainly craft—they call it the Warthog—and there has always been an influential element in the Air Force that would like to see it removed from the inventory entirely. At some point in the country's budget-cutting mood, the critics may get their wish.

Of more concern to special operations leaders than hardware is the constant strain on their aircrews. The command has the highest operating tempo of any unit in the Air Force. That means long family separations, high divorce rate, and aircrews who are just plain tired. For officers, the fact that they are away from home so often, coupled with the fact that they do most of their flying at night, makes it difficult to attend specialized military schools or to gain the advanced degrees that are essential for advancement in today's smaller and highly competitive military.

The air commandos have clearly benefited from their association with the new United States Special Operations Command. It has given them a much more secure source of funds, and that helps to account for the new buildings and its fleet of new and refurbished aircraft. But the parent command is, and will probably remain, dominated by the Army and Army thinking, and many air commandos find that worrisome.

The Pentagon's plans now call for the military to be able to respond to two major contingencies in two parts of the world at the same time—another Gulf War and a war in Korea, for example. But Hobson, for one, doesn't think that is going to happen. Instead, he foresees more small contingencies. Some, like Operation Provide Comfort, the aid for the Kurds in northern Iraq, may involve little or no combat.

It will be the kind of world where military commanders will wonder how to cope with unusual and unexpected situations in unfamiliar parts of the world. And then, as they have so often in the past, they will send in the air commandos to do the job.

Glossary

A-1E Propeller-driven close support aircraft extensively used in Southeast Asia. Known by the nickname of Spad and the call sign of Sandy.

A-26 Invader Twin-engine bomber introduced in World War II. It was known as the B-26 during the Korean War, but again as the A-26 in Southeast Asia.

ABCCC Vietnam-era Airborne Control and Command Center—called AB Triple C. C-47 and later C-130 planes stayed on station twenty-four hours a day. Known in daytime as Cricket, at night as Alley Cat.

Aberdeen Landing zone during Allied incursion into Burma in World War II.

ABF Attacks by fire.

AC-47 Original fixed-wing gunship used in Southeast Asia. Known as Snoopy and Puff, the Magic Dragon.

Air America Airline operated by the Central Intelligence Agency in Southeast Asia.

Air Resupply and Communications Service During the 1950s, used to drop leaflets and insert agents in foreign countries. Known by the acronym of ARCS.

Apache Army helicopter gunship.

AWACS Airborne Warning and Control System, a flying command post with powerful radar.

B-17 Flying Fortress Bomber used to deliver supplies behind enemy lines in World War II.

B-24 Liberator Bomber used by Carpetbaggers in World War II to supply guerrillas behind German lines.

Barrel Roll Area of operations along the Laos–North Vietnam border. Began in December 1964, with Thai-based planes attacking targets in Laos.

Bird Dog Single-engine Cessna aircraft, flown by forward air controllers known in Laos by the call sign of Raven.

Blue Spoon Code word used in planning the invasion of Panama. The operation itself was called Just Cause.

Broadway Landing zone for Allied incursion into Burma in World War II.

Butterfly Call sign for original enlisted forward air controllers in Laos. They were replaced in 1967 by commissioned pilots, using the call sign Raven.

Carpetbaggers Special air operation during World War II delivering supplies and personnel to resistance forces.

CAS Controlled American Source. Code name for CIA operating out of base in northern Thailand into Laos.

CAS Close air support.

Cetniks Forces headed by Gen. Draja Mihailovich, minister of war in the royal Yugoslav government, operating in exile out of Cairo in World War II.

Chalk Term used to distinguish aircraft loads, as in "Chalk One," "Chalk Two."

Chindits Designation for Brig. Gen. Orde Wingate's forces operating behind Japanese lines in Burma. The word is a corruption of the Burmese word *chinthe,* the fierce dragonlike creature whose likeness guards Burmese temples.

Chowringhee A potential landing zone in Burma named for the main thoroughfare in Calcutta.

Combat Skyspot The TSQ-81 radar, a modified version of the Strategic Air Command bomb scoring radar. It was used in Southeast Asia to direct bombers to their targets, especially in bad weather.

Combat Talon MC-130 airplane used to carry special forces behind enemy lines.

Commando Club Code name for a radar system operated from Site 85 on Phou Pha Thi Mountain in northeastern Laos.

Commando Hunt Code name for a series of campaigns using sensors to detect and attack enemy forces and truck traffic on the Ho Chi Minh Trail. They covered the period of November 1968 through October 1971 and were numbered from I to VI.

Credible Sport Code name for a special program to modify an MC-130 transport plane so it could land in a soccer field in Teheran and take off again with hostages held by the Iranians.

Delta Force Army antiterrorist unit.

Dien Bien Phu Site of a 1954 battle in which elite French forces were trapped and defeated by the Vietminh.

FAC Airborne forward air controller.

FAG Forward air guide, controlling air strikes from the ground in Laos.

Farmgate Code name for first air commando units sent to Vietnam in 1961.

FARRP Army acronym for Forward Area Refueling and Rearming Point.

Fulton Recovery System Method in which a person on the ground releases a line attached to a balloon. The line is snagged by an airplane, and the person is then reeled into the plane.

Gee box Radio navigational device used in World War II.

Hmong Mountain people of Laos who cooperated with the United States in resistance to the North Vietnamese. Also known as the Meo.

Ho Chi Minh Trail North Vietnamese supply route through Laos into South Vietnam.

Holloway Commission Investigative body, headed by Adm. James L. Holloway III, set up after the disaster at Desert One.

Honey Badger Code name for preparations for a second effort to rescue American hostages held in Teheran.

Igloo White Code name for a system of sensors designed to detect movement of North Vietnamese troops and supplies along the Ho Chi Minh Trail and across the DMZ in Vietnam. Name changed from Muscle Shoals in 1968.

Joan-Eleanor System used in World War II in which an agent behind enemy lines broadcast a narrow beam detected by a plane flying at high altitudes.

Joe An agent parachuted behind enemy lines in World War II. Female agents were known as Janes.

Joe Hole Opening in the belly of a bomber through which an agent was dropped.

Jolly Green Giant United States Air Force HH-3E helicopter often used for search and rescue in Southeast Asia.

Jungle Jim Code word for Air Force unit set up in the early 1960s to help other nations resist Communist aggression. More formally, it was known as the 4400th Combat Crew Training Squadron.

Just Cause Code word for the invasion of Panama in 1989.

Long Chieng A forward staging area used by the CIA in Laos and headquarters for resistance fighters led by Vang Pao. The base was also known as Lima Site 30, 20 Alternate, or Alternate.

Longcloth World War II operation in which three thousand Chindits of the 77th Indian Infantry Brigade crossed into Burma on foot and penetrated deep in country in February 1943. They suffered from lack of air support and resupply.

Maquis French resistance fighters in World War II.

Mosquito A lightweight British twin-engine bomber used by the Carpetbaggers in World War II. In Korea, the word was used to designate forward air controllers flying T-6 trainers.

Nickels Slang name for leaflets dropped in World War II.

Nimrod Call sign used by A-26 pilots operating out of Thailand from 1966 to 1969.

NVA North Vietnamese Army.

NVG Night-vision goggles.

Office of the Coordinator of Information World War II military intelligence unit formed in July 1941.

Office of Strategic Services World War II military intelligence unit known as OSS, formed from Office of the Coordinator of Information in June 1942. The OSS was the predecessor of the Central Intelligence Agency.

Operation Aviary Agents, code-named Rabbits, were landed by parachute behind enemy lines in Korea.

Operation Buick One of a series of mass drops of supplies to resistance forces in France in July and August 1944.

Operation Cadillac Mass drop to resistance forces on 14 July 1944 as the battle for Saint-Lo was reaching its climax.

Operation Haik Small air unit set up by the CIA in 1958 to provide air support to rebels against the Indonesian government.

Operation Rice Bowl The plan to rescue American hostages from Teheran in 1980.

Operation Thursday The allied incursion into Burma in 1944.

Pave Hawk MH-60 helicopter used by Air Force special operations. Based on Army Black Hawk design and smaller than the Pave Low.

Pave Low MH-53 helicopter developed for use in low-level operations at night and in bad weather behind enemy lines.

Phou Pha Thi Secret radar site in Laos, twenty-five kilometers from the North Vietnam border, that directed air strikes against Hanoi. Also known as Lima Site 85, it was captured by the enemy in 1968.

Picadilly One of the major landing zones during Operation Thursday in Burma in 1944.

Plaine des Jarres Known as PDJ, an area in central Laos distinguished by large pot-shaped burial urns left by earlier inhabitants.

Project 404/Palace Dog A secret Air Force unit that controlled much of the air war in Laos in the 1960s and 1970s.

Project Lucky Tiger Code name for plan to introduce A-26 attack planes into Laos in 1966.

Project Mill Pond Code name for the introduction of unmarked B-26 bombers into Thailand to fly "armed reconnaissance" missions over Laos.

Project 9 Code name for preparations for the Operation Thursday incursion into Burma in World War II.

Project Ranch Hand Program, beginning in 1962, in which C-123 planes flown by air commandos dropped chemicals to burn the leaves off trees in enemy-held areas of Vietnam.

Project Shining Brass Code name for a program of dropping road-watch teams near enemy supply routes in North Vietnam and Laos. The name was changed to Prairie Fire in 1968 and Phu Dung in 1971.

Project Water Pump Code name for program to train indigenous pilots in Thailand.

Quadrant Conference Meeting in Quebec in August 1943 in which Prime Minister Winston Churchill and President Franklin D. Roosevelt discussed the future course of the war.

Raven Call sign for a small group of forward air controllers in Laos.

Rebecca/Eureka World War II system which used radar pulses reflected off the ground system—Eureka—to guide the plane, with its Rebecca device, to the target.

RTB Return to base.

Son Tay Site of raid near Hanoi on 20 November 1970. The suspected prisoner-of-war camp held no prisoners.

Spectre Call sign for the AC-130 gunship.

S-phone A kind of powerful walkie-talkie radio with a range of eight to ten miles, used in World War II.

Starlight scope Night-vision device capable of amplifying light four hundred thousand times.

Stray Goose Code name for an operation in which MC-130 Combat Talon planes flew alone and unescorted to drop leaflets and North Vietnamese currency over Hanoi and Haiphong. Carried on for several years during the 1960s, the operation was ended in 1969.

TACAN Tactical Air Navigation station.

Udorn Base for air commandos operating out of Thailand.

V-22 Osprey Tilt-wing plane.

Vang Pao Leader of Hmong units opposing North Vietnamese in Laos.

Vientiane Administrative capital of Laos.

Vietminh Military units opposing the French in Indochina.

White City Allied base behind Japanese lines in Burma. So named because the area was littered with white parachutes.

Winchestered Slang word used by gunship crews when they have fired all their bullets.

Zebra Code name for mass drop of supplies behind German lines in France in World War II.

Sources

With the exception of interviews conducted by the author, all interviews referred to in the Sources were conducted for the Air Force Oral History program and are available in the Air Force Historical Research Agency library at Maxwell Air Force Base, Montgomery, Alabama. Although many Vietnam-era documents have been declassified, a number of them remain classified, and access is limited to those with the appropriate security clearance. The oral history interviews are also available on microfilm at the library of the Air Force History Office at Bolling Air Force Base, Washington, D.C. However, if a declassified document is on a roll of microfilm that also contains a classified document, the entire roll is considered classified.

PART 1: BIRTH OF THE AIR COMMANDOS

One of the best accounts of Operation Thursday, the airborne invasion of Burma in 1944, is contained in the Air Force Oral History Program interview conducted with the late Col. Philip G. Cochran at Rochester, New York, and Washington, D.C., in October and November of 1975 by James C. Hasdorff.

An overview of the operation is also contained in Herbert A. Mason, Jr., SSgt. Randy G. Bergeron, and TSgt. James A. Renfrow, Jr., *Operation Thursday: Birth of the Air Commandos* (Air Force History and Museums Program 1994) and in R. D. Van Wagner, *1st Air Commando Group: Any Place, Any Time, Any Where*, Military History Series 86–1 (USAF Air Command and Staff College, 1986).

The operation is also covered, with interviews of some of those involved, in Philip G. Chinnery, *Any Time, Any Place, a History of USAF Air Commando and Special Operations Forces* (Annapolis: Naval Institute Press, 1994).

Also available is the Oral History Program interview with Maj. Gen. John R. Alison, conducted at Washington, D.C., 22–28 April

1979 by Maj. Scottie S. Thompson. Permission to cite or quote from this interview must be obtained from the donor.

These documentary sources were augmented with personal interviews I conducted with Stam Robertson, Ray Ruksas, John Dudak, and Richard D. Snyder at the 1st Air Commando Association reunion in Fort Walton Beach, Florida, in October 1994.

A brief overview of special operations is provided in an Air Force pamphlet, *Heritage of the Quiet Professionals*, covering the history of Air Force special operations from World War II through the Gulf War.

PART 2: BEHIND THE LINES IN EUROPE

The best overview I found of special operations activities in Europe during World War II is *Special Operations: AAF Aid to European Resistance Movements, 1943-1945*. Written by Maj. Harris G. Warren for the AAF Historical Office, headquarters, Army Air Forces, this manuscript was published in typescript form in June 1947. It covers not only the activities of the Carpetbaggers in northern Europe but also the aid to the resistance in southern Europe.

A similar but less inclusive account of the special operations war in Europe is provided by Maj. Bernard Victor Moore II, *"The Secret Air War over France": USAAF Special Operations Units in the French Campaign of 1944. A Historical Case Study of the Role of Air Force Special Operations Forces in High Intensity Conflict*, a thesis presented to the faculty of the School for Advanced Airpower Studies, Air University, Maxwell Air Force Base, Montgomery, Alabama, May 1992.

The experiences of the Carpetbaggers are covered in Ben Parell, *America's Secret War in Europe* (Austin: Eakin Press).

A broad overview of Air Force special operations, referring back as far as the campaign against Pancho Villa in 1916, is contained in *AFSOC: The Air Force's Newest Command*, by Lt. Col. Jerry L. Thigpen, USAF (Carlisle Barracks, Pa.: U.S. Army War College, 1991).

Colonel Robert W. Fish, who was intimately involved in Carpetbagger operations throughout the war, has collected a treasury of both official records and personal reminiscences of that period. A group history, with original documents downgraded to unclassified, dates from 1962. In a much more ambitious effort, Fish put together *Memories of the 801st/492nd Bombardment Group, As Told to Col. Robert W. Fish,* 20 September 1990. This collection is especially valuable because it contains a full index. I subsequently interviewed Colonel Fish and his friend, Col. J. W. Bradbury, USAF retired, a Carpetbagger pilot who has contacted a number of Europeans who were on the receiving end of the supply drops by the Carpetbaggers. Both now live in San Antonio, Texas.

PART 3: KOREA AND BEYOND
The history of the air commandos, beginning with Korea, is covered in a readable, heavily illustrated form in Col. Michael E. Haas, with TSgt. Dale K. Robinson, *Air Commando! 1950–1975: Twenty-five years at the Tip of the Spear,* published by the Air Force Special Operations Command at Hurlburt Field in 1994. As an active duty officer, Haas had the advantage of being able to examine material that is still classified and to request declassification of the material he needed for his book.

He was able, for example, to obtain excerpts from the still-classified Air Force Oral History Program interview with Brig. Gen. Henry "Heinie" Aderholt, whose career so closely parallels the history of Air Force special operations. I interviewed Aderholt at his office in Fort Walton Beach, Florida, in December 1993.

The story of the A-26 (known during the 50s as the B-26) is told in fascinating detail in Dan Hagendorn and Leif Hellstrom, *Foreign Invaders: The Douglas Invader in Foreign Military and US Clandestine Service* (Leicester, England: Midland Publishing, 1994).

Richard Snyder told me of his experiences as a B-26 pilot in Korea during the interview cited in Part 1.

My account of the adventures of Lt. Col. Robert A. Madden, who served as an air commando in three wars and was shot down in Korea, is based on his reminiscences as published in the journal of the Air Commando Association, the *ACA Newsletter,* of March 1992.

The material on the Air Resupply and Communications Service comes from my interview with Fish and from files of the *Air Resupply and Communications Association Newsletter.* Carl H. Bernhardt, Jr., provided me with a computer diskette containing the entire file of the newsletter.

PART 4: THE LONGEST WAR

A good background of the early years of the air commando involvement in Southeast Asia is provided in John Hawkins Napier III, "The Air Commandos in Vietnam: November 5, 1961 to February 7, 1965," a Master's thesis submitted to the graduate faculty of Auburn University on 16 March 1967.

The organization of the Jungle Jim unit at Hurlburt Field and the deployment of the Farmgate detachment to Vietnam are described in a letter from Wade Everett in the March 1992 *ACA Newsletter.*

The early Farmgate history is covered by Richard Secord in his biography, Richard Secord, with Jay Wurts, *Honored and Betrayed: Irangate, Covert Affairs, and the Secret War In Laos* (New York: John Wiley & Sons, 1992).

That era is also covered in Oral History Program interviews with Maj. Frank J. Gorski, Jr., conducted by Lt. Col. V. H. Gallagher and Maj. Lyn R. Officer, at Eglin Air Force Base on 5 February 1973; with Lt. Col. Roy C. Dalton, conducted by Majors Victor Anthony, Ralph Rowley, and Riley Sunderland on 8 February 1973; and with Lt. Col. Roy H. Lynn, conducted by Lt. Col. Ray L. Bowers and Major Anthony on 9 September 1970.

Colonel Ronald Jones, USAF retired, told me of his experiences flying an MC-130 on leaflet-dropping missions over North Vietnam in the Stray Goose operation during an interview at his San Antonio home on 4 December 1994.

A rich source of information about air commando activities in Southeast Asia is contained in a series of historical documents prepared during the war for headquarters, Pacific Air Force. Known as CHECO Reports (an acronym for contemporary historical examination of current operations), most of these documents are not specifically concerned with special operations as such. But the air commandos seemed to show up wherever the action was hot and heavy—and dangerous—so the CHECO reports often provide a detailed description of their activities.

Among the CHECO reports that proved particularly valuable were:

Night Close Air Support in the Republic of Vietnam, 1961–1966, prepared by Lawrence J. Hickey. Covers Farmgate, the introduction of the AC-47 gunship, the battles of Song Be, Dong Xoia, Quang Ngai, and Plei Me, the fall of the A Shau Special Forces camp, and deployment of the 4th Air Commando Squadron.

USAF Support of Special Forces in Southeast Asia, prepared by Kenneth Sams and Lt. Col. Bert B. Aton, 10 March 1969.

Kham Duc Special Report, 8 July 1968, prepared by Kenneth Sams and Maj. A. W. Thompson. Describes air support for evacuation of Special Forces camp at Kham Duc on 12 May 1968.

The Fall of A Shau, prepared by Kenneth Sams, 18 April 1966. Covers both the loss of an AC-47, whose copilot fought off the Vietcong while his colleagues were rescued, and the heroic rescue of Maj. Dafford W. Myers, after his plane had crashed on an enemy-held runway, by Maj. Bernard F. Fisher.

The development and use of fixed-wing gunships is described in detail in Jack S. Ballard, *Development and Employment of Fixed-Wing Gunships 1962–1972* (Washington, D.C.: Office of Air Force History, 1982).

The use of the gunships in combat is covered in a series of CHECO reports, among them:

Pave Mace/Combat Rendezvous (u), prepared by Maj. Richard R. Sexton, 26 December 1972, describes the first use of the FC-47, later AC-47, gunship to support a South Vietnamese outpost on a dark night in 1965.

First Test and Combat Use of AC-47, interim report No. 2, prepared by Kenneth Sams with foreword by Col. Edward C. Burtenshaw, 8 December 1965.

Fixed Wing Gunships in Southeast Asia (July 1969–July 1971) prepared by Capt. James L. Cole, Jr., 30 November 1971, gives detailed history of gunships, from AC-47 to the Surprise Package.

Interesting background on the development of the fixed-wing gunship is provided by an article, "How the Gunships Came to Be," in the June 1989 issue of the *ACA Newsletter* by Col. Gilmour Craig MacDonald, USAF retired. He tells how he proposed the idea of side-firing, pilot-aimed gunships in April 1942.

A personal account of the unfortunate deployment of the AC-47 gunships to the Ho Chi Minh Trail is provided in an article in the March 1990 *ACA Newsletter* by Lt. Col. Charles A. Riley, USAF retired. He describes how four aircraft and more than 30 crew members were lost in short order.

PART 5: THROUGH THE LOOKING GLASS

The best overall account of the secret war in Laos, especially as it affected the Hmong people, is contained in Jane Hamilton-Merritt, *Tragic Mountains: The Hmong, the Americans, and the Secret Wars for Laos, 1942–1992* (Bloomington: Indiana University Press, 1993).

A good deal of background on that shadowy phase of the war in Southeast Asia is also contained in Secord's biography, cited in Part 4. His account of the loss of the critical radar base known as Lima Site 85 on Phou Pha Thi Mountain was especially useful.

An official account of the loss of the site is contained in a CHECO report prepared by Capt. Edward Vallentiny on 9 August 1968. An intriguing historical footnote to that battle was provided by author Neil Sheehan in "The Last Battle," an article in *The New Yorker* for 24 April 1995. He located the Vietnamese leader of the commandos who scaled a two-thousand-foot cliff to attack the base.

Background on the air commandos' war in Laos and Thailand was derived from the interview with Henry Aderholt, cited in Part 3; an interview with Clyde Howard, a combat controller who served a number of tours in Southeast Asia, at Navarre, Florida, on 15 October 1994; the Oral History Program interviews with Roy Dalton, cited in Part 4, with Maj. Donald Randle, conducted by Lt. Col. Robert G. Zimmerman at San Rafael, California, in December 1974, with Maj. Jesse E. Scott, conducted by Lt. Col. V. H. Gallagher and Hugh N. Ahmann, at Maxwell Air Force Base on 6 April 1973, and with Col. Robert L. F. Tyrrell, the long-time air attaché in Vientiane, conducted by Colonel Zimmerman in Seattle, Washington, 12 May 1975.

Jim Stanford, one of the enlisted forward air controllers known as Butterflies, told me of his experiences in an interview in Fort Walton Beach, Florida, in October 1994.

A battle in which another Butterfly, Charles Jones—known as

Butterfly 44—played a pivotal role is described in *Second Defense of Lima Site 36*, a CHECO report prepared by Capt. Melvin F. Potter on 28 April 1967.

The story of the Ravens, the commissioned pilots who took over from the enlisted Butterflies, is told in Christopher Robbins, *The Ravens: The Men Who Flew in America's Secret War in Laos* (New York: Crown Publishers, 1987).

Additional background on the Ravens came from Jerome "Jerry" Klingaman, who headed the secret Project 404/Palace Dog, managing the secret air war in Laos, in an interview at Hurlburt Field, Florida, in October 1994. Project 404/Palace Dog is described in a recently declassified five-page document, *History of Participation in Project 404/Palace Dog*, dated 28 January 1971. It was obtained from the Air Force Historical Research Agency at Maxwell Air Force Base.

Fascinating details of Raven operations are provided in Oral History Program interviews with Maj. Michael E. Cavanaugh, conducted by Lt. Col. Robert G. Zimmerman at Randolph Air Force Base, Texas, on 21 November 1974, and with Capt. Karl L. Polifka, conducted by Colonel Zimmerman, in Washington, D.C., on 17 December 1974. Permission to cite or quote from the Polifka interview is required. I obtained permission in a telephone conversation with Polifka, who now lives in Williamsburg, Virginia.

My account of the A-26 operations in Southeast Asia, in both the earlier Mill Pond deployment to Thailand and during the lengthy Nimrod period, is derived from Hagendorn and Hellstrom's *Foreign Invaders*, cited in Part 3; from "'Nimrods'—Truck Killers on the Trail," an article in the July 1988 issue of the *ACA Newsletter*, by Thomas Wickstrom; from interviews with Wickstrom, Tim Black, and Gene Albee at the Nimrods' 1994 reunion in Fort Walton Beach, Florida, and the Oral History Program interview with Major Gorski, cited in Part 4.

Wickstrom, a Nimrod pilot who now lives in Huntington Beach, California, has been most active in gathering information about the long history of the use of the A-26 in various parts of the world.

Further background material concerning the war in Laos was derived from the CHECO reports, *Interdiction at Ban Bak, 19*

December 1970–5 January 1971 (prepared by Maj. John W. Denni-son 26 January 1971); *Pave Aegis Weapon System (AC-130E GUN-SHIP)* (prepared 30 July 1973) and *OV-1/AC119 Hunter-Killer Team* (prepared by Maj. Richard R. Sexton and Capt. William M. Hodgson on 10 October 1972).

Three CHECO reports cover the development and use of Igloo White, the so-called McNamara Barrier of sensors intended to help block movement of North Vietnamese soldiers and sup-plies down the Ho Chi Minh Trail. They are *Igloo White, Initial Phase* (prepared by Col. Jesse C. Gatlin, 31 July 1968), covering the Muscle Shoals project through the operational period of 1 De-cember 1967 to 31 March 1968; *Igloo White, July 1968–December 1969* (prepared by Maj. Philip D. Caine on 10 January 1970), and *Igloo White, January 1970–September 1971* (prepared by Capt. Henry S. Shields, 1 November 1971).

PART 6: SON TAY AND THE *MAYAGUEZ*

A detailed account of the Son Tay raid is contained in Benjamin F. Schemmer, *The Raid* (New York: Harper & Row, 1976).

My research included interviews with Lt. Gen. LeRoy J. Manor, USAF retired, who commanded the operation, in Shalimar, Florida, 10 and 13 October 1994, and Col. Ronald Jones, USAF retired, a C-130 pilot who participated in preparations for the raid, at his home in San Antonio, Texas, on 4 December 1994.

The observations of Col. Royal A. Brown are contained in an Oral History Program interview conducted by Maj. Lyn R. Offi-cer at Eglin Air Force Base on 9 February 1973.

Colonel Gary L. Weikel told me of his part in the *Mayaguez* op-eration in an interview at his office in the Pentagon on 25 Octo-ber 1994.

Details of the capture of the ship, the subsequent rescue at-tempt, and statements issued by officials in Washington were ob-tained from the files of the *New York Times*.

Aderholt, in the interview cited in Part 3, told me of his in-volvement in training Cambodian air force crews as part of Proj-ect Water Pump. Clyde Howard, in the interview cited in Part 5, told me of the mistaken B-52 bombing of a Cambodian village.

PART 7: HOSTAGE RESCUE EFFORTS

The Air Force role in the effort to rescue the hostages from Teheran in 1980 is described in a fascinating account in Col. James H. Kyle, USAF retired, with John Robert Eidson, *The Guts to Try* (New York: Orion Books, 1990).

The postmortem on the failure of the rescue attempt is contained in the report of the Special Operations Review Group, usually referred to as the Holloway Commission Report. The text of the report was printed in the 15, 22, and 29 September 1980 issues of *Aviation Week & Space Technology* magazine. Although portions of the original report were deleted for security reasons before its public release, the report as released accurately reflects the conclusions of the panel.

Colonel John T. Carney, Jr., USAF retired, told me of his survey of the desert landing site in an interview at his office in Fort Walton Beach, Florida, on 6 October 1994.

Colonel Lee Hess, USAF retired, described his involvement in the planning for the raid during an interview at his office at Hurlburt Field, Florida, on 10 October 1944.

Sergeant Mike Hozenbackez described his training as a gunship crew member for the later phases of the operation, which were canceled because of the problems at Desert One. He was interviewed at Hurlburt Field on 14 October 1994.

General LeRoy Manor, who was a member of the Holloway Commission, discussed the hostage rescue attempt and compared it to the Son Tay raid, which he directed, in the interview cited in Part 6.

Colonel Ron Jones, in the interview cited in Part 6, told of his involvement in the deception operation in Egypt before the rescue attempt.

Gary Weikel, in the interview cited in Part 6, told me of his concerns about the failure of the hostage rescue planners to follow the successful model of the Son Tay raid. His views are further spelled out in "Just Cause and Desert Storm—New Paradigms or Aberrations?" a paper presented at the National War College, Washington, D.C., in January 1991.

Honey Badger and the preparations for another attempt to

rescue the hostages in Teheran are described in Richard Secord's *Honored and Betrayed,* cited in Part 4, and in Steven Emerson, *Secret Warriors: Inside the Covert Military Operations of the Reagan Era* (New York: Putnam's, 1988).

I also discussed Air Force preparations for that renewed effort with John F. "Jack" Kelly, Frank Pehr, Lt. Col. Michael E. "Mike" Homan, and Col. Mike Damron in interviews at Kirtland Air Force Base, Albuquerque, New Mexico, in November 1994, and with Col. John Roberts, USAF retired, at his Alexandria, Virginia, office on 22 November 1994.

Pehr was an especially valuable source of information about the development of the Pave Low III helicopter system.

That development is also described in detail in Leo Anthony Gambone, *Pave Low III: That Others May Live* (History Office, Aeronautical Systems Command, undated).

Colonel Ron Jones, in the interview cited in Part 6, told me of Credible Sport, the crash effort to modify a C-130 to land in a soccer stadium in Teheran.

Details of the Grenada invasion are described in detail in Donn-Erik Marshall, *Urgent Fury: The U.S. Military Intervention in Grenada,* a Master's thesis presented to the graduate faculty, Corcoran Department of History, University of Virginia, May 1989, and in Mark Adkin, *Urgent Fury: the Battle for Grenada* (Lexington, Massachusetts: Lexington Books, 1989).

Personal reminiscences of the Grenada operation were obtained in interviews with Maj. Gen. James L. Hobson, Jr., at Andrews Air Force Base, Maryland, on 25 April 1995 and with Carney and Hozenbackez, cited in Part 7.

An account of Hobson's involvement in Grenada, which won him the Mackay Trophy, is contained in "Hobson Takes AFSOC Reins" in Night Flyer, a publication of the Air Force Special Operations Command, for July–August 1994.

General George A. Gray III, commander of the 1st Special Operations Wing at the time of Just Cause—the invasion of Panama—discussed that operation with me in an interview at McGuire Air Force Base, New Jersey, on 9 November 1994.

Other details of the Panama operation were provided in the

interviews with Carney, Weikel, and Hozenbackez, cited in Parts 6 and 7, and in an interview with Maj. Bob Leonik at the Pentagon on 17 October 1994.

The development of the special tactics teams and their involvement in both Just Cause and Desert Storm and Desert Shield are covered in *History of the 1720th Special Tactics Group, January 1990–December 1991. Volume I* by Kenneth N. Rose, USAF historian, and Col. Robert W. Neumann, commander.

The history of the special tactics teams is also covered in Frank Oliveri, "When the LZ Is Hot," *Air Force*, February 1994.

Personal observations of special tactics team involvement were provided in an interview with TSgt. Gordon W. Tully and SSgt. Boyd Bowling at Hurlburt Field, Florida, on 5 October 1994.

Clay McCutchan, a lieutenant colonel in the reserves, described his decision not to fire the guns of his gunship during an interview at Hurlburt Field on 13 October 1994.

In response to a request under the Freedom of Information Act, I received a small collection of papers, mostly newspaper clippings and press releases, concerning the "friendly fire" incident involving another AC-130 gunship. The Air Force response to my request said all other documents concerning the incident had been routinely destroyed.

The incident, first disclosed by *Newsweek* magazine in the issue of 25 June 1990, was described in several news articles: Tracy Wenzel, "Crews Under Fire, 'Friendly Fire' Probe Centers on Gunships," *Northwest Florida Daily News*, 21 June 1990; Christopher Clausen, "Hurlburt Crews Shot at GIs by Mistake," *Pensacola News Journal*, 22 June 1990; Wenzel, "AC-130 Panama Goof Confirmed," *Northwest Florida Daily News*, 22 June 1990, and Wenzel, "Hurlburt Aircrew Spared Discipline for Its 'Mistake,'" *Northwest Florida Daily News*, 1 July 1990.

PART 8: NEW CHALLENGES

A valuable overview of the participation of Air Force special operations forces in Desert Shield and Desert Storm is provided in Chapter V, "Operations Desert Shield and Desert Storm," in *AFSOC History 1990–1991*, prepared by the Command History

Office at Hurlburt Field. That chapter was written by SSgt. Randy Bergeron.

The role of Air Force special operations in the beginning of Desert Storm was described to me in interviews with George Gray and Bob Leonik, cited in Part 7, and an interview with Maj. Ben Pulsifer, at Kirtland Air Force Base, Albuquerque, New Mexico, on 30 November 1994.

Lieutenant Colonel Homan and MSgt. Timothy Hadrych told me of their perilous daytime foray into Iraq to rescue a downed Navy flier. Homan also described delivering a heavy load of Army Special Forces soldiers and their equipment deep in Iraq.

Sergeant Steve D. Jones told me of his participation with British special forces soldiers sent to blow up a communications line near Baghdad. He and Command MSgt. Wayne Norrad also described the scene at the Kuwait International Airport as the Special Tactics teams moved in to restore operations. Both men were interviewed at Hurlburt Field in October 1994.

The hectic scene at the Al Jouf airfield when planes returned from the first strike against Iraq was described by Gordon Tully in the interview cited in Part 7.

My account of the shootdown of *Spirit 03*, the AC-130 Spectre gunship, is derived from the report of the official investigation into the incident obtained under the Freedom of Information Act. The "Spirit 03 Report" is contained in 1SOW AFSOCCENT Deployed (Desert Storm) Part I and II, an undated Air Force Special Operations Command document. Additional information was contained in the interview with George Gray, cited in Part 7. The memorial service for the crew is described in David Tortorano, "Family, Friends Mourn Heroic Hurlburt Crew," *Pensacola Daily News,* 16 March 1991.

The involvement of members of the 24th Special Tactics Team in the fighting in Somalia is described in MSgt. Philip F. Rhodes, "A Soldier's Nightmare," *Night Flyer,* first quarter, 1994.

Major Greg S. "Fritz" Buterbaugh gave me a useful insight into the operations of the MC-130 Combat Talons, and Lt. Col. John Bicket gave a similar description of the use of the MH-60 Pave Hawk during interviews at Kirtland Air Force Base in November and December 1994.

I discussed the future of Air Force special operations in the interview with General Hobson, cited in Part 7. My thoughts on the problems and opportunities facing the command were also heavily influenced by my interviews with Gary Weikel and Lee Hess, cited in Parts 6 and 7, as well as Weikel's National War College paper and a sharply critical, no-holds-barred farewell address delivered by Hess when he retired in December 1994. He provided me with a copy of the address.

Index

Aircraft: Apache helicopter, 291, 314; A-10, 297, 298, 305, 312; A-1E, 144, 147, 211, 212, 314, 319; A-1H, 147; A-20, 15; A-26 Invader, 95-99, 173, 193, 194, 196-200, 314, 317, 322; A-37 Dragonfly, 148; A-7, 178, 255; AC-119G, 159; AC-119K, 159, 201; AC-130 (Spectre), 160, 161, 200, 201, 203, 255, 266, 279, 284, 303, 309, 319, 331; AC-47 gunship, 144, 324; AD-5, 147; AD-6, 147; AWACS, 297, 303-305, 314, 319; Black Hawk, 253, 308; B-17, 45, 62, 83, 314; B-24 Liberator, 45-46, 48, 50, 55-58, 60, 62, 66-68, 70-71, 73-77, 79, 80-81, 84, 86, 91, 93-96, 99, 314; B-25, 5, 23, 29, 32, 45, 84; B-26, 95, 110, 123, 126-128, 134-137, 146, 193, 314, 317; B-26 Marauder, 95; B-52, 179, 224, 327; C-118, 125; C-119, 112, 118, 159; C-123, 139, 194, 318; C-130, 124, 125, 157, 178, 235, 238, 241, 246-250, 259, 314; C-141, 239, 244; C-47, 3, 4, 12, 19, 23, 25, 28, 63, 64, 66, 75, 82, 88-91, 123, 131, 132, 135, 139, 148-152, 155, 157, 174; C-54, 112; DC-6, 125; F-100, 148; F-105, 148, 183, 186, 218, 219; F-111, 178; F-4, 148, 218; F/A-18, 295; FC-47, 150; Halifax bomber, 47; HC-130 tanker, 227; HH-3, 210, 212, 216, 217; HH-53, 210, 212, 217, 256, 272; JU-88, 57; MC-130 Combat Talon, 140, 211-213, 216, 236, 238, 244, 264, 306, 315, 319; ME-110, 57; Mosquito, 95, 98, 99, 108, 317; O-1 Bird Dog, 147, 179; O-2, 147; OV-10 Bronco, 147; P-40, 13; Porter Pilatus, 174; Pave Hawk, 274, 280, 311, 317, 331; Pave Low, 253-257, 259, 261, 270, 272, 274, 279-281, 285, 288, 290, 292, 293, 297, 298, 300, 307, 308, 311, 312, 317-319, 329; P-51 Mustang, 29, 24, 62, 108, 312; SA-16, 112, 115, 304, 305; Skyraider, 147; Spitfire, 15, 92; Super Jolly Green Giant, 210, 225, 229, 254; Tornado, 295, 296; U-10, 140, 194; U-2, 117, 118; V-22 Osprey 311; Waco glider, 88

Air Resupply and Communications Service (ARCS), 104, 113, 115-118, 209, 238, 314, 322

A Shau valley, 143

Aderholt, Brig. Gen. Henry "Heinie," 104-107, 111, 125-128, 154, 168, 169, 176, 179-181, 196, 198, 223, 322, 325, 327

Agent Orange, 139

Air America, 168, 174, 176, 314

Air commandos, 31, 32, 34, 40, 43, 85, 88, 103, 105, 108, 110, 126, 139, 140, 142, 143, 146-148, 153, 157, 161, 166, 172, 174, 201, 203, 204, 209, 211, 249, 254, 257, 265, 267, 268, 284, 285, 299, 302, 306, 307, 310, 313, 318-320, 322, 323

Air Force Cross, 309

Air Force Special Operations, 3, 70, 113, 117, 123, 125, 150, 157, 161, 173, 222, 223, 225, 231, 238, 239, 250, 251, 253, 254, 261, 270-272, 274, 281, 284, 299, 301, 307, 311, 312, 317, 321, 322, 329-332

Air Transport Command, 82

Al Jouf, 294, 331

Alabama Air National Guard, 128

Albee, Lt. Gene, 195-196, 327

Alconbury airfield, 48

Alison, Brig. Gen. John R., 4-6, 13-15, 17-21, 27-29, 34, 85, 215, 320

Allen, Col. Keith, 75, 76

Alternate 20, 166

Ambrose, Lt. George W., 56

An Loc, 161, 203

Antisubmarine warfare, 45

Armed reconnaissance, 126, 317

Army Air Forces, 4, 99, 103, 321

Arnold, General of the Army Henry H., 4, 12-18, 20-21, 26, 34-38, 43, 45, 85, 215

Baghdad, 288, 295-297, 301, 302, 331

Baker, Leo, 129

Baldwin, Air Marshal Sir John E.A., 4
Balkan Air Force, 86, 89
Balkan Air Terminal Service, 89
Ban Leboy ford, 194
Barrel Roll, 169, 219, 314
Bay of Pigs 128-130
Beckwith, Col. Charles, 234, 240, 244,
    246, 269
Bicket, Lt. Col. John, 332
Bien Hoa, 132, 133, 137, 138, 153
Binh Thuy, 153
Black, Tim, 199, 326
Blida airdrome, 84
BLU-82 Daisy Cutter, 306
Blue Spoon, 274, 275, 315
Bosnia, 87, 310
Bovingdon air base, 46
Box-and-one, 235, 245, 283
Bray, SSgt. Jeffrey, 308, 309
Brindisi, 87-91
Brink, Dale, 184
Broadway 4-6, 26-29, 31, 32, 63, 315
Broma airport, 74
Bronze Star, 309
Brown, Col. Royal A., 218, 219, 327
Brunner, Ssgt. Frederick J., 97
Burma, 3, 4, 8-12, 14, 15, 18, 21, 23-24,
    27, 29, 33, 34, 36, 38, 40, 43, 82, 83, 85,
    88, 105, 108, 110, 113, 147, 179, 215,
    238, 300, 312, 314, 315, 317-320
Buterbaugh, Maj. Greg S., 332
Butterflies, 165, 173-176, 180, 186, 187,
    315, 325, 326
Buzz bomb, 75

Callahan, 2nd Lt. Robert, 58, 59, 80
Cambodia, 172, 214, 223, 224
Campell, Dwight S., 198
Carney, Col. John J., 234-236, 238, 240,
    244-248, 262-264, 268-270, 283,
    328-330
Carpetbaggers 40, 43, 48-51, 53, 57, 58,
    60, 61, 63-71, 74, 75, 79-82, 84, 85, 89,
    90, 93-95, 97, 103, 104, 111, 112, 125,
    148, 209, 314, 315, 317, 321, 322
Cavanaugh, Maj. Michael E., 167, 171,
    181, 182, 184, 185, 326
Cavelli, 1st Lt. A.F., 194

Central Intelligence Agency, 44, 77, 107,
    174, 234, 314, 317
Cetnik, 86
Chaophakaow!, 169
Cheney Award, 307
Chiang Kai-Shek, 9
China, 9, 12, 15, 29, 104, 105, 107, 108,
    116, 166, 215
Chindits, 11, 12, 18-25, 28-34, 63, 315,
    317
Chindwin river, 25, 27
Chinnampo, 114
Cho-do, 114
Choisin reservoir, 107
Cholson, 116
Chowringhee, 5, 28, 29, 315
Churchill, Winston, 12, 16, 85, 87, 318
Civil Air Transport, 118, 125
Civil War, 152
Cochran, Col. Philip, 4-6, 13-15, 17-24,
    26, 27, 29, 31, 35-40, 85, 215, 320
Colby, William, 77
Cold War, 104, 113, 289, 308
Collins, Capt. Willard M., 144
Combat Control Teams, 203, 235
Comer, Lt. Col. Richard L., 290, 291,
    293
Commando Club, 188, 315
Credible Sport, 259, 261, 315, 329
Cuba, 128, 129, 131, 267

D-day invasion, 60
Da Nang, 133, 140, 153, 215, 219, 256
Dalai Lama, 125, 126
Dalton, Col. Roy C., 135, 323, 325
Darby, James, 81
Defense Intelligence Agency, 213
Delta force, 234, 236, 238-241, 253, 316
Desert One, 238, 241, 244-246, 249-252,
    257, 267, 275, 282, 283, 290, 310, 316,
    328
Desert Shield, 285, 307, 330
Desert Storm, 307, 308, 312, 319, 328,
    330, 331
Devers, Lt. Gen. Jacob L., 46
Distinguished Flying Cross, 115, 278,
    299
Donovan, William J., 44, 45, 83

Doolittle, Gen. James, 62-64
Dudley, Capt. C.G., 194

Easter offensive, 161
Eisenhower, Gen. Dwight D., 39-40, 60-61, 85, 117
Emmel, Lt. Oliver H., 97, 98
Estes, Capt. James E., 47
Everett, Wade, 131, 323

Fales, MSgt. Scott, 308, 309
Farmgate, 132, 133, 135-138, 143, 165, 169, 174, 193, 252, 316, 323, 324
FARRP, 237, 238, 316
Firefly, 186
Fish, Col. Robert, 46, 48, 50, 51, 55, 66, 72, 77, 78, 84, 97, 111, 112, 117, 321, 322
Fisher, Maj. Bernard F., 144-147, 324
Fitzpatrick, Lt. Ernest B., 57
Flexman, Ralph E., 151
FLIR, 211, 293
Flying Tigers, 15
Ford, President Gerald R., 222
Fort Belvoir, 208
Fort Bragg, 209
Fort Rucker, 179
Fort Walton Beach, 104, 321, 322, 325, 326, 328
Forward air controller (FAC), 108, 134, 143, 147, 161, 165, 167, 168, 170, 176, 177, 179, 180, 182, 187, 195, 198, 277, 314-318, 325
Free French, 52, 83
Freiburg, 81
Fulton Recovery System, 124, 236, 316

Gast, Lt. Gen. Philip, 243
Gee box, 53, 54, 316
Geneva, 59, 64, 73, 84, 133
Geneva accords, 133
Gliders, 3, 5, 6, 19, 21-23, 25, 27, 28, 88, 91
Gorski, Maj. Frank J. Jr., 137, 138, 193-195, 198, 199, 323, 326
Gray, Brig. Gen. George A. III, 278, 288-291, 304, 305, 311, 312, 329, 331
Gray, Wade, 129, 130

Green Berets, 130, 143, 210, 217, 218, 277, 288, 300, 301
Grenada, 262, 263, 267-269, 271, 275, 276, 284, 312, 329
Griffiss, Col. Townsend, 15
Guam, 132, 241

Hadrych, MSgt. Timothy, 299, 307, 331
Haig, Alexander, 213
Hamilton-Merritt, Jane, 325
Hanoi, 118, 141, 188, 202, 204, 208, 209, 212, 215, 220, 318, 319
Hanoi Hilton, 204, 208
Happy Valley, 128, 129
Harman, Lt. Carter, 31
Harrington airdrome, 49
Heddleson, SSgt. James J., 56
Heflin, Col. Clifford J., 46, 48, 50, 51, 64-66, 84
Hellfire guided missile, 289
Henderson, Sgt. George W., 56
Hess, Col. Lee, 237, 241, 328, 332
Hobson, Maj. Gen. James L., 264, 265, 268, 272, 312, 313, 329, 332
Holloway Commission, 248, 249, 310, 316, 328
Homan, Lt. Col. Michael E., 296-301, 329, 331
Honey Badger, 257-259, 261, 316, 328
Hopkins, Harry, 14, 20
Hotel Beau Rivage, 71
Howard, Clyde, 170, 172, 177, 178, 197, 203, 224, 325, 327
Howard Air Force Base, 273-276, 281
Hozenbackez, MSgt. Mike, 266, 267, 328-330
Hudson, Lieutenant William H., 63, 94
Hue, 143
Hurlburt Field, 123, 257, 274, 311, 322, 323, 326, 328, 330, 331

Igloo White, 201, 316, 327
Imphal, 10, 33
Inch'on, 105
India, 3, 5, 6, 9-11, 15, 20, 21, 24-25, 26-30, 33, 36, 108, 126
Indonesia, 124
Iran, 15, 236-239, 250-252

Janes, 51
Japanese, 3, 5-12, 15, 22, 24-26, 27, 29-34, 43, 103, 315, 319
Jedburgh teams, 52, 63
Joan-Eleanor system, 98, 316
Joe, 47, 55, 84, 96, 97, 112, 114, 316
Joe hole, 47, 55, 84, 96, 112, 316
Johnson, President Lyndon, 190, 214
Johnson, U. Alexis, 127
Joint Chiefs of Staff, 44, 46, 83, 213, 215, 237, 248, 310
Jones, MSgt. Charlie, 174, 175, 187,
Jones, Lt. Devon, 298, 299
Jones, Col. Ronald, 140-142, 213, 242, 243, 244, 259, 260, 323. 327, 329
Jones, MSgt. Steve D., 301, 302, 306, 307, 331
Jungle Jim, 122, 123, 129-132, 138, 257, 311, 316, 323

Kassel, 37, 38, 40
Keeny, Lt. Ralph W., 79
Kelly, John F., 258, 329
Kennedy, President John F., 127, 130, 151
Khe Sanh, 190, 282
Khmer Rouge, 223, 225, 226, 229
King, Col. Benjamin H., 131
Kirtland Air Force Base, 257
Kisarazu, 114
Kissinger, Henry, 213, 222
Klingaman, Jerome, 183, 326
Kraljev, Col. Ben, 209
Krause, Lt. Col. James R., 158
K'un-ming, 9
Kurds, 307, 313
Kuwait, 306, 331
Kyle, Col. James H., 241, 246, 247, 328

Laird, Defense Secretary Melvin R., 213, 220
Lake Annecy, 71
Lalaghat, 3, 6, 21, 25, 31, 34
Laos, 124, 126, 127, 139, 143, 156, 160, 161, 164-170, 172, 174-177, 180, 183, 185, 186, 188, 191, 192, 194, 195, 198, 202, 204, 209, 210, 216, 219, 223, 224, 254, 282, 314-319, 323, 325, 326

Leaflets, 69, 89, 115, 116, 140, 142, 165, 306, 314, 317, 319
LeMay, Gen. Curtis, 123, 138, 152
Lentaigne, Maj. Gen. W.D.A., 33
Leonik, Maj. Robert, 290-292, 330, 331
Leuchers, Scotland, 74, 76, 78
Levitow, Airman First Class John L., 157, 158
Libya, 10, 112, 117
Lima Site 30, 166, 317
Lima Site 36, 186, 187, 189, 190, 326
Lima Site 85, 187, 188, 318, 325
Litterbug, 165
Long Chieng, 126, 166, 167, 171, 174, 178, 184, 317
Longcloth, 11, 12, 26, 317
Luang Prabang, 185
Luftwaffe, 39, 81
Ly Leu, 170, 171
Lyon, France, 67, 69, 73, 74, 94

MacCloskey, Col. Monro 86, 91, 116, 117
MacDonald, Gilmour Craig, 151, 324
Mackay Trophy, 268, 299, 329
Madden, Lt. Col. Robert A., 108-111, 322
Mandalay, 11, 29, 24, 32
Manduria, 84
Manor, Maj. Gen. LeRoy, 209-211, 213-215, 217-220, 248, 249, 251, 327, 328
Mansur, John, 183
Maquis, 59, 64-66, 68, 317
Maquis Violette, 68
Marangus, Lt. Stephen J., 80
Marseilles, 73
Marshall, Gen. George C., 17, 85, 329
Martin, Maj. Corby, 300, 301
Masirah, 238, 244
Mayaguez, 222, 225, 226, 229-231, 238, 240, 250, 270, 281, 327
McCain, Adm. John, 215
McCluskey, Capt. James, 198
McCutchan, Maj. Clay, 273-277, 284, 330
McNamara, Defense Secretary Robert S., 201, 327
McNamara Barrier, 201, 327
McRaven, Cdr. William, 220

Mead, Lt. John B., 67-69
Medal of Honor, 146, 157
Mediterranean, 84, 85
Meherabad, 252
Mekong river, 172, 198
Meo, 126, 166, 316
Mihailovich, Gen. Draja, 86, 315
Military Airlift Command, 271, 284
Missiles; SA-2, 203, 242, 243; SA-3, 242,
  243; SA-7 Strela, 203; SAM, 90, 141,
  203, 219, 244, 292, 293; SCUD, 299;
  Stinger 112, 159, 201; V-2, 70
Mogadishu, 221, 308, 310
Molesworth airbase, 112
Momyer, Gen. William W., 155, 176, 177
Monkey Mountain, 215, 218
Moorer, Adm. Thomas, 215, 216
Muong Soui, 171, 184
Murmansk, 76
Myanmar, 8
Myers, Maj. Dafford W., 144-147, 324
Myitkyina, 11, 32

Nakom Phanom (NKP), 172, 193, 194,
  196, 198-200
Nazi, 39, 77, 79, 94
Nha Trang, 153
Nicaragua, 128, 129
Nicoll, 2nd Lt. William W., 56
Nienaber, Cpl. Estil I., 27
Night vision goggles (NVG), 211, 235,
  246, 258, 264, 275, 292, 317
Nimrod, 194, 198-200, 317, 326
Nokateng, 180
Noriega, Manuel, 273, 274, 279
Normandy invasion, 36, 59, 61, 86
Norrad, CMsgt. Wayne, 306, 307, 331
North Korea, 103, 106, 114
North Sea, 76, 78, 79
Norway, 44, 47, 70, 75-77, 79
Numata, Lt. Gen. T., 33

Office of Special Services (OSS), 43-46,
  50-53, 66, 83-84, 96, 107, 317
Office of the Coordinator of
  Information (COI), 43, 317
Old, Brig. Gen. William D., 4, 22
Olivette, Lt. Ralph, 108, 109

Oman, 238
On Mark, 193
Onbauk, 29
Operation Aviary, 105, 317
Operation Buick, 62, 317
Operation Cadillac, 62, 317
Operation Eagle, 223
Operation Just Cause, 274, 280, 315-16,
  330
Operation Provide Comfort, 307, 313
Operation Rice Bowl, 234, 236, 242, 251,
  317
Operation Think, 116
Operation Haik, 123, 124, 317
Operation Thursday, 3, 4, 6, 24-26, 29,
  30, 32, 36, 317, 318, 320

P'yongyang, 115
Padong, 126
Paengnyong-do, 107
Painter, 2nd Lt. Sam O., 90
Panama, 273-275, 279, 281, 284, 315,
  316, 329, 330
Paradise Camp, 89
Pararescuemen (PJ), 269, 284, 308
Partisans, 86-89, 92, 93
Pathet Lao, 126, 127, 165, 168
Patton, Gen. George, 38-40, 70, 94
Pave Aegis, 161, 327
Pearl Harbor, 8
Peenemunde, 74
Pehr, Col. Frank, 254, 256, 329
Pennington, Ben, 299
Peterson, 1st Lt. Delbert R., 144
Phelan, James, 31
Philippines, 112, 113, 118, 124, 132, 220
Phnom Penh, 223-225
Phou Pha Thi, 188, 189, 315, 318, 325
Picadilly, 4, 5, 318
Plaine des Jarres, 127, 164, 173, 182,
  184, 186, 191, 318
Pleiku, 109, 144, 153
Point Salines airport, 262
Polifka, Capt. Karl L., 182-184, 190, 191,
  326
Pope, Allen, 124, 236
PORK-SAUSAGE, 6
Powell, Gen. Colin, 310

Powers, Francis Gary, 118
Prestwick, Scotland, 75
Project 404/Palace Dog, 174, 183, 318, 326
Project 9, 15, 318
Project Lucky Tiger, 173
Project Mill Pond, 126, 317
Project Mule Train, 142
Project Ranch Hand, 139, 318
Project Tailchaser, 151
Project Water Pump, 168, 318, 327
Puerto Cabezas, 128
Puff, the Magic Dragon, 150, 314
Pulsifer, Maj. Ben, 292, 293, 331
Pusan, 104, 107

Quadrant Conference, 12, 318
Qui Nhon, 144

Rabbits, 105, 106, 317
Rangers, 173, 239, 241, 245, 264-270, 274, 282, 284, 309, 310
Rangoon, 8, 9, 35
Ravens, 165, 168, 173, 180-184, 190, 191, 198, 326
Ray, Thomas W., 129
Rebecca/Eureka system, 54
Rhine River, 37
Riley, Lt. Col. Charles A., 153, 156
Rio Hato, 282
Roberts, Capt. John, 187
Roberts, Col. John, 329
Robertson, Stam, 30, 31, 33, 321
Roosevelt, President Franklin D., 12, 13, 16
Rose, Rich, 184
Royal Air Force, 11, 12, 46, 80
Ruksas, Ray, 32, 33, 321

S-phone, 54, 68, 319
Samp, SSgt. Lloyd I., 33
San Antonio, 48, 140, 322, 323, 327
Sanders, 2nd Lt. Robert L., 58, 59, 80
Sasaki, 1st Lt. Edwin, 153
Sato, Lt. Gen. K., 33, 34
Schiller, Ralph, 79
Schlesinger, Defense Secretary James, 222, 230

Scholl, Robert L., 199
Schreiner, Maj. Dave, 75, 76
Schwarzkopf, Gen. H. Norman, 285, 288-291
Schweinfurt, 45
Scruggs, Lt. Mike, 198
SEALs, 130, 210, 220, 223, 263, 270, 279, 280
SEAL, Team SIX 263
Secord, Richard, 122, 133, 134, 174, 177, 188, 197, 252, 253, 257, 323
Seoul, 104, 105, 113
Shamburger, Riley, 129
Shank, Capt. Edwin G., 146
Shernak, 1st Lt. Tom, 137
Silver Star, 69, 115, 183, 299, 309
Simon, Lt. Murry L., 67
Simons, Lt. Col. Arthur D., 209, 214, 217
Skyspot, 188, 189, 315
Slim, Maj. Gen. William J., 4, 9, 10, 33
Snyder, Richard D., 30, 32, 34, 110, 111, 321, 322
Snyder, Capt. Robert H., 90
Soc Trang, 133, 137, 138, 146
Son Tay, 209, 210, 214, 216, 217, 220, 221, 226, 230, 238, 248-251, 290, 319, 327, 328
SONNIE project, 74
South Korea, 104
Soviet Union, 87, 104, 113, 117, 123, 202, 308
SOYA-LINK, 6
Spaatz, Lt. Gen. Carl A., 83-85
Special Forces, 67, 130, 142, 143, 198, 209, 234, 237, 271, 285, 288, 289, 306, 315, 324, 331
Spirit 03, 303-305, 331
Stanford, Jim, 174-176, 325
Stapel, Capt. Wilmer L., 64, 65
Starlight Scope, 158, 196, 197, 319
Stilwell, Lt. Gen. Joseph W., 9
Strategic Air Command, 111, 123, 179, 188, 224, 315
Strategic Air Force, 85
Stratemeyer, Maj. Gen. George, 4
Stray Goose, 140, 142, 319, 323
Sullivan, Maj. Robert F., 114-116
Surprise Package, 159, 160, 324

Swarts, Lt. Robert, 74
Sweeney, Gen. Walter C., Jr., 154
Syngman Rhee, 105

Tabas, 236
Taegu, 104
Takhli, 125, 127, 177, 214
Tan Son Nhut, 153
Tang Island, 222, 225, 227, 229
Task Force Ranger, 308, 310
Teheran, 15, 234, 236-239, 245, 251-253,
  259, 315-317, 328, 329
Tempsford, 46
Terrain following radar (TFR), 212
Terry, Ronald W. 151-152, 155, 157-158,
  160, 255, 256, 259
Texas Instruments, 255, 256
Thailand, 8, 125, 127, 167, 172, 173,
  176, 177, 184, 193, 196, 198-200, 203,
  208-210, 214, 219, 222-225, 227, 228,
  315, 317-319, 325, 326
Tibet, 125, 126
Tonkin Gulf Resolution, 214
Trask, Capt. Thomas J., 296-299
Tresemer, Maj. Edward C., 64, 65, 97, 98
Trondheim, 76
Tully, TSgt. Gordon W., 282, 283,
  294-296, 330, 331
Tunisia, 83
Tyrrell, Col. Robert L.F., 181, 325

U Tapao, 225-227, 229, 230
U.S. Special Operations Command, 271,
  284, 285, 312, 313
U-Go, 25, 33
Ubon, 200
Udorn, 168, 177, 204, 214, 216, 218, 319
United Nations, 104, 106, 308, 310
Upham, Col. Hudson H., 94, 96, 97
USS Coral Sea, 225, 228-230

USS Holt, 226

Vandenberg, Gen. Hoyt S., 111
Vang Pao, 126, 167-169, 171, 173, 174,
  177, 187, 191, 223, 317, 319
Vaught, Maj. Gen. James, 236, 237, 240,
  241, 252
Vientiane, 127, 165-167, 174, 181, 187,
  319, 325
Vietcong 135-137, 139, 150, 152, 153
Vietminh, 119, 167, 316, 319
Vietnam, 95, 109, 110, 118, 127, 131-133,
  136-140, 142, 143, 146, 147, 150-153,
  156-158, 160, 161, 164-166, 169, 176,
  180, 186, 188, 190-194, 196, 201-203,
  208, 211, 214-216, 220, 230, 239, 240,
  242, 250, 254, 271, 282, 290, 308, 312,
  314, 316, 318, 320, 323

Wadi Kena, 239, 242, 244
Walker, Douglas D., 73, 76, 77, 79
Walsh, Maj. John W., 97
Weaver, Maj. Paul J., 303
Weikel, Col. Gary, 226-230, 250, 270-272,
  279-282, 310, 327, 328, 330, 332
Welch, Gen. Larry D., 240
West Point, 122, 174
Westerman, Frank, 114, 115
Weyland, Gen. O.P., 38
White City, 63, 319
White, Ross D., 95
Wickstrom, Maj. Tom, 198, 201, 327
Wild Weasel, 218
Wilkinson, TSgt. Timothy, 309, 310
Wingate, Brig. Gen. Orde C., 4-6, 10-13,
  16-18, 24-25, 28, 29, 32, 33, 38
Wolfe, Lt. Tom, 195

Yangon, 8
Yazd, 236